The PRINCES
in the TOWER

The
PRINCES
in the
TOWER

ALISON WEIR

Ballantine Books • New York

Library of Congress Catalog Card Number: 93-70004

ISBN: 0-345-38372-9

Manufactured in the United States of America

First American Edition: January 1994

This book is dedicated to
my cousin,
Christine Armour,
and in loving memory of
Joan Barbara Armour

'. . . look back with me unto the Tower. —
Pity, you ancient stones, those tender babes,
Whom envy hath immured within your walls!
Rough cradle for such little, pretty ones!
Rude, ragged nurse, old sullen playfellow
For tender princes . . . '

Richard III, Act IV, Scene I

'Ah me, I see the ruin of my House!
The tiger now hath seiz'd the gentle hind;
Insulting tyranny begins to jet
Upon the innocent and aweless throne:—
Welcome destruction, blood and massacre!
I see, as in a map, the end of all.'

Richard III, Act II, Scene IV

Contents

Illustrations

Author's Preface

This is a book about the deaths, in tragic circumstances, of two children. It is a tale so rich in drama, intrigue, treason, plots, counter-plots, judicial violence, scandal and infanticide, that for more than five centuries it has been recounted and re-interpreted in different ways by dozens of writers. And it is easy to see why: it is a mystery, a moral tale, and – above all – a gripping story. More compellingly, it is the story of a crime that has never been satisfactorily solved.

There are few people who have not heard of the Princes in the Tower, just as there are few people who do not relish a good murder or mystery story. In the case of the Princes, we have an especially fascinating mystery, not only because they were royal victims who lived in a particularly colourful age, nor because there are plenty of clues as to their fate, but because speculation as to what happened to them has provoked controversy for so many hundreds of years. Even today, the battle still rages between those who believe that the Princes were murdered by their uncle, Richard III, and the revisionists, who have forwarded several attractive theories to the contrary.

It has to be said, at the outset, that it is unlikely that the truth of the matter will ever be confirmed by better evidence than we already have. We are talking about a murder that was committed in the strictest secrecy half a millennium ago in a period for which sources are scanty and often evasive. It is true that documents occasionally come to light which add yet another tiny piece to this extremely complex jigsaw-puzzle, but a historian can rarely hope to produce, in such a case, the kind of evidence that would convince a modern court of law of the identity of the murderer. The historian's job is to weigh the evidence available, however slender and circumstantial, and then – on a balance of probabilities – reconstruct what probably happened. Thus are history books written, and we should not hope for anything better.

For three centuries and more, the revisionist view of Richard III has prevailed, and in recent years the efforts of the Richard III Society have ensured that textbooks are now being cautiously rewritten to present a kinder view of the last Plantagenet king. Yet since the discovery in 1934 of Dominic Mancini's contemporary account of Richard III's usurpation, which corroborated many details in the *Croyland Chronicle* and other contemporary works hostile to Richard, the majority of serious historians have rejected the revisionist view and stressed the huge amount of circumstantial and other evidence against Richard III.

I have therefore tried to approach this book with as open a mind as possible. I have studied all the contemporary works on the subject, as well as dozens of modern ones, and I have collated all the evidence available. I am now confident that the solution to the mystery presented here is the only plausible one. In my research, I have analysed every sentence written about the disappearance of the Princes in original sources, even rearranging information into its correct chronological sequence, and I have found – somewhat to my surprise – that it is indeed possible to reconstruct the whole chain of events leading up to the murder of the Princes, and to show, within the constraints mentioned above, how, when, where, and by whose order, they died. The truth of the matter is there in the sources, for those who look carefully enough. We are dealing here with facts, not just speculation or theories, which I have tried very hard to avoid.

I realise, of course, that my claims are highly contentious, but I am confident that they can be substantiated by good evidence, as I will demonstrate in the text. Thus I hope to entertain, inform, and convince all those who read this book.

Alison Weir

Acknowledgements

I should like to acknowledge my gratitude to the following: Pamela Tudor-Craig (Lady Wedgwood) for permission to use material from her splendid and informative catalogue for the National Portrait Gallery's 1973 exhibition on Richard III; Mr Brian Spencer, for allowing me to use information printed in that catalogue and deriving from his unpublished manuscript about the inmates of the Minories: the Archaeological Resource Centre in York for allowing me to use the services of their textiles expert.

I should also like to acknowledge my indebtedness to the works of the late Professor Charles Ross and that of Mr Desmond Seward, which were a constant inspiration. I must also express my gratitude to my editor, Jill Black, for her constant encouragement and for some extremely helpful suggestions on chronology and dates, especially in relation to Gloucester's coup of April 1483. Gratitude is also due to my agent, Julian Alexander, for his unflagging enthusiasm, and to my husband Rankin and children John and Kate for their forbearance over the last two years.

Lastly, I must stress that, while all these good people have given valuable assistance with this book, the end product is entirely my own and reflects my conclusions, not theirs.

I

Richard III and
the Chroniclers

Modern writers on the subject of the Princes in the Tower have
tended to fall into two categories: those who believe Richard III
guilty of the murder of the Princes but are afraid to commit themselves
to any confident conclusions, and those who would like to see Richard
more or less canonised. It is time therefore for the evidence to be
re-evaluated and the events surrounding the disappearance of the
Princes in 1483 to be reconstructed with greater confidence, because
there does exist a considerable amount of contemporary evidence for a
solution to this mystery.

It has been said by several writers that both the traditionalist and
revisionist views of Richard III fit the known facts, but this is not the
case: there are many blind alleys in this mystery, and many authors
who have made the mistake of wandering up them. There also exist a
great number of misconceptions about Richard III and the Princes, and
because the subject still provokes furious debate, one gains the impression that to venture a firm view on the matter is to step into a
minefield. However, this book was not written with the intention of
fuelling the controversy, but because there is a need for the subject to be
dealt with from an objective viewpoint based on common sense and
sound research.

The subject of the Princes in the Tower cannot be studied without
first evaluating the reliability of the few surviving original sources –
virtually all we have to rely on. The late fifteenth century is a poorly
documented period of English history. Few contemporary chronicles

survive and some official records still await examination. Thanks to a growing interest in the period, however, much research has been done over the last century and many excellent books have been published. Nevertheless, the second half of the fifteenth century remains in some respects very much a twilight world to the historian.

This book is mainly about the years 1483–5, the period spanning the reigns of Edward V and Richard III. Nearly all the narrative sources for this period have a partisan bias: most were written in the south of England and reflect anti-northern sentiment, for Richard III was identified very much with northern interests.

Few royal letters survive, and of the great collections of letters of the period – the *Paston Letters*, the *Cely Letters* and the *Stonor Letters* – fewer than ten refer to Richard III's usurpation of the throne in 1483. Much of what we know about the period comes from later sources, because for the years 1483–5 there are very few reliable contemporary narrative sources, and only two major ones.

The first of these is Dominic Mancini's account of the events leading up to July, 1483 – *De Occupatione Regni Anglie per Riccardum Tercium* (*The Occupation of the Throne of England by Richard III*). Mancini was an Italian monk who lived in France and died after 1494. *De Occupatione* was his only prose work. Mancini came to England late in 1482 in the suite of the French ambassador. His brief was to report back to the Archbishop of Vienne on English affairs. He remained in London until July, 1483, leaving England the week after Richard III's coronation.

Mancini's book, which he completed on 1st December, 1483, at Beaugency, was an official report on recent events in England. His stated intention was 'to put in writing by what machinations Richard III attained the high degree of kingship', and he fulfilled this in the most vivid and objective manner. It is Mancini's objectivity that makes his book an invaluable source; he had no reason to write anything hostile to Richard III. A man of integrity, he confined himself only to the facts, and avoided falling into the habit affected by so many contemporary writers, that of using historical facts to illustrate a lesson in morality. Furthermore, he avoided referring to Richard's accession as a usurpation: 'occupation' is his preferred word.

Mancini's credibility as an historian is further reaffirmed by independent corroboration of his account by other sources, notably the *Croyland Chronicle* and the later accounts of Polydore Vergil and Sir Thomas

More, none of whom had access to Mancini's book. Indeed, it was lost for centuries; no one knew of its existence until 1934, when it was discovered by Professor C.A.J. Armstrong in the archives of the Bibliothèque Municipale at Lille, and subsequently published.

Mancini was reluctant to name his sources, but his account suggests that he had contacts at court, some of whom were apparently hostile to Richard III. The only source mentioned by name is Dr John Argentine, physician to Edward V, who could speak Italian. Mancini could also have made use of Italians living in London, in particular Pietro Carmeliano, a court poet to both Edward IV and Henry VII.

There are flaws in Mancini's book, of which he himself was aware, stating his reluctance to commit his account to paper as he did not know the names of some of those mentioned nor their motives. He admitted his account was incomplete in details. He lacked an understanding of English and a knowledge of English geography, and he paid little regard to chronology, although, in fairness to him, this was a period when recording dates was not considered of prime importance by historians. Nor is there in his book any physical description of Richard III – perhaps we should assume he never saw him. This, and the fact that the latter part of the account is less detailed, suggests that Mancini was no longer able to make use of some of his former court informants.

The second major source for the period 1483–5 is the *Second Continuation of the Croyland Chronicle*. The magnificent Abbey of Croyland (now spelt Crowland) in Lincolnshire was at this time the most important and wealthiest religious foundation in the east of England, and its mitred abbot ranked with the bishops. Royal visitors to the abbey in the late fifteenth century included Henry VI, Edward IV, and Richard III when he was Duke of Gloucester. Several chronicles detailing the history of England and of the abbey were written at Croyland. Those prior to 1117 are spurious, but the three anonymously written continuations, spanning the periods 1144–1469, 1459–86 and 1485–6, are genuine.

The author of the *Second Continuation* (1459–86) states that it was written in the ten days ending on 30th April, 1486. The last events he describes are the marriage of Henry VII and the northern uprising of that spring. His work is without doubt the best source for the period. Where verifiable, it is highly accurate, and its author was a man who could write authoritatively and from personal knowledge of many of the events he describes. It is clear too that he withheld information that was politically sensitive: his silence on certain subjects sometimes speaks volumes. Much of what he did write is substantiated by other writers, such as Mancini, Vergil and More, who never read his manuscript.

The author of the *Croyland Chronicle* did not approve of Richard III. As a churchman, he was shocked by Richard's behaviour, denouncing him for sensuality, holding an execution on a Sunday, and overspending. However, he declared his intention of writing his history 'in as unprejudiced a manner as we possibly can', asserting that he was presenting the reader with 'a truthful recital of the facts without hatred or favour'. And he was indeed a surprisingly objective, if ironic, observer for his time.

Who was he, this anonymous author to whom we shall refer merely as 'Croyland'? He described himself as a doctor of canon law and a member of the royal Council. We know also, from the text, that he was a southerner who resented northern interlopers in the government. He was a cultivated man who was well acquainted with the workings of Council, Parliament, Convocation and Chancery. Thus there is every reason to identify him with John Russell, Bishop of Lincoln (1480–94), Keeper of the Privy Seal (1474–83), and Lord Chancellor of England under Richard III (1483–5), an erudite and wise man who earned the praise of Sir Thomas More. Croyland Abbey lay within Russell's diocese, and the *Third Continuation* of its *Chronicle* records his month-long visit there in April, 1486, when the *Second Continuation* was written. The Bishop could well have dictated his history to a member of his retinue of twenty persons or to a monk living in the abbey. Most telling is the fact that the Bishop's own involvement in the events described is never referred to.

Croyland's manuscript was immediately suppressed when Henry VII, in the interests of dynastic security, ordered the destruction of all copies of the Act of Settlement known as 'Titulus Regius' (1484), which set forth Richard III's title to the throne: the text of this was incorporated in Croyland. Several copies of the manuscript were destroyed. A few survived, being hidden, but Croyland was not used as a historical source until 1619. The earliest surviving copy is that in the Cottonian Library (British Library MS. Cotton Otho B. XIII), which was seriously damaged by fire in 1731. There is a seventeenth-century transcript in the Bodleian Library (Corpus Christi College MS. B. 208). The full Latin text was published by W. Fulman in 1684, and the standard translation remains that by H.T. Riley (1854).

Several Tudor sources provide accounts of the period 1483–5. The main problem facing any historian studying Richard III is how much to rely on these Tudor accounts, which are so rich in detail and so hostile to Richard, and which sometimes contradict each other. This problem may be solved by evaluating each on its own merits, taking into account the circumstances in which it was written and the sources used, if known. We must also consider the difficulties Tudor historians faced in gaining access to sources and information.

The earliest Tudor writer of note was John Rous (1411–91), an artistic Warwickshire chantry priest and antiquarian. He was clearly not an eyewitness to most of the events he describes, and not averse to recording gossip as fact. Rous's writings show with striking clarity how the accession of Henry VII in 1485 affected the recording of contemporary history. Rous was first and foremost a chronicler of the Beauchamp and Neville families, earls of Warwick, to whom he was devoted. In 1483–5, he compiled the *York Roll*, an illustrated history in English of these families, which is now in the British Library. Richard III appears in this as the husband of Anne Neville, to whom the *Roll* was dedicated and given, and is referred to by Rous as 'a mighty prince and especial good lord; . . . a most virtuous prince'.

Rous made two copies of the *York Roll*; he could not retrieve the first after Richard III's death, but he altered his own Latin copy (now in the College of Arms, London), mutilating it wherever a picture of Richard appeared. His laudatory description of him was deleted and in its place were just the words '*infelix maritus*' – the 'unhappy spouse' – of Anne Neville. Rous also wrote a history of England dedicated to Henry VII, which was completed in 1490; in it, he portrays Richard III as a deformed monster and tyrant, likening him to the antiChrist. It has been suggested, however, that Rous's hostility towards Richard derived not so much from his desire to win the favour of Henry VII as from his conviction that Richard had murdered his heroine, Anne Neville.

Pietro Carmeliano of Brescia (d.1527) was an Italian cleric who came to England in the reign of Edward IV and became a court poet, later earning the approval of the great humanist scholar, Erasmus. In 1483–5

Carmeliano wrote a *Life of St Catherine* (Bodleian Library, Oxford, Misc. 501), which he dedicated to Sir Robert Brackenbury, then Constable of the Tower of London. In its introduction, he praised Richard III lavishly, but in September 1486, under Henry VII, he wrote a poem to mark the birth of Henry's son Arthur, in which he savagely accused Richard of murdering the Princes in the Tower and Henry VI, amongst other crimes. This seems to have won him the King's favour, for that same month Henry granted him a pension and made him his Latin secretary, chaplain and lute player.

The third writer of note of the early Tudor period was Bernard André (who died after 1527), a blind poet from Toulouse who became Henry VII's official historian and tutor to his sons after coming to England in 1485. From 1500–1502, André worked on a life of Henry VII which he never completed. This undoubtedly presents the official version of recent history, as approved by the King, but it seems that André also used earlier works which are now lost. He portrays Richard III as an utter villain and Henry VII as God's messenger come to avenge his predecessor's crimes. Erasmus knew André but was unimpressed with his work.

The chief foreign source for the Yorkist period is the *Mémoires* of Philippe de Commines, a French politician and diplomat who moved in the highest circles of the courts of France and Burgundy. He compiled his memoirs after his retirement in 1490, and they cover the period 1464–98. After 1480, however, Commines no longer enjoyed the confidence of those who ruled France, although he had met Edward IV and later knew Henry Tudor during his exile. There are obvious flaws in his work, yet he did record the gossip then circulating on the Continent and may well have had access to more reliable sources of information for the later period.

The so-called *London Chronicles* provide us with an observant and detailed record of events in the late fifteenth century. The first is that chronicle known as B.L. Cotton MS. Vitellius AXVI, written during the early years of Henry VII's reign and published by C.L. Kingsford as *Chronicles of London* in 1905. Then there is a fragment from the commonplace books of a London merchant which was discovered in the College of Arms in 1980, and published as *Historical Notes of a London Citizen, 1483–1488* in 1981. The other *London Chronicles* were written, at least in part, by Robert Fabyan (d.1513), a wealthy London clothier and alderman of the City of London. He made a compilation of several London chronicles (the originals of which are now lost) which is known as the *Great Chronicle of London* and is in the Guildhall Library. This is a major source for the period, for all its errors and confused chronology. It is an eyewitness account, clearly based on first-hand knowledge of some of the events described and reflecting the public opinion of its day. The section dealing with the period ending 1496 was written before 1501–2 and possibly earlier. Although the *Great Chronicle* is pro-Lancastrian in sympathy, it is unlikely that its author had access to the works of Rous, André and Carmeliano.

Fabyan also wrote *The Book of the Concordance of Histories*, a history of England from the Conquest to his own time, which was printed in 1516 as *The New Chronicles of England and France*. It was based in part on Fabyan's own diaries but is not as comprehensive as the *Great Chronicle*.

One controversial source is the *Song of the Lady Bessy*, a colourful and proven to be mainly fanciful account in verse of the conspiracy that led to Richard III's overthrow. It was probably written before 1504 by Humphrey Brereton, a squire to Lord Stanley, and while it grossly exaggerates the role played by Elizabeth of York in the plot, it contains some apparently authentic details.

The chief narrative source dating from Henry VII's time is the *Anglica Historia* of Polydore Vergil. Vergil, a cleric from Urbino, Italy, came to England around 1501–2 and stayed. He was a renowned Renaissance scholar and humanist, and a friend of Erasmus and Thomas More. He quickly attracted the attention of Henry VII, who made use of his talents and rewarded him with benefices. After the accession of Henry VIII, however, he made an enemy of Cardinal Wolsey and fell from favour. He left England in 1551 and died in Italy in 1555.

In 1507, Henry VII commissioned Vergil to write an official history of England. Vergil spent six years researching this project, and wrote the first draft in c.1512–14. But it took him a further nineteen years to complete and revise all the twenty-six books in the *Anglica Historia*. The finished work, dedicated to Henry VIII, was published in 1534 in Basle. Vergil's was therefore the first account of Richard III's usurpation to appear in print: in fact, it is the most detailed extant account of his reign.

Vergil followed the Renaissance tradition of using history to teach a moral lesson, whereby the reader might benefit from learning about the past. A skilful historian and writer, he used an innovative approach that had a profound influence on later Tudor writers. He could be maddeningly vague at times, and selective about what he wrote, yet he was no sycophant. He was criticial of Henry VII in places, and raised a storm by his rejection of the time-honoured notion that the Arthurian legends were based on fact. Thus he was no mere propagandist, but an objective writer who drew his own conclusions.

Vergil seldom states who his sources were, but Henry VII gave him unrestricted access to official records and personally imparted details of his exile and early years as king. Vergil tells us that other contemporaries also passed on their recollections of previous reigns, some of which they may, of course, have deliberately falsified. He also says he consulted a great number of chronicles and other documents; in 1574 it was alleged by John Caius of Cambridge that Vergil had destroyed cartloads of ancient manuscripts so as to ensure that the flaws in his history would not be detected. This may well be the reason why so few sources for Richard III's reign have come down to us – those that have survived were either hidden or abroad. However, Vergil himself says that he could find very few written sources for the period after 1450.

There is no proof that he ever saw the *Croyland Chronicle*; it had been suppressed long before his time, but the two accounts do corroborate each other to a great extent. Vergil's account of recent times also substantiates in many respects that of Sir Thomas More (see below), but is less detailed. Vergil never saw Mancini's history, yet again the two accounts often agree.

Vergil worked under constraints. He was capable of suppressing the truth where it was politic to do so, and was well aware that certain subjects were highly sensitive. He claimed he was presenting a truthful picture, yet he had to be tactful and avoid offending his royal patron and other powerful persons. He may well have been briefed to follow the 'least said, soonest mended' policy adopted by Henry VII himself. In the circumstances, therefore, he wrote, to his credit, a remarkably balanced work.

The first – and the most controversial – biography of Richard III was written by Sir Thomas More. Entitled, *The History of King Richard III*, it was written around 1514–18 and revised in the late 1520s. More's account is rich in compelling, authentic, eye-witness detail – which in itself argues its reliability – and shows familiarity with the workings of the royal household in Richard's time. Approximately one-third of it contains eloquent speeches invented by More for his characters but based on authentic source material. This was an accepted practice in an age when history and literature were almost indivisible.

More's history has its obvious flaws: some names and dates are incorrect or missing, and some of its content may well be based on inaccurate sources or – as More admits – the result of 'divining upon conjectures'. Nevertheless, it has been verified in so many respects, and by so many other sources – such as Mancini and Croyland, who were not known to More, and Vergil, who was – that there is little reason to doubt its overall authenticity.

Sir Thomas More was a lawyer, a humanist scholar, and a politician, a man whose reputation for integrity was famous throughout Christendom. He served for a short time as Henry VIII's Lord Chancellor before resigning because his conscience would not allow him to condone Henry's break with Rome. He was executed for his defiance in 1535, and later made a saint by the Roman Catholic Church.

More brought to his history of Richard III the benefit of his fine legal mind, his truthfulness and his intellectual judgement, and there is little doubt that he went to great trouble to find out the truth about the Princes in the Tower, whose fate was the central theme of his book. Roger Ascham, the great Elizabethan scholar, described the book as a model of historical writing, and there is no evidence that he or his contemporaries ever considered it satirical, which it has been called by at least one modern writer.

It was never More's intention to write propaganda for the Tudors, although many have accused him of doing just that. In fact, he had good reason to hate Henry VII: in 1504 he had risked a charge of high treason when he opposed the King in Parliament. Henry VII realised that Thomas could not pay the fine his offence merited, so he imprisoned and fined his father, Judge Sir John More. Nor was More any sycophant to Henry VIII, who for many years valued his opinion because he knew it was an honest one. More also risked offending his powerful friend, the third Duke of Norfolk, by his brief portrayal of the roles played by the first and second dukes under Richard III. With More, the truth came first.

More's work was never intended for publication but was written purely for private intellectual recreation. Nor was it finished. It may be that More was persuaded by someone influential to abandon it because of things in it that could have proved embarrassing to those of Richard's contemporaries who were still alive, or their descendants. Or More may simply have lost interest in the project or lacked the time in which to complete it.

More's work has value, therefore, because it was relatively objective. He had no motive for lying. He used a wide variety of sources and obtained first-hand information from those courtiers and others who had been alive in Richard III's time. These people are not named, but we may hazard a guess as to who they were.

It has been asserted by numerous writers that More's chief source of information was Cardinal Morton, Henry VII's Lord Chancellor, who suffered imprisonment and exile under Richard III. More was in Morton's household from the age of twelve to fourteen, but it is hardly likely that the great Cardinal would have favoured such a young boy with so many confidences. This is not to say that More did not pick up some information at that time from Morton; he greatly admired him, and must have had some personal contact with him. And Morton was the one man who could have known the truth about some of the events of which More writes: More speaks of his 'deep insight into political worldly drifts'. However, the notion that More's information came from Morton was not mooted until 1596, when Sir John Haryngton suggested in *The Metamorphosis of Ajax* that Morton might even have been the author of More's book. This theory was later embellished by Richard III's apologist, Sir George Buck, but both Buck and Haryngton incorrectly assumed that More was an adult when he was in Morton's service. There is no contemporary evidence to suggest that Morton had anything to do with the work, and no serious historian nowadays believes that anyone other than More wrote it. The style of the work alone argues strongly in favour of his authorship.

There were many other sources that More could – and probably did – make use of. His own father, a judge of the King's Bench, had been a keen political observer in Richard's reign. Thomas Howard, third Duke of Norfolk, More's 'singular dear friend' according to More's son-in-law William Roper, could have told More about the involvement of his family in the events of the time. It is perhaps significant that More makes hardly any reference to these important persons in his book, even though they had been prominent at court: to have done so would have been to compromise both the Duke and More's friendship with him. More may also have obtained information from Dr John Argentine, Robert Fabyan, Polydore Vergil (whose work he knew in manuscript form), Richard FitzJames, Bishop of London – Edward IV's chaplain and friend – Sir Thomas Lovell, Speaker of the Commons under Henry VII and a friend of More, Sir John Cutte – Richard III's receiver of crown lands in six counties and More's predecessor as Under Treasurer – Sir John Roper, Richard's commissioner of array for Kent, and Sir Reginald Bray and Christopher Urswick, both of whom were involved in the plot to depose Richard and set Henry Tudor on the throne; Urswick was another friend of More's. As a lawyer and Under-Sheriff of London, More had access to the legal records of Richard III's reign. He also used the *Great Chronicle*.

More wrote both English and Latin versions of his history. A 'corrupt and altered version' was first printed by Richard Grafton in 1543 in *Hardyng's Chronicle*; it appeared again in *Hall's Chronicle* in 1548. The full Latin text was printed by More's nephew William Rastell in 1557, with a note that it was taken from a holograph manuscript found by Rastell amongst More's papers; the original text is in the College of Arms, London (MS. Arundel 43). More's *Richard III* was widely read and became very popular, and it was the chief inspiration for Shakespeare's *Richard III*, with which, of course, dramatic liberties were taken.

Above all, More gives a credible and consistent portrayal of Richard that can hardly have been based on fiction; anyone reading his manuscript, which was privately circulated amongst his friends, some of whom had known Richard III, could have spotted any inconsistencies. And More himself had several means of checking his facts.

Later Tudor chroniclers such as Hall and Holinshed all relied on Vergil and More. But in 1611 the antiquary John Speed discovered a draft of the suppressed Act 'Titulus Regius', which outlined the grounds on which Richard III had claimed the throne. This discovery shed what appeared to be new light on the fate of the Princes. Speed printed the original draft of the Act that year, and six years later Sir William Cornwallis published *The Encomium of Richard III*, the first of the revisionist works, which was in effect a defence of Richard against the charge that he had murdered the Princes.

Cornwallis's theme was taken up even more enthusiastically in 1619 by Sir George Buck, who was described by William Camden as 'a man of distinguished learning'. Buck was of an old Yorkist family, the great-grandson of John Buck, a member of Richard III's household who was executed after having supported Richard at Bosworth. The Howard family had later used their influence to prevent his family from losing everything, and more than a century later Sir George was still grateful to them. He had risen to prominence at the court of Elizabeth I, and became Master of the Revels to James I, licensing several of Shakespeare's plays in this capacity. Tragically he went insane in 1621 and died the next year.

Buck's *The History of King Richard III* was written in 1619. It was a vast work, carefully researched from early manuscripts preserved in the Tower of London, Sir Robert Cotton's library – which contained an original copy of the *Croyland Chronicle* – the College of Arms, and the private collection of Thomas Howard, Earl of Arundel, to whom the work was dedicated. It is also possible that Buck used family information handed down from Richard III's time.

Buck's aim in writing his book was to proclaim Richard III's innocence of the crimes laid at his door by earlier writers. He was not entirely impartial – his family had supported Richard and he felt this needed justification. He claimed that More's biography was too full of errors to be reliable. Many people found Buck's portrayal attractive and credible, and it was at this point that the controversy over Richard III that persists to this day began in earnest.

Buck's holograph MS. (Cotton MS. Tiberius E.xf.238) – 'corrected and amended on every page' – was damaged in the Cottonian fire; only fragments remain in the British Library. Another version of the first two books of the manuscript is British Library Egerton MS. 2216–2220, but this is a copy. Buck's nephew, another George Buck, printed an abridged and censored version of the work in 1646, the only version available until 1979, when A.N. Kincaid published his splendid edition of the original text, which revealed several convincing details and exposed the deficiencies in the 1646 edition.

The last of the 'original' narrative sources was *The History of Henry VII* by Sir Francis Bacon (1561–1626), published in 1622. This excellent, erudite work by a lawyer, statesman and Lord Chancellor, was for centuries the standard biography of Henry; well-researched, objective, and advanced for its time. Even today it stands up well in the face of modern research. Placed as he was, Bacon had access to official records, some no longer extant, and his work has value for this alone.

The sources discussed above are so integral to the subject of the Princes that, as will be seen in the following chapters, they are indeed part of the plot. All these writers have, in their various ways, influenced the controversy about the Princes, and so we need to know about them, and their loyalties and prejudices, before we can consider what weight to give to their evidence. This is a crucial factor, because in that evidence lie the vital clues to the fate of the Princes.

2

The Sanctuary Child

In the fifteenth century the succession to the English crown was never stable. The Plantagenets had ruled England since 1154, and until 1399 the succession had generally passed fairly peacefully from father to son. But Edward III, who died in 1377, had several sons whom he endowed with dukedoms, thus calling into being a race of magnates or aristocrats related by blood to the King, some of whom ultimately became intent on claiming the throne. The first was Henry of Bolingbroke, son of John of Gaunt, Duke of Lancaster, fourth surviving son of Edward III. In 1399, Bolingbroke deposed, and later murdered, his childless cousin Richard II and usurped the throne himself as Henry IV, thus founding the royal House of Lancaster and overlooking the claim of Richard's designated heir, his third cousin Edmund Mortimer, then a child of seven, who was descended from Lionel of Antwerp, Duke of Clarence, second surviving son of Edward III.

Henry IV's title to the throne was therefore dubious, but what he had taken he held on to, and the reputation of his successor, Henry V, seemed to ensure that the House of Lancaster would continue to reign gloriously after his death. But Henry V died young unexpectedly in 1422, leaving as his heir a baby, Henry VI. Henry survived his minority, but he was, as Philippe de Commines tells us, 'a very ignorant and almost simple man', who cared little for the riches and show of this world. His reputation was saintly rather than regal, and as a ruler he was weak, possibly even mentally defective, being easily manipulated by his strong-minded queen, Margaret of Anjou, and his factious magnates.

rival by force. Civil war broke out again and in September, 1460, after several indecisive battles, York marched on London and, in a move unpopular with both sides, claimed the crown for himself, basing his claim on the right of the heir-general over the heir-male. Parliament would not agree to his demand, but in October passed an Act of Accord which disinherited Prince Edward and recognised York as the King's heir.

This provoked an incensed Queen Margaret to decisive action, and on 30th December, 1460, York, his son Edmund, Earl of Rutland, and Salisbury were slain at the Battle of Wakefield. Two months later the Lancastrians scored another victory at St Albans, but York's claim had been inherited by his nineteen-year-old son, Edward, Earl of March, who secured London, had himself proclaimed king on 4th March, 1461, and annihilated the Queen's army at the bloody and decisive Battle of Towton on 29th March; Henry VI remained a fugitive until he was captured and imprisoned in the Tower in 1465. Edward returned to London where he was crowned King Edward IV on 28th June. The magnates willingly offered him fealty, and he quickly established himself as ruler of England, the first sovereign of the House of York.

The Wars of the Roses undoubtedly weakened the position of the Crown and created a political climate in which treachery flourished. Edward IV, however, would provide England with strong government, and during his reign trade and the arts flourished and many of his subjects grew prosperous. The conflict had touched the lives of the participants only, and had barely affected the country at large. Contemporary architecture was becoming less militaristic, as defensive castles were replaced by domestic manor houses around which moats were built for ornament rather than to keep out intruders. Only seven of the great aristocratic families became extinct as a result of the Wars of the Roses: there was no mass annihilation of the nobility, as has often been claimed.

Just one-tenth of the population lived in towns, for society was mainly rural. About 75,000 people lived in London, the largest city, which was by then firmly established as the political, commercial and cultural capital of England. In 1483 Dominic Mancini noted that

London merchants were extremely wealthy; this wealth came mainly from the importing of luxury goods from abroad. England's chief sources of foreign revenue were the wool and wool cloth trades with Flanders.

The English, however, hated foreigners, particularly the French. Their insularity was reflected in the growing sense of nationalism which during the fourteenth and fifteenth centuries had resulted in English replacing Norman French as the chief language of the realm. This in turn led to an increase in literacy amongst the people, so that in the early years of the sixteenth century Sir Thomas More could claim that more than 50 per cent of the population could read and write.

The late fifteenth century also saw a renewal of interest in the visual arts, particularly architecture, which led to the last flowering of the perpendicular style in England, to which St George's Chapel, Windsor, Eton College, King's College Chapel at Cambridge and the Henry VII Chapel in Westminster Abbey all bear witness.

While the aristocracy hankered after the old feudal ideals of order in society, the middle classes were rising in prominence and affluence and beginning to intermarry with the gentry classes. Most people, however, lived in mean dwellings and subsisted in poverty. Foreign observers described the ordinary working Englishman as gluttonous, work-shy and treacherous. Unfortunately, the law that required every able-bodied man to keep a weapon in readiness to assist his sovereign in an emergency frequently led to those same weapons being used on that sovereign's tax collectors, though there was no more violence or law-breaking in this period than at any other time in English mediaeval history.

From the beginning, Edward IV was a popular king. 'I am unable to declare how well the commons love him,' wrote one Londoner. 'Thus far he appears to be a just prince, and to mean to mend and organise matters otherwise than has been done hitherto.'

Edward was tall – his skeleton, found in 1789, measured 6 feet 3½ inches – brown-haired, broad-chested, well-built, always fashionably and extravagantly dressed, and, in the opinion of all observers, extraordinarily good looking. He was something of an exhibitionist, loving to show off his fine physique to onlookers. Yet he was courageous in battle, energetic, intelligent, witty, genial and unusually accessible to his subjects. Those who crossed him found that he was also ruthless, violent and terrifying when his temper was roused. His chief vices, according to the unanimous opinion of contemporary chroniclers, were avarice, extravagance and lechery.

Edward's promiscuity was notorious. Mancini tells us he was 'licentious in the extreme'. He would seduce a woman, use her, and then carelessly abandon her, often passing her on to his friends or other courtiers. 'He pursued with no discrimination the married and unmarried, the noble and lowly.' But he 'took none by force'. Money, promises and his own sex-appeal were invariably enough to conquer all resistance, 'and having conquered them, he dismissed them'. The names of his mistresses are rarely recorded but in the early 1460s he had an intermittent affair with Elizabeth Lucy (née Wayte), who bore him one, possibly two, children.

With his youth, looks and reputation, Edward IV was a prize for any princess in Europe and his marriageability was a considerable political asset. Warwick, now his chief magnate and councillor, urged a marriage alliance with France, whose king, Louis XI, had been lending support to Queen Margaret. But in September 1464, when the royal Council met at Reading Abbey to discuss a match with Louis' relative Bona of Savoy, whom Warwick had suggested as a bride, Edward stunned everyone present by announcing that he had been married since May to an English commoner whose name was Elizabeth Wydville.

Elizabeth was described by her enemies as being of lowly origins. The Wydvilles, who claimed descent from a Norman called William de Wydville and his wife Emma, a Saxon, were in fact an old family of minor gentry who had settled in Northamptonshire during the reign of Henry II. Their name is usually – and incorrectly – spelt Woodville, but that is a rare form in contemporary documents, in which it almost always appears as Wydville, Wydeville, Wydvil and Wydevile; on Elizabeth's tomb it is spelt Widville.

Elizabeth's grandfather, Richard Wydville I, distinguished himself fighting for Henry V in France, and his 'very greatly notable services' were rewarded with lands in that country, lucrative high offices, a knighthood and a seat on Henry VI's Council. His son, Richard Wydville II, born around 1405 and said by the French chronicler

Monstrelet to be the handsomest man in England, was knighted by Henry VI in 1426 and given his own command in France three years later. His family's chief residence at this time was a house called The Mote (rebuilt in the eighteenth century and now a Cheshire Home), east of Maidstone, Kent, and not far from Ightham where his aunt, Joan Wydville and her husband, Sir William Haute, owned a fine twelfth-century manor house still to be seen today.

In 1436 Sir Richard took the enormous liberty of marrying the Princess Jacquetta of Luxembourg, widow of Henry V's brother, the Duke of Bedford. Aged twenty and 'an exceedingly handsome woman', according to Monstrelet, she was the daughter of the French Count of St Pol and a descendant of Charlemagne. Bedford had married her two years before his death in 1435 because he wanted her brother's friendship. In 1436 she was therefore a desirable and rich widow, having inherited all her childless husband's estates. Her marriage to Sir Richard Wydville caused a resounding scandal. Her brother refused to have anything further to do with her, and Monstrelet says she and Richard 'could never visit the continent or her brother would have slain them both'. In England they were fined £1,000 for marrying without the King's consent, and raised the money by selling Bedford's lands. But Jacquetta still retained her title of Duchess of Bedford and ranked as first lady in the realm until Margaret of Anjou married Henry VI in 1445, at which time some of Jacquetta's lands were restored to her, including the manor of Grafton, Northamptonshire, where she and Richard settled. In 1449 he was raised to the peerage and created Baron Rivers.

Jacquetta and Richard had a large family – eight boys and eight girls, of whom Elizabeth, born around 1437, was the eldest. The family's loyalties had always been to the House of Lancaster; Elizabeth served as a maid-of-honour to Margaret of Anjou, and when she was about fifteen she was married to a well-born Lancastrian knight, Sir John Grey of Groby, and went to live with him on his estate at Bradgate, near Charnwood Forest, in Leicestershire. Here, probably, their two sons were born, Thomas around 1455 and Richard about a year later. When the Wars of the Roses broke out, Sir John was given command of Henry VI's cavalry but was killed at the Battle of Towton in 1461. Fortunately he escaped attainder and his lands were not confiscated, although his widow was not left comfortably off. Lord Rivers and his eldest son Anthony had also fought for Henry VI but had the presence of mind to change sides and declare for Edward IV, who, despite having taunted Rivers the year before about his lowly birth and his scandalous marriage, welcomed and pardoned them.

No-one knows when Edward IV first became attracted to Elizabeth Wydville, but all commentators agree that the marriage was based on lust. For years afterwards, rumours about the King's courtship persisted. Sir Thomas More stated that Elizabeth waylaid Edward in Whittlebury Forest, kneeling with a child on either side and begging for financial help so enchantingly that he was quite overcome with desire for her. Fabyan said that Duchess Jacquetta, reputedly a witch, had cast a spell on the King. It was even rumoured that when Elizabeth refused to become Edward's mistress he had threatened rape, whereupon she had made to kill herself with a dagger; appalled, the King had offered her marriage. None of these tales are substantiated by contemporary evidence. Polydore Vergil sums up the truth when he says that Edward was led into wedlock 'by blind affection and not by the rule of reason'. The fact that he arranged to marry Elizabeth in secret proves that he knew he was making an unsuitable match and boycotting a major political advantage. He must certainly have been aware that no king since the Conquest had married a commoner and that Warwick was deep in negotiation for a French marriage. But these things counted for very little against his passion for Elizabeth Wydville.

In the spring of 1464 Edward was on his way north to put down successfully a rising in favour of Henry VI. On the way he stayed at Stony Stratford, from whence he rode – on the pretext of going hunting – to Lord Rivers's manor at Grafton. Here, early in the morning of 1st May, he was married to Elizabeth, with only the priest, the Duchess of Bedford and three others as witnesses. Then the King went back to Stony Stratford and only returned late at night when, with her mother's connivance, Elizabeth came secretly to his bed. A little known contemporary French chronicler called du Clercq implies that this was not the first time they had slept together, but the English chroniclers are silent on the subject.

The marriage, predictably, proved to be very unpopular. Lord Wenlock told the Burgundian ambassador that the King's announcement of it had been the cause of 'great displeasure to many great lords, and especially to the larger part of all his Council'. Jean de Waurin, the

French chronicler, says the Council told the King to his face 'that she was not his match, however good and however fair she might be, and he must know well that she was no wife for a prince such as himself, for she was not the daughter of a duke or earl, but her mother had married a simple knight, so that though she was the child of a duchess and a niece of the Count of St Pol, still she was no wife for him'.

The marriage also caused divisions within the royal family. Mancini even asserted, some years later, that the King's own mother, the Duchess of York, 'fell into such a frenzy that she offered to submit to a public enquiry and asserted that Edward was not the offspring of her husband but was conceived in adultery, and therefore in no wise worthy of the honour of kingship'; this tale, however, features nowhere in contemporary accounts. Mancini says that both the King's younger brothers, the Dukes of Clarence and Gloucester, were 'sorely displeased at the marriage', especially Clarence, the King's heir-presumptive, who 'vented his wrath more conspicuously by his bitter and public denunciation of Elizabeth's obscure family'. Gloucester, 'being better at concealing his thoughts', kept quiet.

The person who was offended most by the marriage was Warwick, who had urged the French alliance. The Earl soon had further cause for anger because the King rapidly promoted Elizabeth's large and rapacious family, 'to the exaltation of the Queen and the displeasure of the whole realm'. This led to the creation of a powerful new faction at court which quickly came to rival the influence of the Nevilles.

The Wydvilles were never popular. Mancini says they were 'detested by the nobles because they, who were ignoble and newly-made men, were advanced beyond those who far excelled them in breeding and wisdom'. Elizabeth's father was created Earl Rivers, her son Thomas Grey was married to the King's niece and later made Marquess of Dorset, and her brother Lionel was appointed Bishop of Salisbury. Another brother, John, aged only twenty, made – according to a contemporary letter quoted in James Gardner's *Letters and Papers Illustrative of the Reigns of Richard III and Henry VII* – 'a diabolical marriage' with the aged Duchess of Norfolk, 'a slip of a girl' of sixty-seven. Most of Elizabeth's sisters made brilliant marriages amongst the nobility, including Katherine, whose resentful bridegroom was the Queen's ward, Henry Stafford, Duke of Buckingham, a descendant of Edward III. All of these marriages and elevations were made 'to the secret displeasure of the Earl of Warwick and the magnates of England'.

The divisions created by Edward IV's marriage to Elizabeth Wydville were therefore critical; they not only helped to bring about the eventual rift between Edward and Warwick, but they would also split the Yorkist party and lead directly to the downfall of the dynasty.

As for the woman who was the cause of all this havoc, her contemporaries observed that she was outwardly 'lovely looking and feminine smiling, neither too wanton nor too humble'. Humble she most certainly was not, but Mancini thought her 'an undistinguished woman promoted to exalted rank', while Sir Francis Bacon had no doubt that she was 'a busy and negotiating woman'. She was also wily, vengeful, arrogant, greedy and ruthless. All commentators, however, are agreed on her beauty: she was 'moderate of stature and well made', having very long pale gold hair and ice-blue eyes. Two remarkable portraits of her survive: one is a wooden panel in Queen's College, Cambridge (which she co-founded), which is a copy after an original of c.1464, possibly by John Stratford. The other is a stained-glass portrait, one of a series of Edward IV's family, in the Great North Window of Canterbury Cathedral. Crafted by William Neve around 1482, it was badly damaged by the Puritans in 1642, and the faces of the King and Queen are the only surviving originals; those of their children have been restored. Elizabeth's is striking in its beauty.

Elizabeth was crowned in 1465, and bore three daughters in succession – Elizabeth in 1466, Mary in 1467 and Cecily in 1469. Throughout these years relations between the King and Warwick deteriorated steadily, the situation worsening after 1468 when Edward, far from concluding the French alliance that Warwick still urged, made a treaty with the Duke of Burgundy, who married Edward's sister Margaret that year. Warwick, seeing his power corroded, began to intrigue against his master, and in 1469 he allied himself to Clarence, initially with a view to gaining control of the King and ruling through him.

Clarence was then twenty, tall, fair and regal. He had a surface charm and, according to Mancini, 'a mastery of popular eloquence', but these barely masked a weak, discontented and vicious character. Edward had been very generous to his brother, but Clarence was jealous of him and hungry for power. Warwick now bolstered Clarence's pretensions by offering to overthrow Edward, make him king, and marry him to Isabella, one of his two daughters who, as Warwick had no son, were the greatest heiresses in England. Edward had consistently refused requests to marry them by both his brothers, foreseeing that such alliances would enhance the already disconcerting power of the Nevilles, and naturally this had given Warwick further cause for grievance. In July 1469 Clarence openly defied the King and married Isabella in Calais. Then he and Warwick sailed back to England, where Edward IV was defeated and taken prisoner at the Battle of Edgecote. After this battle, Warwick had the Queen's father, Lord Rivers, and her brother, John Wydville, beheaded, and spread the story that Edward IV was a bastard, the son of Duchess Cecily and an archer called Blaybourne.

In late 1469, problems on the Scottish border engaged Warwick's attention and his resources and forced him to release Edward IV. By the spring of 1470 the King had regained control of the government and denounced Warwick and Clarence as traitors. They fled abroad and began plotting with Louis XI for the restoration of Henry VI. Warwick made an unlikely alliance with Margaret of Anjou, and together they invaded England on 13th September.

At that time, Queen Elizabeth was in the Tower of London, seven months pregnant with her fourth child. She had prepared a luxurious chamber in the royal apartments for her confinement, but was destined never to use it, for on 1st October she learned that the King and his brother Gloucester had fled to the Low Countries. Four days later Warwick and Clarence entered London, and the Queen secretly left the Tower to take refuge in the Sanctuary at Westminster Abbey. The feeble Henry VI was restored to the throne that same day and transferred from his prison in the Tower to the opulent rooms prepared for the Queen.

The Sanctuary was almost deserted when Elizabeth arrived with her three daughters and her mother, 'in great penury and forsaken of all friends'. But the Abbot of Westminster, Thomas Millyng, into whose charge the Queen entrusted herself, was a kindly man, placing the three best rooms in his own house at her disposal and providing her with several things 'for her comfort'. A London butcher, John Gould, donated half a beef and two muttons each week 'for the sustention of her household', and her Italian physician, Dr Serigo, visited regularly. These details are recorded in a letter written by Edward IV to the Lord Privy Seal in 1473. Yet for all these comforts Elizabeth was painfully aware that she was in what the chronicler John Warkworth called 'great trouble', and that there was an ever-present threat from the new régime.

It was not the most auspicious time to give birth, but on the night of 2nd November, 1470, 'she was lighted of a fair prince' whom she named Edward after his father. The Council had magnanimously paid Lady Scrope £20 to assist at the birth, and Old Mother Cobb, the Sanctuary midwife, delivered the child. His birthdate is verified by a later grant to him of the issues of the duchy of Cornwall, backdated to 2nd November, 1470, 'on which day he was born'. Edward came into the world, says Commines, 'in poor estate', and his baptism by the Sub-Prior of Westminster in the Abbot's House was carried out 'without pomp' and with no more ceremony than if he had been a poor man's son. The Abbot and Prior were godfathers, and the Duchess of Bedford and Lady Scrope godmothers.

The Queen and her children remained in the Sanctuary 'in the greatest jeopardy that ever they stood', according to the French chronicler Jean de Waurin, for five more months until, in March 1471, Edward IV, with financial aid from Burgundy, invaded England. Many rallied to his cause and, through the good offices of their mother, Edward was reconciled to his brother Clarence, who had now realised that there was little to be gained from supporting Henry VI. When he reached Dunstable, Edward sent a message to his wife to comfort her. Then he marched on London, which, on 11th April, opened its gates to him and declared its loyalty. Henry VI was deposed that same day and returned to prison in the Tower.

By the King's order the Queen and her children were brought that day from the Sanctuary to the Palace of Westminster, where they were reunited with him. *Fleetwood's Chronicle* describes how he comforted the Queen, who carried their son, 'wherewith she presented her husband, to his heart's singular comfort and gladness'. Edward kissed all his daughters 'full tenderly', and took the infant Prince, 'his greatest joy', in his arms, weeping as he did so. Then, after a night spent at Baynard's Castle, he had his wife and children escorted to the Tower for their own safety, for the realm was not yet won back. Warwick, Margaret of Anjou, and the heir to Lancaster were still at large.

On 14th April, Easter Sunday, Edward scored a victory at the Battle of Barnet, in which Warwick lost his life. Then the King marched west in pursuit of Queen Margaret, whose army he encountered at Tewkes-bury on 4th May. A bloody battle ensued, which resulted in the deaths of the last of the male Beauforts and the 17-year-old Prince Edward of Lancaster. Most contemporary sources state the Prince was killed in the battle, but Croyland says he died 'either on the field or after the battle by the avenging hands of certain persons'. Vergil says that Gloucester, Clarence and Lord Hastings killed him in the King's presence. This may well be true, and would explain Croyland's reticence in naming names, especially that of Edward IV.

After the battle Margaret of Anjou was taken prisoner, being later ransomed by Louis XI. She returned to France, where she died in poverty in 1482.

On 21st May Edward IV entered London in triumph, to an enthusi-astic reception. Commines says this was due to three things: the birth of an heir to York, the hopes of the City merchants that he would now be able to repay the loans he had forced them to give him, and the efforts of 'the ladies of quality and rich citizens' wives, with whom he had formerly intrigued', who 'forced their husbands to declare them-selves on his side'.

Edward had come into his own again; the immediate threat from Lancaster had been removed and all was set fair for a period of stable government. Later that year he would create his son Prince of Wales and Earl of Chester (he had been Duke of Cornwall at his birth), and would handsomely reward Abbot Millyng, Butcher Gould, Mother Cobb and Dr Serigo, all of whom had succoured his queen during her stay in sanctuary.

When Edward IV returned to London that May there was just one unpleasant task remaining to be done – one that could not wait.

3
Richard of Gloucester

In May, 1471, Henry VI was still a prisoner in the Tower of London, and it was here, according to the reliable contemporary chronicler John Warkworth, that he was 'put to death, the xxi day of May, being a Tuesday night, between eleven and twelve of the clock, being then at the Tower the Duke of Gloucester, brother to King Edward, and many other. And on the morrow he was chested and brought to [St] Paul's, and his face was open that every man might see him, and in his lying he bled on the pavement there. And afterwards at the Black Friars was brought, and there he bled new and fresh. And from thence he was carried to Chertsey Abbey in a boat, and buried there in Our Lady's chapel.'

The murder of Henry VI was committed in strict secrecy, and it was given out officially by the Government that, upon learning of the death of his son and the capture of his wife, he had taken 'to so great despite, ire and indignation that, of pure displeasure and melancholy he died'. This fooled no one. A corpse that bled profusely on the pavement had not died of displeasure, as anyone could see. And that Henry VI died violently was borne out by the examination of his remains in 1910: the medical report in *Archaeologia* states that his skull was 'much broken', as if it had been crushed by a blow, and still had attached to it some hair, 'apparently matted with blood'. There was, both in 1910 and in 1471, little doubt in anyone's mind that Henry VI had been murdered. The Milanese ambassador in England informed the King of France almost at once that Edward IV had 'caused King Henry to be secretly assassinated at the Tower. He has, in short, chosen to crush the seed.'

Croyland, writing in 1486, says, with his usual reticence: 'I shall say nothing about the discovery of King Henry's lifeless body in the Tower of London. May God have mercy upon, and give time for repentance to, him, whoever he may be, who dared to lay sacrilegious hands on the Lord's Anointed! Let the doer merit the name of tyrant.' Croyland's use of the word 'tyrant' must mean that he is referring to a ruler, namely Edward IV, who had without doubt given the order for Henry VI's murder. But, as the Great Chronicle states, 'the common fame went that the Duke of Gloucester was not altogether guiltless', and Warkworth's significant mention of Gloucester's presence in the Tower on the night of the murder seems to infer that the Duke was somehow implicated – otherwise, why mention him at all? Commines says that Gloucester 'killed this good man with his own hands, or at least had him killed in his presence in some hidden, obscure place'; Carmeliano, in 1486, made a similar accusation, and John Rous, writing before 1490, stated that Gloucester 'caused others to kill the holy man, or, as many think, did so by his own hand'. Fabyan has Gloucester stabbing Henry with a dagger, while Vergil says he 'killed him with a sword, whereby his brother might be delivered from all fear of hostility'. And More says that Richard slew Henry VI 'without commandment or knowledge of the King'. All these writers found it credible that Gloucester had been guilty of committing the murder.

Bernard André alone stated what was probably nearest the truth – that Gloucester arranged the murder of Henry VI at Edward IV's command. Only the King himself could have given the order for the killing in cold blood of a crowned and anointed monarch, whose death would give him such a political advantage. Gloucester, as Constable of England, would have had the duty of conveying those orders to the Tower and ensuring that they were carried out. Thus far he was almost certainly involved in the murder.

We should pause now to consider why people believed that this young duke was capable of regicide, and to trace his early life and the development of his character. Richard Plantagenet, youngest son of the Duke of York, was born on 2nd October, 1452, at Fotheringhay Castle. John Rous's hostile account of his life describes him as coming into the world, after two years in his mother's womb, with teeth, long hair to his shoulders, a humped back, and his right shoulder higher than his left. More repeats these details, adding cautiously that 'either men of hatred report the truth, or else nature changed her course in his beginning'. It is of course quite possible that Richard was born with teeth and long hair and deformities, and that there was some truth in what Rous and More wrote, but it seems likelier that over the years some embroidery had been added to the tale for dramatic effect.

The new baby seems to have been a weakling: 'Richard liveth yet,' recorded the anonymous annalist in the *Chronicle of William of Worcester*, with apparent surprise. However, Richard survived the perils of early childhood and seems to have spent his younger years in the company of his elder brother George, in the care of their mother at Fotheringhay. After Edward IV's accession in 1461, Richard was created Duke of Gloucester and sent to receive a knightly education in the household of the Earl of Warwick, which was based mainly at Middleham Castle in Yorkshire. Here, Richard's companions included Warwick's daughters, Isabella and Anne, and the Earl's ward, Francis Lovell, who would remain a lifelong friend. Here, too, Richard learned the arts of warfare and the skills required by a nobleman, as well as receiving some rudimentary training in law.

During the 1460s Edward IV did little for his youngest brother, heaping honours instead upon George, whom he had created Duke of Clarence and brought to court. But it was Richard who stayed loyal to the King when Warwick and Clarence turned traitor in 1469. Richard was then appointed Lord High Admiral of England, Chief Justice of the Welsh Marches, and Chief Constable of England, a post he had held briefly in childhood. He was also given other honours and offices in Wales and the duchy of Lancaster. The following year he replaced the disgraced Warwick as Chief Steward and Chamberlain of South Wales, thus becoming the King's chief representative in the principality. Later that year Richard accompanied Edward IV into exile, and after Edward's restoration in 1471 was rewarded for his loyalty with yet more offices, replacing Warwick as Great Chamberlain of England and becoming Chief Steward of the duchy of Lancaster.

Richard was essentially the child of a violent age, born to a legacy of civil war. His childhood and formative years were overshadowed by battles, treachery and violent death. When he was eight his father and his brother Edmund were killed in battle. He grew to maturity in an uncertain and insecure world, and twice suffered the agony of exile. He saw his brother the King betrayed by their brother Clarence and by Warwick, who had been as a father to Richard. It is therefore fair to say that by the age of eighteen he had become hardened to violence and treachery, and had developed a ruthless streak in his character.

Gloucester first saw battle himself at Barnet in 1471, where he acquitted himself well leading the vanguard of the royal forces, showing considerable ability in warfare whilst in the thick of the fighting. He also fought brilliantly at Tewkesbury, for which he received yet more lands by way of reward. It was after Tewkesbury that Gloucester's ruthlessness first became apparent, when, as Constable of England, he exercised his right to sentence to summary execution, without trial or witnesses, the last Beaufort Duke of Somerset and other Lancastrians, including one in holy orders who was entitled to immunity from the death penalty. These unfortunate men had been forcibly dragged from sanctuary in Tewkesbury Abbey on Gloucester's orders. Some writers have also implicated Gloucester in the death of Prince Edward of Lancaster, as we have seen. Within a month of this, the Duke had assisted in the murder of Henry VI. Whether he struck the fatal blow or not, Gloucester, at the impressionable age of eighteen, must have learned from this a useful lesson about the advantages of political murder, and would have been shown a clear precedent for the elimination of a king by violence.

Richard of Gloucester was typical of the magnates of the period: acquisitive, hungry for wealth, land and power, brave in battle, tough, ruthless, energetic, and keenly interested in warfare, heraldry, and the manly pursuits such as hunting and hawking. He was staunchly loyal to the King and to his own supporters and followers, but did not scruple to ride rough-shod over the rights of other people. Ambition drove him. Mancini, writing in 1483, says that from the first 'there were those who were not unaware of his ambition and cunning, and who had misgivings about where they would lead'.

Gloucester also courted popularity, and worked hard all his adult life to win it. He was an able man, and had some good qualities: he was hard-working and conscientious in his duties. He also had that in him that inspired the loyalty of others, and his fair share of the charisma of the Plantagenets. Croyland states he had a quick, alert and 'overweening' mind, that he was courageous and daring, and that he had 'a sharp wit [and] courage high and fierce'.

In his youth he was amorous; he acknowledged two bastards, who were probably born before 1472. One was John of Pontefract, or of Gloucester, knighted in 1483, who was still under age in 1485 when his father appointed him Captain of Calais, calling him 'our dear son, whose quickness of mind and agility of body, and inclination to all good customs give us great hope of his good service for the future'. The other was Katherine, who was generously dowered by Richard when she married William Herbert, Earl of Huntingdon, in 1484. A mysterious Richard Plantagenet of Eastwell in Kent, of whom more will be heard later, is also thought to have been a bastard son of Richard's, and there may have been four others, including one Stephen Hawes, but the evidence for these is unreliable.

Conflicting descriptions of Richard left by his contemporaries have given rise to yet another controversy surrounding him – what did he look like? The consensus of opinion was that, unlike Edward IV and Clarence, he resembled his father, being dark-haired and short of stature. This lack of height is attested to by most writers, as is the slightness of his body. The Scots envoy, Archibald Whitelaw, who saw Richard in 1484, noted he had 'such a small body', while the Silesian knight, Nicholas von Poppelau, who also met Richard that year, commented on how lean he was. Later, John Rous would sneer at his 'little body and feeble strength', while Vergil, whose description was said to be based on the testimony of those who had known Richard, said he was 'deformed'.

It is this question of deformity that has long puzzled historians. In Richard's lifetime no writer made reference to any: Croyland, Commines and the *Great Chronicle* make no mention of deformity, neither do the two earlier eyewitnesses, Whitelaw and von Poppelau. The Elizabethan antiquarian John Stow told Sir George Buck 'he had spoken with old and grave men who had often seen Richard, and they had affirmed he was not deformed but of person and bodily shape comely enough', which is slightly at variance with the eyewitness reports. In 1491, moreover, York Civic Records record that in the course of a fight a schoolmaster called John Payntour called Richard a 'Crouchback', the first instance of him being referred to by what later became a popular nickname. Richard had often been in York and was well-known there. Perhaps Master Payntour was merely being provocative, but it is quite possible that he had seen Richard and knew there was no longer any need for tact.

As the Tudor period drew on, so the legend of the deformed king was elaborated upon. Rous, writing before 1490, stated that he had 'unequal' shoulders, 'the right higher and the left lower', and a humped back. In Vergil's account it is the left shoulder that is 'higher than the right'. More, who also claimed one shoulder was higher than the other, echoed Vergil. The eyewitness von Poppelau wrote of Richard's 'delicate arms and limbs'; by More's time it was believed that he had been 'ill featured of limbs' and 'crook-backed', with a 'shrivelled withered arm'.

To contemporary eyes, physical deformity was the outward manifestation of evil character. Thus portraits of Richard, held to have been painted with the aim of flattering him, were altered in Tudor times to reflect what people believed he had really looked like. The earliest representation of him is the line drawing by John Rous in the first *York Roll*, which shows no deformity. Then there are three portrait types, of which several versions exist. The earliest is in the collection of the Society of Antiquaries of London, a masterful and evidently faithful copy of an original believed to have been from life, which has been tree-ring dated to c.1516–22. In this, Richard has no apparent deformity.

The second portrait type is that in the Royal Collection, which has been tree-ring dated to c.1518–23. This is the most important of the three as it was the one on display in the royal palaces, which is probably why it was radically altered. X-rays taken in the 1950s and 1973 show that the right shoulder has been overpainted above the still-visible original shoulder line by a later hand, and that the eyes have been narrowed. About thirty copies of this portrait are in existence, including that in the National Portrait Gallery, and all show the added deformities.

The third likeness is also in the collection of the Society of Antiquaries, and is entitled the 'Broken Sword' portrait; this has been tree-ring dated to c.1533–43. Again, X-rays show drastic alterations. The portrait originally had a much-raised left shoulder and deformed left arm, but in the seventeenth or eighteenth centuries, it was altered to show Richard with a more normal appearance. A copy of this portrait, unaltered and showing the left arm ending in a stump, was sold in 1921 in Brussels to a private collector.

Richard's face in his portraits matches the descriptions given by Rous and Vergil, the latter writing that he had 'a short and sour countenance', and also More, who said he was 'hard-featured of visage'. It is a stern face, with cold eyes and a thin-lipped, tightly pursed mouth, a portrait of a man looking older than his years.

So what was the truth about Richard's appearance? It would appear that he did have some slight deformity which eyewitnesses either did not notice or were too tactful to refer to overtly. It is possible that he suffered a mild form of Sprengel's deformity, or under-development of the right or left scapula leading to inefficient flexing of the shoulder muscles. There must, after all, have been some grain of truth in what the early Tudor chroniclers wrote, for there were many people still alive who could have pointed out any gross anomalies in their works, people who remembered Richard well. Nevertheless, as memories faded and the years passed, the truth became more distorted, until by 1534 it was generally accepted that he had been a villainous hunchback with a withered arm. And there were then few of his contemporaries still alive to pour scorn on such nonsense.

In 1471, Gloucester and Clarence were reconciled to each other, but not for long. In Clarence's household lived his wife's younger sister, Anne Neville, who, with Isabella, was co-heiress to their father, the late Earl of Warwick. Warwick had not been attainted, and his titles and estates should therefore have passed to his widow, Anne Beauchamp, who was entitled to a third share, and to his two daughters, the remainder being divided equally between them. But Edward IV had seized control of the Warwick inheritance and divided it up, giving some lands and offices to Clarence, in right of his wife, and some to Gloucester, whilst ignoring the rights of the Dowager Countess. Clarence, who had received the lion's share, felt he should have all, and was therefore mortified when in 1471 Richard made it plain that he wanted to marry Anne Neville and claim half her patrimony. 'This, ' wrote Croyland, 'did not suit the plans of the Duke of Clarence, since he feared a division of the Earl's property.' He knew very well that marriage to Anne would entitle Richard to half the Warwick inheritance, and this made him determined to prevent the marriage. 'In consequence of this, violent dissensions arose between the brothers.'

Anne Neville was then fifteen. She had been briefly married, almost certainly in name only, to Prince Edward of Lancaster, and since his death she had been living in Clarence's great London house, The Erber, in Downegate Street near the Thames. 'In presence she was seemly, amiable and beauteous, and in conditions full commendable and right virtuous and, according to the interpretation of Anne her name, full gracious,' wrote Rous, who revered Anne as Warwick's daughter. There is a drawing of her in royal heraldic robes in the Rous *Roll*, which shows a slender woman with long fair hair. Richard had known Anne in youth at Middleham, and the Flemish chronicler Majerres claims he became close to her then, yet his motive for marrying her was not so much love as the desire to acquire her lands. Neither Richard nor Clarence would show any regard at any time for the vociferously voiced claims of the Countess of Warwick, who had been illegally deprived by the King of her dower. To men like these, she simply did not count.

Croyland tells us that Clarence was so determined that Gloucester should not marry Anne Neville that he 'caused the damsel to be concealed in order that it might not be known by his brother where she was. Still, however, the craftiness of the Duke of Gloucester so far prevailed that, having discovered the girl dressed as a kitchen maid in London, he had her moved to the Sanctuary of St Martin's', near Newgate. Clarence demanded that Anne be returned to his house, but he was not her legal guardian and was powerless to prevent Richard from placing her in the care of her uncle, the Archbishop of York.

'At last,' wrote Croyland, 'their most loving brother the King agreed to act as mediator, and the whole misunderstanding was set to rest.' A private war, however, had only just been averted. A seething Clarence had to agree to the carving-up of the Warwick estates, even though he received the greater share of them and was created Earl of Warwick and Salisbury in right of his wife. Gloucester, in turn, was, on marriage, to receive Warwick's estates in Yorkshire, Northumberland and Cumberland, where he would inherit the loyalty and service of those who had served the Nevilles.

Richard and Anne were married in the spring or summer of 1472 at Westminster, either in the Abbey or in St Stephen's Chapel. Richard was so anxious for the marriage to go forward that he did not wait for a papal dispensation – which was necessary, as he and Anne were second cousins. After the wedding the couple lived chiefly at Middleham Castle, a massive eleventh-century stronghold on high ground over-looking the River Ure in Yorkshire, which had been previously owned and enlarged by the Nevilles. Although primarily built for defence, the castle was in Richard's day extremely comfortable, with luxurious private apartments, fireplaces in the domestic ranges, and communal latrines. The Duke himself built a new great hall with spacious windows above the old keep. There was a chapel, and plenty of accommodation for the many scores of retainers a royal duke needed in his retinue. Middleham is now a ruin, but enough remains to give a good impression of the splendour that once earned it the name 'the Windsor of the North'.

We know nothing at all about Richard and Anne's personal life, nor whether they were happily or unhappily married, nor what they felt about each other. Anne's health seems to have been delicate, and they had one child only, named Edward of Middleham after the place of his birth, who was probably born in the spring of 1476, as Rous states he was seven and a half in August 1483. He seems to have been a frail boy as he rarely left Middleham, where he was nursed as a baby by one Jane Collins, who earned 100s. per annum, and he was later tutored by a Master Richard Bernall.

In the summer of 1473 Gloucester arranged for his mother-in-law, the Countess of Warwick, to join the household at Middleham. This unfortunate lady, still in her forties, had been living in the Sanctuary at Beaulieu Abbey in Hampshire since Warwick's death, occupying herself by sending urgent petitions for the restoration of her lands to the King, the Queen, the King's mother the Duchess of York, and even the young Princess Elizabeth, but to no avail. On 13th June, 1473, the *Paston Letters* record that 'the Countess is now out of Beaulieu sanctuary, and Sir James Tyrell conveyeth her northward, men say by the King's assent'. Tyrell was one of Richard's most trusted retainers. Rous later stated that the Countess had fled to Gloucester 'as her chief refuge', only to find herself 'locked up for the duration of his life'. As Rous had always taken such a particular interest in the Beauchamp and Neville families, and made it his business to record their deeds, it is quite possible that this was the Countess's fate. Certainly she made no public appearances after this time. Indeed, both Gloucester and Clarence were instrumental in bringing about the passing, in 1474, of an Act of

35

Parliament settling all the Warwick estates upon themselves in right of their spouses, and ignoring the rights of the Dowager Countess, who was deemed to be 'naturally' and legally dead. Gloucester had now learned another valuable political lesson: that Parliament could be manipulated to pass legislation that took no account of the principles of established law.

4

Clarence and the Wydvilles

Edward IV may have been a licentious man, but his court was decorous and ceremonious. From the beginning his aim was to emulate Burgundy, whose court was then the model for Europe. Thereafter, for several decades, Burgundian influence was to be detected in all aspects of court life.

Visually, Edward's court was magnificent – a Bohemian visitor, Gabriel Tetzel, described it in 1466 as 'the most splendid court that could be found in all Christendom'. The King favoured and refurbished the palaces of the Thames Valley – Westminster, the Tower, Greenwich, Sheen, Eltham and Windsor. In all of these he made extravagant improvements, patronising architects, stonemasons, sculptors, glaziers, silversmiths, goldsmiths, jewellers and merchants dealing in luxury goods such as tapestries and fabrics. Hence the royal palaces were supplied with everything 'in such costly measure', says Tetzel, 'that it is unbelievable that it could be provided'. Rich cloth of Arras adorned the walls, the tables were set with fine napery and gold, silver and gilt plate, chairs and cushions were upholstered in velvet and damask, beds covered with sheets of fine holland cloth and counterpanes of crimson damask or cloth of gold trimmed with ermine. In summer there were elaborate picnics by the river, with tables set up in the gardens under the trees; courtiers could shade themselves in silken tents, and watch the King and his guests glide past along the river in gilded barges: from these issued the music for which Edward's court was renowned. Croyland tells us that the court presented 'no other appearance than such as fully befits a most mighty kingdom filled with riches'.

Court etiquette was very formal and a strict code of courtesy prevailed. Banquets could last three hours and more, and on one occasion the Queen kept her ladies on their knees throughout while she and her guests ate in silence. Even her own mother had to stand until the Queen had been served the first course. On state occasions, and at the Christmas and Easter courts, the King and Queen always appeared wearing their crowns.

All of this had to be paid for. Although the expenses of his court were actually less in real terms than those of any previous mediaeval English monarch, Edward IV borrowed thousands of pounds from financiers of the City of London and Italian merchant bankers, and pawned some jewels, but in the end stringent economies had to be enforced. These were laid down in the *Black Book of the Household* in 1471–2 and made Edward rather unpopular, for from thenceforth household supplies such as wood for fires, torches, candles, rushes for floors, straw for mattresses, food, wine and ale were rationed, the duties of servants strictly delineated, and restrictions placed on the number of servants a nobleman might bring to court: a duke was allowed twelve, a baron only four.

By the early 1470s Edward IV was already carrying out the duties of kingship in a suitably magnificent setting. He was well aware of the political value of lavish display, but during the latter years of his reign there were fewer extravagant ceremonies at court and in public.

The King's needs were looked after by the officers of the royal household, which was at the core of the court, but many of these posts were sinecures held by the great magnates and delegated to lesser mortals. Then there were in attendance the royal councillors, the civil servants, the domestic servants, visiting nobles, foreign ambassadors and visitors, the ladies and officers of the Queen's household, and a whole army of petitioners seeking favours from the King. The purchasing and purveying of influence, grace and favour were the main business of the court. Thus ambitious magnates battled for supremacy in an atmosphere charged with vicious competitiveness and ruthless ambition.

At the centre of this circle of patronage was the King, to whom all sought access. This was usually granted only after receipt of a written request. The King was seen as the fount of all honours and benefits, but Edward was shrewd and only rewarded those who were prepared to serve him well; there were few time-servers at his court. To his credit, he did not allow his many mistresses any political power, nor did he advance his bastards, but he had promoted and favoured the Wydvilles and in the eyes of many that was thought just as bad, especially since, in the years after 1471, their influence was extended to encompass the heir to the throne.

In June 1471, Elizabeth Darcy was appointed Lady Mistress of the newly-created Prince of Wales' nursery, and Avice Welles was given the post of nurse. On 3rd July, the King commanded his chief magnates to swear an oath of allegiance to the Prince as 'the very undoubted son and heir of our sovereign lord'. Forty-seven lords gave their oath, foremost amongst them being the Dukes of Clarence, Gloucester and Buckingham. Five days later the King issued Letters Patent appointing a council that would be responsible for the administration of his son's household and estates until he reached the age of fourteen, his expected majority. Its members comprised the Queen, Clarence, Gloucester and a panel of bishops. Sir Thomas Vaughan was given the office of Prince's Chamberlain; his duty was to walk behind the King, carrying the young Edward in his arms, on ceremonial occasions. Vaughan would remain with Edward for most of his life, offering him dedicated service, and it appears that his charge became very close to him.

In 1473, when he was three, the Prince of Wales' household was permanently established at Ludlow Castle on the Welsh Marches. On 23rd September that year a series of ordinances governing the Prince's upbringing and education were drawn up. Although the régime was rather strict for so young a child, these ordinances reveal the tender love felt by the King for his son, and in some respects they show an enlightened approach to child-rearing. The Prince was to rise each morning 'at a convenient hour according to his age', and attend Matins and mass before breakfast. Before dinner he was to be instructed 'in such virtuous learning as his age shall suffer to receive'. This included listening to 'such noble stories as behoveth a prince to understand and know'. Afternoons were to be spent in physical activity and the acquiring of the knightly arts such as horsemanship, swordsmanship, tossing the quintain and 'such convenient disports and exercises as behoveth his estate to have experience in'. After Vespers and supper, the Prince was allowed some time for play, when he could indulge in 'such honest disports as shall be conveniently devised for his recreation'. Until he was twelve, he was sent to bed at 8.00 pm; from 1482, he was allowed to stay up until 9.00 pm. His tutors and servants were sensibly exhorted 'to enforce themselves to make him merry and joyous towards his bed', and once he was asleep a watch was kept over him throughout the night in case sudden illness carry off 'God's precious sending and gift' and the King's 'most desired treasure'. No 'swearer, brawler, backbiter, common hazarder or adulterer' was ever to be allowed into the household; Edward IV was taking no chances.

On 10th November, 1473, the Prince's maternal uncle, Anthony Wydville, Earl Rivers, then aged thirty-one, was appointed his Governor, a post which made him effective ruler of Wales; Rivers was also preferred to the Prince's newly-formed Council, commissioned in the names of Edward and his mother to govern and restore order to the Welsh Marches on behalf of the King. The Council was nominally accountable to the Prince, but the man with real power was its Lord President, John Alcock, Bishop of Worcester (later Bishop of Ely), who had served briefly as Lord Chancellor of England in 1475 and was a founder of Jesus College, Cambridge. Alcock had also been given responsibility for the Prince's education, and tutored him personally. The faithful Sir Thomas Vaughan was appointed Treasurer to the Prince, and continued to care for the child's daily needs, there being no women at Ludlow. Edward's half-brother, Sir Richard Grey, was also on his Council, as was his mother's relative, Sir Richard Haute.

For the next ten years, says Mancini, the growing Prince lived at Ludlow, and 'devoted himself to horses and dogs and other useful exercises to invigorate his body'. The castle was his chief residence, but he spent time also at the manor of Tickenhill at Bewdley, which his father had had prepared as a kind of holiday retreat for him. He was exceptionally lucky in his governor and uncle, who was not only as powerful a figure in the Welsh Marches as Gloucester was in the north, but also, states Mancini, 'a kindly, serious and just man, and one tested by every vicissitude of life. Whatever his prosperity, he had injured nobody, though benefiting many, and therefore he had entrusted to him the care and direction of the King's son.' Rivers and his late father, reported the Milanese ambassador, were 'men of very great valour'. More thought Rivers to be a man of honour. To his contemporaries, he was indeed the very mirror of Chaucer's 'parfait, gentil knight' – brave, chivalrous, cultivated, elegant, charming, pious and well-educated, and his feats in the jousting lists were renowned.

Rivers was a very religious man, even an ascetic one, for he wore a hair shirt beneath his rich robes. During his early years at Ludlow he translated three devotional works from Latin to French; this work, entitled *The Dictes and Sayings of the Philosophers*, was in 1476 the first book to be printed in England by William Caxton, whose patron Rivers was. Rivers' piety also led him to write poetry about the seven deadly sins, and to go on several pilgrimages abroad. He had travelled all over Europe, visiting several Italian cities including Rome, and the shrine of St James of Compostella in Spain; Pope Sixtus IV had been sufficiently impressed by him to appoint him Defender and Director of Papal Causes in England.

Rivers added to these talents his abilities as a military and naval commander and as a diplomat. But he was first and foremost a Wydville, loyal to his sister and her faction, and his appointment as Governor of the Prince, together with the careful selection of the members of the Council of the Marches, meant that young Edward would grow to maturity firmly under Wydville control, influenced by his mother's supporters throughout his formative years. As More commented, 'In effect, everyone as he was nearest of kin unto the Queen, so was planted next about the prince, whereby her blood might of youth be rooted in the Prince's favour.' And that is exactly what happened.

On 17th August, 1473, Queen Elizabeth bore a second son at the Dominican Friary in Shrewsbury (a fourth daughter, Margaret, had died in infancy the previous year). This new prince was called Richard, and he was created Duke of York in 1474, thus setting a precedent for the tradition that the second son of an English monarch is usually given this title. Soon, more children joined the royal nursery: Anne in 1475, George (who died at the age of two) in 1477, Katherine in 1479, and Bridget in 1480. This last princess was dedicated to religion from her infancy, and entered Dartford Priory at the age of seven.

In 1475, Edward IV appointed the Prince of Wales Guardian of the Realm during his coming absence in France which was to last from 4th

July to 20th September; the Queen was granted £2,200 yearly for the maintenance of her eldest son whilst he lived at court. The Prince made a state entry into London on 12th May, and was knighted by his father on Whitsunday at the Palace of Westminster. In France, Edward IV concluded with Louis XI the Treaty of Picquigny, which provided for the betrothal of Edward's eldest daughter Elizabeth of York to the Dauphin of France. Commines says that the King and Queen were delighted with the match, anticipating that Elizabeth would have a glorious future as queen of France. Henceforth they had her dressed in the French style and addressed as Madame la Dauphine.

A year later the Prince of Wales' marriage came under consideration, when Edward IV opened negotiations with Ferdinand and Isabella, the joint sovereigns of a newly-united Spain, for the hand of their daughter and heiress, the Infanta Isabella. These dragged on for two years until Isabella was superseded in the succession by her brother Juan, born in 1478; seeing her political value diminished, Edward IV lost interest. His next choice was the daughter of the late Duke of Milan, but the Duke's widow, Bianca of Savoy, was against the match, so the King had to abandon it.

The Prince of Wales and his younger siblings were not the only children born into the House of York during the 1470s. The Duchess of Clarence's first child had died at birth, but in 1473 she bore a daughter Margaret, and in 1475 a son Edward, who was styled Earl of Warwick in right of his mother. A fourth child, Richard, arrived on 6th October, 1476 in the new infirmary at Tewkesbury Abbey in Gloucestershire, but – according to the *Tewkesbury Abbey Chronicle* – his mother never recovered from the birth. By 12th November she was so ill that she was taken home to Warwick Castle to die. She lingered until 21st December, and her infant son followed her to the grave on 1st January. After lying in state for thirty-five days, the Duchess's body was buried in a new vault behind the high altar of Tewkesbury Abbey, near her Beauchamp forefathers.

The loss of his wife merely added to Clarence's woes. He was royal, he was wealthy, he had been given by the King his splendid London house, The Erber, and his household numbered nearly 300 persons and cost £4,000 yearly at that time to run. Yet all this was not enough. He still burned with resentment because Gloucester had received so much of the Warwick inheritance; it was Gloucester who held sway in the north where once the Nevilles had ruled, whereas Clarence was baulked of power by the King, who would not even let him go to Ireland to fulfil his duties as Lord Lieutenant. It does not seem to have occurred to him that he had given Edward no cause to trust him, and that he had been lucky to be forgiven for his earlier treachery.

Gloucester's power was not the only reason for Clarence's dissatisfaction. At court, the Wydvilles held sway, and in Wales, that other potential power base, their influence was paramount. It was obvious to Clarence that he was politically isolated and that the King had no intention of allowing him more than the semblance of power. In 1477, to make matters even worse, Edward IV thwarted Clarence's attempt to marry the young Mary of Burgundy, whose father, Duke Charles the Bold, had been killed at the battle of Nancy, leaving her sole heiress to that great duchy. As Mary's husband, Clarence would be Duke of Burgundy and ruler of a powerful continental principality. Edward IV had no intention of allowing this to happen, and urged Mary's marriage to Maximilian of Austria. Croyland says that this 'increased Clarence's displeasure still further' and that from now on the brothers 'each began to look upon the other with no very fraternal eyes'.

What really lay behind Edward's aversion to the match was his knowledge that Mary of Burgundy had a claim to the English throne through her grandmother Isabella of Portugal, a granddaughter of John of Gaunt. There was also, according to Rous and Vergil, a popular prophecy then in circulation, which foretold that 'G' should follow 'E' to the throne. Both writers say that Edward was much troubled by this prophecy, since Clarence's name was George. Then Queen Elizabeth added fuel to the fire when she proposed her brother Rivers as a husband for Mary of Burgundy, a proposal that was treated with contempt by the Burgundian court. But when Clarence, abandoning his suit, proposed to marry a Scottish princess, Edward refused to grant permission for that also.

Clarence was not the man to take this kind of treatment meekly. He retaliated by striking at the Queen, and the Rolls of Parliament record how he set about doing this. In the spring of 1477, Elizabeth Wydville had in her service a woman called Ankarette Twynho, a respectable widow of good family who had previously served the late Duchess of

Clarence. On 12th April, without any warrant, 100 of Clarence's retainers dragged Ankarette from her home near Frome in Somerset, seized her valuables, and shut her up in the jail at Warwick. Three days later she was brought before the justices at Warwick Guildhall and accused of having administered 'a venomous drink mixed with poison' to the Duchess, and also of being the means whereby the Queen had used sorcery to bewitch her sister-in-law and so help to bring about her death. The jury, intimidated by Clarence, duly found the helpless Ankarette guilty as charged, and she was taken that same day to the public gallows and hanged, pitifully protesting her innocence. With her suffered John Thoresby of Warwick for allegedly poisoning the Duchess's baby.

The allegations made by Clarence against Ankarette Twynho were so patently fabricated, and so touched the Queen's reputation and honour that retribution was inevitable. Furthermore, Clarence had debased royal justice by his unlawful arrest and murder of his victims. Yet the Council, well aware that his real target was the Queen and at the same time fearful of scandal, did its best to suppress the truth.

The Wydvilles had never had any reason to love Clarence. He had denounced the King's marriage, and been responsible with Warwick for the executions of the Queen's father and brother John in 1469. It was hardly surprising therefore that the Wydvilles quickly retaliated with a counter-charge of sorcery against Clarence, and that the King decided to give his brother a taste of his own bitter medicine as a warning.

Early in May, 1477, Edward IV ordered the arrest of Dr John Stacey, an Oxford clerk and astronomer of sinister reputation. After lengthy questioning and torture, Stacey revealed that Thomas Burdett, a member of Clarence's household, had asked him to cast the horoscopes of the King and the Prince of Wales, with a view to predicting when they might die. Evidently the forecast was unsatisfactory, as before long the two men were allegedly 'moulding leaden images' of Edward and his son in order to bring about their deaths by black magic. Of course, the implication was that Clarence was the prime mover in the plot, but the King did not as yet go so far as to arrest his own brother. Stacey and Burdett were arraigned and condemned as a warning to him, and were executed on 20th May at Tyburn, Burdett declaring, 'Behold I die, but I did none of these things.' Clarence, by-passing the

King, had protested their innocence before the Council but was ignored; instead, the Council declared that the evidence against Ankarette Twynho would be re-examined.

Clarence should have been warned, but rushed headlong into further trouble. He began by publicly denouncing the King as a bastard and a necromancer, and alleging that Edward's marriage to Elizabeth Wydville was null and void because tradition forbade kings of England to marry widows. Clarence then incited, or became involved in, a minor rebellion in the eastern counties against the King, and rumour had it in Europe that he was plotting with Louis XI to help Margaret of Anjou invade England. There may have been no truth in this, but it did not help matters. Finally, Clarence attacked the Queen, openly accusing her of having murdered his duchess by poison and sorcery, and pointedly refusing to eat or drink anything at court.

The King, with astonishing forbearance, turned a blind eye on all these things, probably realising that Clarence would soon enough become the victim of his own follies. Few took him seriously, and he had very little real power. But when Edward went to Windsor in June, Clarence went beyond the point of no return. Storming into the council chamber at Westminster, he insultingly denounced the King's justice and the sentences on Stacey and Burdett, and had their written declarations of innocence read aloud by a priest who was with him.

When he heard what Clarence had done, the King's patience gave way. Honour demanded that Clarence be punished for this crowning act of *lèse-majesté*. The Queen was insisting upon it. Mancini says she 'remembered the insults to her family and the calumnies with which she was reproached, namely that she was not the legitimate wife of the King. Thus she concluded that her offspring by the King would never come to the throne unless the Duke of Clarence were removed, and of this she easily persuaded the King. The Queen's alarm was intensified by the comeliness of the Duke of Clarence, which would make him appear worthy of the crown.' Elizabeth's fear of Clarence was, it seems, far greater than the King's, and this has led some writers to conclude that he knew something about her past that she did not want revealed. There is, however, no evidence that this was so, and we should remember that Clarence's allegations in respect of the King's bastardy and the validity of his marriage were alarming enough in the circumstances. Logically speaking, given his state of mind at that time, if

45

Clarence had known any secrets about the Queen that could be used to his advantage, he would certainly not have hesitated to make them public. Instead, he had fallen back on old, baseless rumours about his brother and invented grounds for the invalidity of the royal marriage that were entirely nonsensical.

Edward IV left Windsor immediately and went to Westminster, where he summoned Clarence and the Mayor and aldermen of London. In the presence of the latter, 'with his own lips', he accused Clarence of 'going above the law' and 'conduct derogatory to the laws of the realm and most dangerous to judges throughout the kingdom', as well as usurping the royal prerogative by acting 'as though he had used a king's power'. Clarence could not deny that he had done these things, and he was arrested and incarcerated in the Tower of London on a blanket charge of 'committing acts violating the laws of the realm'. There was no doubt in anyone's mind that Clarence was a danger to his brother and to the succession. He languished in his prison, traditionally in the Bowyer Tower, until in November 1477 Edward IV made up his mind to try him publicly for his offences. Parliament was then summoned, chiefly for this purpose.

On 15th January, 1478, the day before Parliament was due to convene, a royal wedding took place. The bridegroom was the King's younger son, the four-year-old Duke of York, and the bride was six-year-old Anne Mowbray, Duchess of Norfolk in her own right since the death in 1476 of her father, John Mowbray, fourth and last Duke of Norfolk in the Mowbray line. The wedding, celebrated at St Stephen's Chapel, Westminster, was a splendid state occasion, with almost the whole royal family and court attending. After the marriage, the King induced Parliament to pass an Act declaring that York should enjoy the dukedom of Norfolk and the Mowbray inheritance for life, in right of his wife, even if she predeceased him. This proviso overlooked the superior claim that Anne's coheirs, the Howards and the Berkeleys, would have to the inheritance in the event of her death. The King had come to an accommodation with them, but there was no avoiding the fact that what he had done was against all legal precedents governing the laws of inheritance and there were many who blamed the Queen's influence for this.

On the day following his son's marriage, Edward IV opened Parliament and Clarence was brought to the House of Lords to be indicted

46

on a new charge of high treason. He faced a hostile chamber, whose members had been well-briefed and even bribed by the King, as Croyland infers, with regard to the verdict they should deliver. Many were only too eager to acquiesce to the King's wishes, for Clarence had made many enemies and few friends during his turbulent career. Others, though, were shocked to see the King's brother on a capital charge.

It was an extraordinary hearing. The King himself read out the long indictment, the text of which was incorporated into the Act of Attainder afterwards brought before Parliament. The indictment accused Clarence of 'new treasons to exalt himself and his heir to the regality and crown of England', stressing that these were 'much higher, much more malicious treasons than had been found at any time previously during the reign'. The King stated that he had 'ever loved and cherished [Clarence], as tenderly or kindly as ever creature might his natural brother', giving him 'so large portion of possessions that seldom hath been seen. The Duke, for all this, no love increasing, but growing daily in more and more malice', had 'falsely and traitorously intended and purposed firmly the extreme destruction and disinheriting of the King and his issue'. He had 'spread the falsest and most unnatural coloured pretence that man might imagine, that the King our most sovereign lord was a bastard, and not begotten to reign upon us'. He had not only kept his copy of a document drawn up in 1470 naming him Henry VI's heir, but was now claiming also to be the heir to York. Finally, he had plotted to send his infant son to Ireland, 'whereby he might have gotten him assistance and favour against our sovereign lord'; a child resembling young Warwick was to have been substituted for him during his absence.

These were all quite specific charges, and all equally damning; every one attracted the death penalty. There was silence as the King read them out. Croyland recalled: 'Not a single person uttered a word against the Duke except the King; not one individual made answer to the King except the Duke.' But Clarence's protests availed him not at all, nor did his offer to have the case decided by 'wager of battle'. Edward IV meant to have a conviction for high treason, and Croyland says he did not give Clarence a chance to defend himself properly.

The Act of Attainder against Clarence became law on 8th February 1478. On the previous day the Duke of Buckingham had been appointed Seneschal of England in place of Gloucester, and in that capacity he pronounced sentence of death upon the prisoner. It may be that Gloucester had asked to be spared this duty. Buckingham also sentenced the condemned man to the forfeiture of his honours, titles, lands and estates to the Crown. Croyland felt that the King had secured his brother's condemnation 'on dubious grounds', but there was no doubt that Clarence had committed the crimes of which he had been accused.

Both Croyland and Vergil place the responsibility for Clarence's condemnation solely on the King, and they were probably right to do so, but it was widely believed at the time that the Queen and her faction had been the prime movers in the matter; they had a motive for doing so, and had probably been waiting for an opportunity to eliminate their enemy. In 1483, Mancini heard that the Queen's brother, Edward Wydville, and her sons, Dorset and Grey, had been instrumental in securing Clarence's conviction.

Gloucester certainly believed that the Wydvilles had brought about his brother's condemnation, perceiving that it was a triumph for them, but while this must have been galling in the extreme to him, he did not lift a finger to save Clarence. He may well even have acquiesced in his fall, for there is some contemporary evidence that Gloucester was involved in the proceedings against Clarence. He was at court at the time, for his nephew's wedding, and had attended the Council meetings at which Clarence's fate was discussed. He also played his part in ensuring that Parliament was obedient to the King's wishes: five members at least were his own men. Gloucester also benefited more than anyone else from Clarence's fall. The Attainder against Clarence left Gloucester next in line to the throne after the King's issue; on 15th February his son Edward of Middleham was created Earl of Salisbury, a title that had been borne by Clarence; and on 21st February, Gloucester himself was given Clarence's high office of Great Chamberlain of England. More says that, while Gloucester was opposed to his brother being executed, 'some wise men' were of the opinion that he was not displeased by Clarence's fall.

Edward IV was understandably reluctant to put his own brother to death, and he refused for over a week to give his assent to Clarence's execution. Before long, the Commons were clamouring for justice to take its course, as with any other traitor, and the Speaker came to the

Bar of the Lords, requesting that what was to be done should be done at once. Finally, a deputation of members went to the King, who had no alternative but to accede to their demand for Clarence's death. At the request of their mother, the Duchess Cecily, the sentence was commuted from the full horrors of a traitor's death by hanging, drawing and quartering to beheading or, according to the French chronicler Molinet, any other method preferred by Clarence. The Duchess also begged that the execution take place in private, to avoid some of the scandal that publicity would lend to what was perceived primarily as an act of fratricide.

On 18th February, 1478, Clarence was informed that he was to die that day in the Tower. The *Calendar of Patent Rolls* records that he asked for compensation to be paid to Lord Rivers 'in consideration of the injuries perpetrated on him and his parents' by Clarence and Warwick. Then, according to the *Great Chronicle of London*, 'the Duke of Clarence offered his own mass penny in the Tower, and about twelve of the clock at noon made his end in a rondolet of Malmsey'. Being drowned in wine was an unusual method of execution but Molinet says that Clarence himself had suggested it once in a joke to the King, adding that the Duke had lately expressed a real wish to end his days in this manner. Many contemporary chroniclers, including Commines, Mancini, and the Frenchmen Jean de Roye and Olivier de la Marche, corroborate the details given by Molinet and the author of the *Great Chronicle*; only Croyland is noncommittal, saying: 'The execution, whatever its nature may have been, took place in the Tower of London.' A portrait of Clarence's daughter Margaret, painted around 1530, shows her wearing a miniature wine-cask on a bracelet at her wrist – a poignant memento of her father's fate.

Two days after Clarence's death, Ankarette Twynho's heir Roger petitioned the King to reverse the verdict and sentence on his mother, and his petition was granted.

Clarence was buried beside his wife in Tewkesbury Abbey, where his skull and a few bones are now displayed in a wall-niche near the high altar. He was given a noble funeral, the King bearing the cost and providing 'right worshipfully for his soul'. A beautiful tomb, surmounted by effigies of the Duke and Duchess, was raised to their memory, but has long gone, and the site of their vault is marked merely by a grille in the floor behind the high altar.

Clarence's attainder meant that his orphaned children could not inherit his titles or lands, which had reverted to the Crown. Warwick, however, held his earldom in right of his mother, and the King allowed him a portion of her estates. The Queen's eldest son, Lord Dorset, bought the wardship and marriage of Warwick, and he and his sister Margaret were sent to Sheen to be brought up with Edward IV's children.

Many modern writers have linked the subsequent brief imprisonment of Robert Stillington, Bishop of Bath and Wells, with the fall of Clarence. Stillington was a doctor of civil law, a brilliant intellectual with a great capacity for intrigue. He had been Chancellor of England from 1467–73, and had always enjoyed the favour of Edward IV. But between 27th February and 5th March, 1478, Stillington was arrested on a charge of 'violating his oath of fidelity by some utterance prejudicial to the King and his estate'. We do not know what he had said to give offence, nor is there any evidence that his misdemeanour was in any way connected with Clarence. It is possible that Clarence had allied himself with Stillington; his West-Country estates bordered upon Stillington's diocese. It may be that the Bishop had helped to spread Clarence's slanders about the King's bastardy and his marriage, but there is no proof of this. If Stillington's offence had been treasonable, or if he had posed any real danger to the King's security or the royal succession, he would have been permanently removed from the scene, as Clarence had been. Yet he was released on 20th June, 1478, on payment of a fine, and later given several respectable positions at court without, however, regaining his former influence.

Vergil and More both asserted that Edward IV came to regret having executed Clarence, and Croyland, who knew the King, wrote: 'As I really believe, [he] inwardly repented very often of this act.' Vergil says Edward frequently lamented that no-one had interceded on Clarence's behalf; yet the removal of Clarence had been seen by the majority as a necessary evil that made good political sense. Nevertheless, it had set a precedent for violence within the royal family itself, and demonstrated how ruthless a king sometimes had to be if he wished to remain securely on his throne.

Gloucester was certainly one who learned this lesson well, even as he was bitterly lamenting his brother's death. Only three days after it he procured the King's licence to set up two chantries at Middleham and

Barnard Castle, so that prayers could be said in perpetuity for his dead siblings and all those of his House. According to Mancini, he blamed the Wydvilles for Clarence's execution. 'Richard was so overcome with grief for his brother that he could not dissimulate so well but that he was overheard to say that he would one day avenge his brother's death.' The Duke knew how ruthless the Queen could be, and must have recalled how, in 1467, she had stolen the King's signet ring and given the order for the execution of the Earl of Desmond, in revenge for his having made disparaging remarks to the King about his choice of bride. Unfortunately, the infamous John Tiptoft, Earl of Worcester, who carried out the execution in Ireland, exceeded his brief by murdering also two of Desmond's young sons, an atrocity for which Elizabeth Wydville must bear some responsibility.

This tale has often been dismissed as a Tudor fabrication: the Queen's role in the executions was first publicly referred to in a petition to the Privy Council of her grandson, Henry VIII, made by Desmond's heirs in 1538. Falsely slandering King Henry's grandmother was hardly the way to secure a favourable answer to the petition, and there was no reason why the Desmond family should fabricate such allegations. Moreover, the deed is attested to in the Register of the Mayors of Dublin: 'This year, the Earl of Desmond and his two sons were executed by the Earl of Worcester at Drogheda,' and it is also referred to by Gloucester himself in a letter to Desmond's surviving son, in which he says that they shared a common grief, and that those responsible for Desmond's death and the death of his two sons were the same as had brought about Clarence's death.

Gloucester now had the measure of the Wydville faction, and would remain acutely aware that they were capable of removing by fair means or foul any member of the royal House who stood in their way. 'Thenceforth,' wrote Mancini, 'he came very rarely to court.'

5
'Deadly Feuds and Factions'

On 26th November, 1481, the *Cely Letters* recorded: 'My young lady of York is dead.' Anne Mowbray had died a week earlier at Greenwich Palace, aged only nine. She was buried in the Chapel of St Erasmus, Elizabeth Wydville's own foundation in Westminster Abbey, but when this chapel was demolished in the early sixteenth century to make way for the Henry VII Chapel, Anne's remains were moved to the Minoresses' convent in Stepney. Workmen excavating its site in 1964 found her coffin, buried eleven feet deep. Her remains were examined by medical experts, and then reburied as near as possible to her original resting place in Westminster Abbey.

When Anne Mowbray died, her husband, the eight-year-old Duke of York, retained the dukedom of Norfolk in accordance with the terms of their marriage contract. His right to his wife's estates was confirmed by Act of Parliament in January 1483. To appease Lord Berkeley, one of the rightful coheirs, Edward IV excused him payment of a large debt owed to the Crown, and provided that the Mowbray inheritance should revert to Lords Berkeley and Howard if York died without male issue. Howard, however, received nothing, not even money owed him for supplying plate for the Queen's coronation in 1465. Many lords were angered by the King's treatment of Lord Howard, and concerned at Edward's failure to respect the ancient laws of inheritance upon which their power was built, though there is no evidence that Howard himself expressed any grievance.

The King's elder daughters were now of marriageable age. Mary was betrothed in 1481 to the King of Denmark, but tragically died a year later, before the wedding could take place. At around the same time Cecily was betrothed to the Duke of Albany, brother of James III of Scotland, while preparations were still going ahead for the marriage of Elizabeth of York to the Dauphin. The King's children were described collectively by Croyland as 'sweet and beauteous', and by the French chronicler Jean de Waurin as 'fine looking and most delightful. There were five beautiful girls.'

Edward IV, however, was no longer the magnificent specimen of manly beauty he had been in his earlier years. In 1475, while describing him as 'a very handsome king' and 'a prince of noble and majestic presence', Commines stated he was already 'a little inclining to corpulence'. Croyland says that by 1482, when he was forty, Edward IV was 'a man of such corpulence, and so fond of boon companionship, vanities, debauchery, extravagance and sensual enjoyments'. Mancini tells us that the King 'was most immoderate with food and drink. I have heard that he used to take purges just for the pleasure of gorging his stomach again. Because of his indulgence and idleness he developed a huge stomach, although previously he had not only been tall but lean as well, and led a strenuous life.'

Edward's excesses had already undermined his health, and had also prompted hostility between influential members of the court. 'Although he had many promoters and companions of his vices,' wrote Mancini, 'the more important and especial were three of the relatives of the Queen, her two sons and one of her brothers.' These were Dorset, Grey and Rivers. The cultivated Rivers was popular with the people, although Dorset and Grey had 'earned the hatred of the populace on account of their morals, but mostly because of a certain inherent jealousy which arises between those who are equal by birth when there has been a change in their station'.

Mancini adds that Edward had another boon companion, Lord Hastings, who 'was also the accomplice and partner of the King's privy pleasures'. William, Lord Hastings, was fifty in 1482; he came from a family of Yorkshire gentry who had loyally served the House of York through four generations. Hastings' rise to power began when, as a youth, he was placed in the household of the Duke of York. In 1461 he fought for Edward IV at Towton and was rewarded for his loyalty over the years with a knighthood, vast lands, a seat on the royal

Council, the office of King's Chamberlain, and a baronage. Mancini says that 'from an early age' Hastings had been 'a loyal companion of Edward'; he had also managed to maintain good relations with Clarence, and was well thought of by Gloucester. He was, after all, married to Katherine Neville, a first cousin of the royal brothers.

Hastings had charm and great qualities. His contemporaries, with whom he was exceedingly popular, praised his loyalty, his upright character, his sense of honour and duty, his liberality, his many charities and benefactions, and his patronage of the arts. His closeness to the King meant that he enjoyed great influence, wealth and power – more, indeed, than many of those of higher rank. This, however, together with Hastings' participation in Edward's debaucheries, earned him the jealousy and hatred of the Queen and her faction, which was exacerbated in 1482 by a dispute over the governorship of Calais, then an English possession. Hastings was appointed to this post by the King in preference to Earl Rivers. Rivers, piqued, accused Hastings of intriguing to sell Calais to the French, at which Hastings, knowing his neck was in jeopardy, retaliated by levelling the same accusation at Rivers. He now, to his dismay, discovered the extent of the power of the Wydvilles, who managed to have his informers against them executed for treason, conspiracy and sedition. Hastings fortunately convinced the King of his own innocence, but from then on he would maintain a deadly feud with Rivers and remain on bad terms with the Queen.

Hastings was also engaged in a bitter rivalry with Lord Dorset, which, according to Mancini and More, was on account of the women they were continually trying to seduce from each other. In particular, they were rivals for the favours of Elizabeth Shore, the most famous of Edward IV's many mistresses.

Elizabeth, who is usually – but incorrectly – called Jane, was born around 1450, the daughter of John Lambert, a prosperous London mercer. More says she was married 'ere she were well ripe' to another mercer, 'an honest citizen, young and godly and of good substance', called William Shore, but 'she not very fervently loved' her husband, who was 'frigid and impotent' in bed. There is an unsubstantiated tradition that during her marriage Elizabeth served as a waiting woman to the Duchess of Gloucester whenever that lady came to London; if true, this may have been how she became acquainted with the King, whose mistress she became prior to 1476. More says that her loveless marriage 'the more easily made her incline unto [his] appetite', while the accommodating Shore discreetly left for a long business trip to Antwerp. The Shores' marriage was annulled in 1476, on the grounds of non-consummation.

More, who knew Elizabeth Shore at the end of her long life, gives a fine pen-portrait of her, saying she had 'a soft, tender heart' and was beautiful yet diminutive in stature. 'Yet men delighted not so much in her beauty as in her pleasant behaviour', for she was witty, literate, cheerful, intelligent and playful. More calls her 'the merriest of the King's harlots', and tells us that, while 'many he had, her he loved, whose favour she never abused'.

It is clear that Edward IV made a practice of sharing his mistresses with his friends, and that both Hastings and Dorset were in competition for Elizabeth Shore. More says that Elizabeth attracted the enmity of the Queen, and this may well have been so. No other source mentions it, but Edward's wife can hardly have felt very warmly towards the woman who had replaced her in his bed.

The rivalry over Elizabeth Shore was just one factor dividing the major factions in a court where, according to Mancini, the magnates were greedy for both power and pleasure. On the one hand there were the Wydvilles, loyal to the King but ambitious for themselves and determined to retain a grip on their power; there was Lord Hastings, who led the faction that was staunchly loyal to the Crown while detesting the upstart Wydvilles; and then there was the Duke of Gloucester, who was apparently of this latter faction but who was rarely at court. He had consistently demonstrated his loyalty to his brother the King, and his personal motto was 'Loyaultié me lie' ('Loyalty binds me').

Gloucester was not well-known in the South. Mancini says, 'He kept himself within his own lands, and set out to acquire the loyalty of his people through favours and justice. The good reputation of his private life and public activities powerfully attracted the esteem of strangers. By these acts, Richard acquired the favour of the people, and avoided the jealousy of the Queen, from whom he lived far separated.' Having distinguished himself in two early battles, he won further renown for his command of the expeditionary force which re-took Berwick from the Scots in 1482; after this, Edward IV wrote to the Pope, saying that the victory of 'our loving brother' was 'so proven, that he alone would suffice to chastise the whole of Scotland'. Wrote Mancini: 'In warfare, such was his renown that any difficult or dangerous task necessary for the safety of the realm was entrusted to his direction and generalship.' This was something of an exaggeration, but it is worth noting that even hostile chroniclers praised Richard's bravery and courage in the field of battle.

From 1472–83, Gloucester governed England north of the River Trent for his brother the King. His power in that region was more or less absolute, and the success of his administration was due in no small part to the loyalty of his followers and deputies, whom he treated well and rewarded handsomely, creating a widespread network of support based on patronage and the fact that Gloucester had married a Neville heiress: as Anne's husband, he was looked upon as the rightful successor to that great northern family. As a whole, the North had, in the past, supported the House of Lancaster, but thanks to Richard's strong and stable government which brought peace to the region and rid it of much of its lawlessness, many loyalties were transferred to the House of York; by the 1480s, the scales were tipped firmly in its favour.

Gloucester's power stemmed not only from his wide-ranging responsibilities but also from the fact that he owned vast lands in the North. The city of York was his power-base, where he had his own council, the forerunner of what would later be called the Council of the North. In May 1480 the King appointed him Lieutenant General of the North, broadening his powers. Most sources praise Gloucester's abilities as an administrator, lauding his justness and fairness, but occasionally there is a discordant note: in 1482, the Council of the Duchy of Lancaster complained to the Duke that he was too lax in his duties as its Chief Steward. But such criticisms were few. In January 1483 the King created a great hereditary palatinate lordship for Gloucester, extending over Cumberland and Westmorland, and making him, in effect, more powerful in those shires than the King. He now enjoyed unprecedented power, greater than any other magnate to date; this reflected both his record of loyal service and Edward's complete trust in Gloucester's integrity.

The Civic Records of the City of York give us a fascinating insight into Gloucester's relations with the city council and the people of York. His seat at Middleham was some fifty-odd miles away, but he visited York often, sometimes keeping Easter and Christmas there, where he

was well-known. His relationship with the corporation was a mutually
beneficial one. He safeguarded, and obtained from his brother confirmation of, 'the liberties of this city'; he decreased taxes, and defended
York against its enemies when necessary. In return, he received the
loyalty of the citizens, troops free of charge when he needed them, and
frequent gifts. There is no doubt that he was popular with many of the
citizens, particularly those noblemen on the council of York who
benefited from his patronage and favours and who promoted his
interests in return. To them, he was 'our full tender and especial good
lord' in whom they placed 'a singular confidence', and for whose
prosperous estate they would 'evermore pray to Almighty God'. In
1482, the Civic Records noted that the Duke of Gloucester 'at all times
hath been benevolent, good and gracious lord to this city', and a year
later Gloucester himself, in a letter to the citizens of York, spoke of
'your kind and loving dispositions to us at all times showed, which we
né can forget. Ye shall verily understand we be your especial good and
loving lord.'

Yet those same Civic Records show that the council of York stood
also in some awe of Gloucester and feared to cross him; he was a man
who had to be handled gently. There is evidence that many of the
common citizens of York neither liked nor trusted him. On more than
one occasion his decrees provoked riots, and there were those who
voiced adverse opinions on the Duke in public. We have already seen
that it was a citizen of York who was the first recorded person to
nickname Richard 'Crouchback'.

In the South, and at court, Gloucester was a comparative stranger.
Here, the Wydvilles dominated, because the King had allowed them to
gain control, not only of the heir to the throne and the other royal
children, but had also made them powerful by advantageous marriages,
lands, honours, and titles – even those, such as the Mowbray inheritance (which they administered and enjoyed), to which they were not
entitled but had gained through flagrant disregard for the laws of
England. Such deeds, along with their rapacious greed and humble
origins, had not improved their stock with the magnates over the years.
In 1483, Mancini was amazed at the power of the Queen, who had
'attracted to her party many strangers, and introduced them to court,
so that they alone should manage the public and private business of the
Crown, give or sell offices, and finally rule the very King himself'.

There was rank corruption in high places, and the Wydvilles were at the very centre of it. Edward himself showed special favour to his wife's sons, Dorset and Grey, and her brother, Lord Rivers. He saw nothing ominous in making Rivers guardian of the Prince of Wales, just as he saw nothing ominous in giving Gloucester absolute power in the North; nor was he wary of having Rivers in charge of the Prince's household at Ludlow Castle, with its strategic command of the Welsh Marches.

Edward did not perceive that his policy of entrusting the upbringing of his heir to the Wydvilles was at variance with his making an over-mighty subject of Gloucester, their enemy, whose hatred and fear of them was well-known since it was that which kept him from court. It seems not to have occurred to the King that such a division of power did not augur well for the future. He trusted Gloucester implicitly, just as he had no reason to doubt the loyalty of Hastings to himself nor of the Wydvilles to his son, who was of their blood.

It was, however, Edward IV's failure to envisage what the consequences would be to his kingdom and his heir if he were to die young and leave a minor on the throne that led directly to the tragedy of the Princes in the Tower.

In 1482, says Croyland, 'King Edward kept the Feast of the Nativity at his Palace of Westminster, frequently appearing clad in a great variety of most costly garments'. Jean de Waurin tells us that this Christmas court was 'worthy of a leading kingdom, full of riches and men from almost every nation'. All the King's children were present, even the Prince of Wales.

Young Edward had rarely been seen in London. In 1481 he had come from Ludlow and toured Kent with his father, visiting the shrine of St Thomas à Becket at Canterbury and reviewing the fleet at Sandwich. At this time, the King was negotiating his marriage with Anne, the four-year-old heiress of Brittany, which was agreed upon on 10th May that year. The marriage treaty provided that Anne would be sent to England when she reached the age of twelve, bringing with her a dowry of 100,000 crowns, and that the eldest son of the marriage should inherit England and the second son Brittany. On his marriage, Edward would become Duke of Brittany in right of his wife.

In November, 1482, the Prince reached the age of twelve himself. We have only a vague idea of his appearance, as the extant representations of him cannot be accepted as accurate portraits: they only give an impression of what he looked like. A coloured miniature in the Lambeth Palace manuscript of *The Dictes and Sayings of the Philosophers* shows Edward with his parents, Lord Rivers and other courtiers; the artist appears to have made a crude attempt at the likenesses of these persons, and it would seem that the Prince, with his fair, wavy, collar-length hair, resembled his mother rather than his father. The stained-glass representations of Edward and his brother York in Canterbury Cathedral are not original and cannot be said to be accurate copies of the heads that were smashed during the English Civil War. There is another stained-glass portrait which may be an authentic likeness; it was commissioned by the Prince's tutor, Bishop Alcock, in 1481, and is to be found in the priory church of Little Malvern in Worcestershire. It depicts Edward at prayer, wearing royal robes and coronet. The worn delineations of the face show perhaps fleeting resemblances to both parents. Finally, the wooden panel portrait in St George's Chapel, Windsor, dates from the reign of Henry VII, and we have no way of knowing if the anonymous artist had ever seen Edward. However, the face is suggestive of his father's features, although this may have been deliberate, since the picture was obviously painted for propaganda purposes.

In character, the Prince was said to have taken after Edward IV, and to have had talent and remarkable learning. In June, 1483, John Russell, Bishop of Lincoln and Lord Chancellor of England, preparing his speech for the state opening of Parliament, wrote of Edward's 'toward and virtuous disposition, his gentle wit and ripe understanding, far passing the nature of his youth'. The French chronicler Molinet was less enthusiastic, describing the boy as 'simple and very melancholy' in temperament, but Mancini, who may have seen the Prince and certainly spoke with those who knew him, wrote: 'In word and deed he gave so many proofs of his liberal education, of polite, nay, rather scholarly attainments far beyond his age.' Mancini also noted 'his special knowledge of literature, which enabled him to discourse eloquently, to understand fully, and to declaim most excellently from any work, whether in verse or prose, that came into his hands. He had such dignity in his whole person, and in his face such charm that however much they might gaze, he never wearied the eyes of beholders.'

The Prince was very much his mother's child and under the influence of her faction, to which he naturally inclined. But, as John Rous later commented, he had been 'brought up virtuously by virtuous men', and was 'remarkably gifted and well-advanced in learning for his twelve years'.

At the Christmas court the Prince, appearing in a gown of white cloth of gold, drew comments on his charm, intelligence and abilities. but the festivities were to be ruined by appalling news from France. Mary, the young Duchess of Burgundy and wife of Maximilian of Austria, had recently been thrown from her horse and killed, leaving two children: Philip, her heir, and Margaret, then aged three. Louis XI of France had quickly decided that Margaret would be a better match for the Dauphin than Elizabeth of York, and on 23rd December, 1482, he and Maximilian concluded the Treaty of Arras which provided for such a marriage. The news that his daughter had been ignominiously jilted reached Edward IV early in 1483, and had a devastating effect, provoking in him such anger and disappointment that he was afterwards said to have never got over it. Parliament was summoned, and war was declared on France.

This was the state of affairs when, in March 1483, the King was 'taken in a small boat with those whom he had bidden go fishing, and watched that sport too eagerly'. Mancini adds that Edward, 'being a tall man, and very fat, though not to the point of deformity, allowed the damp cold to strike his vitals' and 'therefore contracted the illness from which he never recovered'. There are indications that the King's health had already given cause for concern that month, for on 8th March, Lord Rivers had sent to his London attorney, Andrew Dymmock, for a copy of the patent appointing him Governor of the Prince of Wales (which authorised him to move the Prince at will), and for the patent empowering him to raise troops in the Welsh Marches. It is likely that Rivers' action was prompted by the need to ensure his continued control over the Prince of Wales and conserve the power of the Wydville faction in the event of the King's death. It is tempting to speculate that Rivers had been warned by his sister that Edward's health was failing, but there is no proof of this.

The King's illness first became apparent at Easter, when he took to his bed. His contemporaries were baffled as to what was wrong with him. Vergil described it simply as 'an unknown disease', and today we are little the wiser as to its nature. Croyland says the King was neither 'worn out with old age, nor yet seized with any known kind of malady, the cure of which would not have appeared easy in the case of a person of more humble rank'. The contemporary Norman chronicler, Thomas Basin, believed that Edward had severely upset his digestive system by eating a surfeit of fruit and vegetables. Commines was sure that his illness 'was caused by Louis XI rejecting the Princess Elizabeth for his little Dauphin Charles', an indication of how deeply aggrieved Edward had been by Louis' perfidy. Dr John Rae, in his book *Deaths of the English Kings*, published in 1913, offered the opinion that Edward IV suffered an attack of pneumonia: contemporary descriptions of the King lying 'on his left side' are perhaps evidence that he was suffering from pain in his left lung.

The royal physicians gathered by their master's bedside, but they could do nothing for him. Commines says that the King then suffered a stroke, which the chronicler attributed to the excesses of his life, but it cannot have been unduly severe as it did not affect his speech. By 7th April, Edward 'perceived his natural strength so sore enfeebled that he despaired all recovery', and summoned his wife and his magnates to his bedchamber. He then commanded Hastings and Dorset to be reconciled with one another, at which the two lords outwardly made their peace. Hastings and the Queen put on a similar charade for the King's benefit, but, as Mancini says, 'there still survived a latent jealousy'.

Two days passed, and on the 9th it became obvious that the King was going to die very soon. The *Song of the Lady Bessy* asserts that on his deathbed he commended the care of his daughter Elizabeth to Thomas, second Lord Stanley, one of his trusted councillors. Stanley, then forty-eight, had been married to the sister of Warwick the Kingmaker, and was therefore cousin-by-marriage to the King and brother-in-law to Lord Hastings. But Stanley's allegiance had not always lain with the House of York. He came from a newly prominent Cheshire family, and owned large estates in that country as well as in Derbyshire and Lancashire, but throughout his life he served his own interests first and foremost, and had on one occasion during the Wars of the Roses remained neutral and aloof during a battle in which both sides besought him to aid them with his men. In 1461 he decided it was prudent to offer his allegiance to Edward IV, but he had happily switched to

Henry VI during the latter's brief return to power in 1470–71. Edward forgave him for this, and made him Steward of the Royal Household in 1472 and a privy councillor in 1477. In 1482, Stanley had married as his second wife Margaret Beaufort, widow of Edmund Tudor, Earl of Richmond, a lady whose sympathies were decidedly Lancastrian, and whose descent from John of Gaunt made her a fine match for any aspiring lord.

Why Edward IV should single out Stanley, and not Hastings or a member of the Wydville faction, as Elizabeth's guardian is a mystery, and the probable truth is that he did no such thing, for the princess remained with her mother and it was not until two years later that Stanley saw fit to act on her behalf.

The Queen was not present at her husband's bedside when, on 9th April, 1483, Edward IV, in the words of Croyland, 'rendered his spirit to his Creator at the Palace of Westminster'. More tells us that 'he left this realm in quiet and prosperous estate', and it is true that when he died he was rich, powerful, and esteemed throughout Christendom as a strong ruler. But he had made one fatal mistake: he had failed to unify the rival factions in his kingdom, and by this omission had placed his son's peaceful succession to the throne in jeopardy. He had also created two mighty power centres in his realm, the Wydvilles and the Duke of Gloucester, and these two were in opposition to each other. Even as Edward's body was being prepared for its lying-in-state at Westminster, it was dawning upon many that a new era of uncertainty had arrived, and that the next weeks would prove crucial. How crucial no-one could yet tell; a few could have foreseen that the survival of the Yorkist dynasty itself would be dependent upon what happened now.

At this time, Judge John More, father of Thomas, was living near Cripplegate in Milk Street, which was in the same ward of the City of London as Redcross Street. In that street lived Richard Pottyer, a retainer of the Duke of Gloucester who held the post of attorney of the Duchy of Lancaster in Chancery; he may even have been Gloucester's own attorney. Judge More knew Pottyer and later learned how, on 9th April, Pottyer received a visit from one William Mistlebrook, who told him of the King's death. Pottyer's response was as chilling as it was incongruous: 'By my troth, man,' he said, 'then will my master the Duke of Gloucester be king!'

6

'Those of the
Queen's Blood'

Edward IV left his kingdom to his eldest son, who was proclaimed King Edward V in London on 11th April, 1483, at which time he was at Ludlow, 200 miles from the capital.

Edward IV's only surviving will dates from 1475. In it, he entrusted the care of his son to 'our dearest wife the Queen', his chief executor. No provision was made for a minority. The Queen was to have any household goods she wanted and power to dispose of the rest. Her daughters were also to be governed and ruled by her in their choice of husbands.

When he was on his deathbed, however, Edward IV either drew up a new will, or added codicils to the first. These documents do not survive, but their existence is attested to by the fact that the executors who met after the King's death were not those listed in the 1475 will, the Queen being the most notable omission. Rous states that Gloucester was named Protector of the Realm by this deathbed 'ordinance', and Mancini 'heard men say that in the same will [Edward IV] appointed as protector of his children and realm his brother, Richard, Duke of Gloucester'. Both André and Vergil repeat these details. It appears that Edward intended that Gloucester should govern the kingdom while the King was a minor, and have care and control of the royal children: this is implied in the Lord Chancellor's draft speech for the state opening of Parliament in June, 1483. Rivers, it seems, was to be removed from his office of Governor, and the Queen was apparently given no power at all. What probably prompted the late

King's change of heart was his realisation of the need to mitigate the rapaciousness and unpopularity of the Wydvilles.

Mancini tells us that on 9th April, the day the King died, 'the Queen, with her second son, the Duke of York, and the rest of her family [*sic*], were in London, where was also the chamberlain, Hastings, with the Bishops of York and Ely, friends of the King. The royal treasure, the weight of which was said to be immense, was kept in the hands of the Queen and her people' at the Tower. In March 1483 the office of deputy constable of the Tower of London had been transferred from Rivers to Dorset, who was now in effective control of both the late King's treasure and the royal ordnance at the fortress. The Queen and her supporters held sway over the court, and Rivers had the young King in his charge. The Wydvilles were firmly entrenched and meant to stay that way, having determined to resist all attempts to make Gloucester protector. Their intention was to ignore Edward IV's will and use Edward V as a puppet, whose strings they themselves would pull.

England, just then, was in a critical situation, having recently declared war on France, and it was essential that a stable regency government be established without delay. According to Croyland, on 9th April the late King's councillors 'were present with the Queen at Westminster'. Almost their first act was to decree that a new bidding prayer be said in churches 'for our new prince, our dread King Edward V, the Lady Queen Elizabeth his mother, all the royal offspring, the princes of the King, his nobles and people'. There was no direct reference to Gloucester, the protector-designate.

Over the next two or three days, the councillors held several important and sometimes heated discussions, and there was some in-fighting between factions now that the firm hand of Edward IV was no longer there to control them, but the Queen, says Croyland, 'most beneficently tried to extinguish every mark of murmur and disturbance'. Very soon, it became clear that the councillors were divided into three camps: the Queen's party, which was the largest and included her kinsmen and most of the bishops, Archbishop Rotherham of York in particular; the smaller anti-Wydville faction led by Lord Hastings with the support of Lord Stanley; and a group including the Archbishop of Canterbury and John Russell, Bishop of Lincoln, who would not commit themselves either way. No-one declared openly for Gloucester.

Croyland says that the only common cause between these factions was loyalty to the son of Edward IV.

Lord Hastings was under no illusion as to what the Wydvilles were trying to do. Their hostility towards him and the older nobility was palpable, and Croyland knew 'he feared that if supreme power fell into the hands of those of the Queen's blood, they would most bitterly revenge themselves on himself for the injuries which they claimed he had done to them'. According to Mancini, Hastings, in turn, 'was hostile to the entire kin of the Queen, on account of the Marquess of Dorset'. This was exacerbated by Hastings' precipitate action in making Elizabeth Shore his mistress as soon as the King was dead. Nevertheless, concerned as he was about the Wydvilles' power and the threat they posed to him, Hastings stayed his hand for the time being.

The Wydvilles now sought by legal means to prevent Gloucester from becoming protector. They had discovered that this office was, according to precedent, purely an interim one, its purpose being to ensure the security and protection of the realm until the sovereign was safely crowned, at which time it would lapse. In 1429, during the minority of Henry VI, his uncle Humphrey, Duke of Gloucester, had relinquished his office of lord protector as soon as the young King (then aged seven) had sworn to protect and defend the Church and his realm at his coronation.

Edward V was now twelve years old, and there was no reason why he should not be crowned immediately. Indeed, the Wydvilles urged this, seeing an early coronation as a way of thwarting Gloucester's claim to be protector, an office they knew would cease to exist after this had taken place. The government then would be in the hands of the Wydville-dominated Council.

At a meeting of the councillors which must have taken place around the time the King was proclaimed on 11th April, the Queen and her party had little difficulty in convincing those present that the coronation should take place without delay. The date was fixed for Sunday, 4th May, and the decision made to summon Edward V to London at once. The Queen, who was taking no chances, demanded that her son be escorted by an army of soldiers, but at this Hastings, who foresaw trouble and bloodshed, exploded with anger and threatened to retire to Calais – of which he was governor – unless a smaller escort was provided. His threat was implicit: it was in Calais that Warwick had plotted against Edward IV in 1470, and Hastings made it quite clear that he would not scruple to plot in the same manner against the Wydvilles. Hard words followed, but in the end, according to More, it was the Queen who backed down, agreeing to limit the King's escort to 2,000 men. Hastings signified his approval, and Dorset wrote at once to Rivers and also, says Mancini, 'to the young King Edward, that he should reach the capital three days before the date appointed' for the coronation.

Hastings was by no means reassured by the Queen's capitulation over the King's escort. He was no fool, and had easily divined the real reason why the Wydvilles were eager to get the King crowned. He had enjoyed, says Mancini, 'a friendship of long standing' with Gloucester, of which the Wydvilles were well aware. Consequently, the present situation was particularly menacing to him. For this reason, and from sincere loyalty, he was anxious to see Edward IV's wishes respecting the protectorate implemented.

At the time of the King's death, Richard of Gloucester was 200 miles from London at Middleham Castle in Yorkshire. No-one had had the courtesy to inform him of his brother's demise, and it appears that the Wydvilles intentionally withheld news of it from him for their own purposes. Hastings, discovering this, was appalled, and took it upon himself to write to Gloucester with the sad tidings. He also sent an urgent warning to the Duke that the Queen's party meant to oust him from power. Mancini heard later that Hastings 'had advised the Duke to hasten to the capital with a strong force and avenge the insult done him by his enemies. He might easily obtain his revenge if, before reaching the City, he took the young King Edward under his protection and authority, while seizing, before they were alive to the danger, those of the King's followers who were not in agreement with this policy.' Hastings added that he was alone in the capital and not without great danger, for he could scarcely escape the snares of his enemies since their old hatred was aggravated by his friendship for the Duke of Gloucester. Mancini says that 'according to common report', this letter was sent by Hastings after a Council meeting on 20th April, but Gloucester had received it by that date, and it is more likely that Hastings wrote to the Duke very soon after the meeting of councillors that took place around 11th April.

Croyland implies that Hastings also confided his fears in a letter to the Duke of Buckingham.

Henry Stafford, second Duke of Buckingham, was one of the most important noblemen in England. He came from an old and respected family that had risen to prominence in the mid fourteenth century, having enriched and advanced itself since that time by a succession of advantageous marriages with heiresses, the greatest of which was that between the fifth Earl of Stafford and Anne, daughter of Thomas of Woodstock, the youngest son of Edward III. Buckingham was twice descended from this lady, who had brought to her husband not only her father's wealth but also half the great Marcher inheritance of the Bohuns, which had been shared between two sisters: Anne's mother, Eleanor de Bohun, and Mary de Bohun, the mother of Henry V. Henvy VI had further advanced the Staffords and in 1444 had rewarded the devoted service of Humphrey Stafford with the dukedom of Buckingham and an income of £5,500 per annum, which was greater than that of any other magnate at the time. Humphrey styled himself 'the high and mighty Prince Humphrey', and he and his race were known to their contemporaries as 'sore and hard-dealing men'. They were loyal to the House of Lancaster during the Wars of the Roses, and the first duke died fighting for Henry VI at the Battle of Northampton in 1460. As his son had predeceased him in 1458, his inheritance passed to his five-year-old grandson, Henry Stafford, who became the second duke and a royal ward.

Although he was a minor the young Buckingham was fabulously wealthy and could look forward to a future that held influence, power and a brilliant marriage. He owned vast lands, manors and castles in twenty-two counties, centred mainly upon Wales and the Midlands, and himself had a claim to be in the line of succession to the throne by virtue of his descent from Edward III. In recognition of this he was granted in 1474 the right to display a coat of arms 'near to the King and of his royal blood', which emblazoned the undifferenced heraldic device of Thomas of Woodstock, whose heir-general he was.

Buckingham was only six when Edward IV became the first king of the House of York, but young as he was his loyalties remained with Lancaster. In 1464, the new queen, Elizabeth Wydville, was granted his wardship, but this was little to the liking of this proud child who looked disdainfully upon his new guardian as an upstart parvenue. He was horrified, therefore, when, in 1466, the Queen betrothed him to her sister Katherine, one of those matches which so infuriated Warwick; Mancini says Buckingham was 'forced' to the marriage and despised his bride, 'whom he scorned to wed on account of her humble origin', and Buckingham himself, years later, complained he had been 'disparaged' by the union. However, he did his duty and sired three sons and two daughters, though there are indications that the marriage was never happy.

Buckingham was eleven when he married Katherine Wydville. He spent the last years of his childhood with his brother under the unwelcome authority of the Queen, who received from the King £500 per annum for their keep, and who engaged a master scholar, John Giles, to teach them grammar.

As he grew to maturity, the young Duke remained loyal to Lancaster, nurturing a festering hatred for the Wydvilles, whom, says Mancini, he 'loathed'. His mother having been a Beaufort, he was Lancastrian by descent as well as by family tradition. But while the deaths of Henry VI and his heir put an end to the Duke's hopes in one respect, they gave birth to a new cause in his life, that of laying his hands on the other half of the Bohun inheritance, which had belonged to Henry VI. Buckingham claimed it by reversionary right, but Edward IV had seized all Henry VI's estates and possessions, saying they were the property of the Crown. Thereafter, the Duke harboured a grudge against the King for depriving him of what he considered to be rightfully his; it was probably because of this, and his ill-concealed resentment of Lord Rivers' power in Wales, which he felt should have been his by right of his being the greatest landowner in the region, that Buckingham did not gain much advancement at court during Edward IV's reign. He graced state functions and entertainments, and supported the King in the prosecution of Clarence, himself pronouncing the death sentence in Parliament, but this benefited him very little, and he was not granted the great offices that a man in his position could expect to receive.

This may also have had something to do with Buckingham's personal character, for he was not popular at court, nor with his tenants on his estates. He was a proud man, jealous of the power of others, and ruthlessly ambitious. He lacked judgement and often acted on impulse. His friends found him to be bluff and hearty, witty and talkative – in fact he was gifted, says More, with marvellous eloquence and had a real talent for persuasive speaking and public oration. More also tells us that Buckingham was strikingly handsome and impressive in appearance. He spoke, it appears, with a northern accent, signing himself phonetically, 'Harre Bokynham'. His motto was *'Souvente me Souvene'* ('Think of me often'), a suitably egotistical device.

By writing to Buckingham, whose hatred of the Wydvilles was famous, Hastings had good reason to believe he would secure an ally.

The news of Edward IV's death reached his son at Ludlow on 14th April, as did the letter asking Rivers to bring his charge to London by 1st May. The news of his father's death was broken to the young King by his uncle, and as the news spread, says Rous, 'his father's friends flocked to him', to pay their respects. Rivers does not seem to have regarded the summons to London as urgent: he had made plans to celebrate St George's Day at Ludlow, and saw no reason to alter them. He also needed time to assemble the escort of 2,000 men for the journey. Mancini records that on 16th April Edward V wrote to the burghers of Lynn in Norfolk (which was near Middleton, a manor owned by Rivers) that he intended 'to be at our City of London in all convenient haste, by God's Grace to be crowned at Westminster'.

On that same day Edward IV's body was taken to Westminster Abbey for the commencement of his funeral ceremonies, the chief mourner being his sister's son, the young Earl of Lincoln. Three days later the late King's body was buried, as he had directed in his original will, in St George's Chapel, Windsor. Gloucester, at Middleham, learned of his brother's death from Hastings' messenger, who probably arrived around 16th/17th April at the latest. The news provoked in the Duke not only grief but also alarm, for he perceived at once that if he did not act urgently and decisively he would be ousted from power by the Wydvilles. His very life might even be in danger, bearing in mind the recent precedent for eliminating a royal duke, and the Wydvilles had shown themselves to be ruthless in the past; certainly Gloucester held them responsible for his brother's execution.

The Duke was also aware that his office of protector-designate would lapse with the coronation, and that the Wydvilles were arranging an early crowning with precisely this in mind. Gloucester could foresee a Wydville-dominated Council ruling through an acquiescent king who, as his mother's son, would be no friend to himself. Nor, if this happened, was it likely that the Duke would be allowed to retain his power and vast lands in the North, for the Wydvilles could only view that as a threat to themselves. Everything that Gloucester held dear was at stake. In fact he had no choice but to act to bring about the overthrow of the Wydvilles and seize the reins of government himself. More and other later writers did not believe that the Duke stood in any real danger at this time, but the weight of contemporary circumstantial evidence indicates strongly that the Wydvilles posed a very real threat to him and that he believed his political and personal survival were both in jeopardy.

Gloucester began planning his coup immediately. Hastings had warned that the key to success was gaining control of the King's person, the Wydvilles' most important political asset, and the Duke recognised the good sense in this. Careful planning was essential to ensure a successful outcome, and sound support was vital. The Duke wasted no time and sent secret messages to Buckingham, Hastings and others, warning them they would be in danger if 'our well-preserved ill-willers' were allowed to remain in control of the King and the government, and asked for their help. He also wrote to many northern lords who could be counted upon to offer loyal support, and commanded them to rendezvous with him at York around 20th April.

To outward appearances, what Gloucester was planning was the political elimination of the Wydvilles. Yet Mancini believed that from the moment he learned of Edward IV's death, Gloucester was plotting to take the throne for himself, and Croyland was of the opinion that such a plot was hatched in the North at this time. Vergil agreed with Mancini, stating he had learned that 'Richard began to be kindled with an ardent desire for sovereignty' immediately he heard that his brother was dead, while More went so far as to assert that he had had designs on the throne even before that event, which is hardly likely as no-one expected Edward IV to die so young while his heir was still a minor.

It was vital that, whatever he was really planning, Gloucester led the Queen and the Council to believe that his intentions were honourable and posed no threat to themselves. Croyland states he immediately wrote 'the most pleasant letter to console the Queen; he promised to come and offer submission, fealty and all that was due from him to his lord and king, Edward V'. Mancini, corroborating this, adds that he said he was willing to take on the office of protector entrusted to him by his brother. Vergil observes wryly that the Duke's 'loving' letters to the Queen promised her 'seas and mountains'.

Gloucester next sent a formal letter to the Council, saying – according to Mancini – that 'he had been loyal to his brother Edward, and would be, if only permitted, loyal to his brother's son and to all his brother's issues, even female, if perchance, which God forbid, the youth should die. He would expose his life to every danger that the children might endure in their father's realm. He asked the councillors to take his desserts into consideration when disposing of the government, to which he was entitled by law and his brother's ordinance, and he reminded them that nothing contrary to law and his brother's desire could be decreed without harm.' In fact, Edward IV had had no legal right to name Gloucester as protector; a dead king's wishes held no force in law. In 1422 both Parliament and Council had rejected the late Henry V's choice of Humphrey of Gloucester as protector during Henry VI's minority, on the grounds that the King's will had been made 'without the assent of the three estates'. Only the Council and Parliament had the right to decide who should govern the realm during a royal minority.

If Gloucester was aware of such legal niceties, he had no time for them. He left Middleham for York around 20th April on the first stage of his journey south. With him were 300 gentlemen of the North, all wearing deepest black like the Duke. It was a sizeable but not an alarming retinue. The plan was that the Duke would intercept Lord Rivers and the King on their journey to the capital.

Gloucester arrived in York around 21st April. He came, says Croyland, 'all dressed in mourning, and held a solemn funeral ceremony for the King, full of tears. He bound by oath all the nobility of those parts in fealty to the King's son; he himself swore first of all.'

Buckingham had learned of the death of Edward IV around 14th April, when he was on his estates at Brecon on the Welsh Marches. A week later he received Gloucester's letter, in which the Duke, says Mancini, complained 'of the insult done to him by the ignoble family of the Queen. Buckingham, since he was of the highest nobility, was disposed to sympathise, because he had his own reason for detesting the Queen's kin.' It was his burning desire to see the Wydvilles crushed, and his hope that once in power Gloucester would grant him the position he had hitherto been denied and hand over the Bohun inheritance, that made Buckingham decide, more or less immediately, to ally himself with the Duke, even if it did mean pitching his fortunes in with those of the House of York.

More says that Buckingham sent his most trusted agent, a man called Humphrey Persivall, to carry the Duke's pledge of support to Gloucester and tell him that Buckingham was ready to march with 'a thousand good fellows, if need be', because he agreed with Hastings that securing the person of the King was the most effective way of executing a coup against the Wydvilles. According to More, Persivall saw Richard at York, but this cannot have been so because Buckingham could not have received Gloucester's letter until 21st April at the earliest and even if he had despatched Persivall that same day, it would have taken the man at least four days to ride from Brecon to York. York Civic Records confirm that Richard had left York for Nottingham by 23rd April. More says that Persivall went back to Brecon and then rode to Nottingham for a second interview with Gloucester, but it is clear that there could only have been one meeting between the Duke and the agent due to the speed of events and that it must have taken place at Nottingham. Buckingham, his decision made, instructed Persivall to inform Gloucester that he would rendezvous with him at Northampton. Then, after Persivall had gone, his master spent a few days gathering together an escort of 300 men and preparing for the journey before setting out from Brecon by 26th April at the latest.

In London, meanwhile, according to Mancini, 'on completion of the royal obsequies, and while many peers of the realm were collecting in the City, a Council assembled', summoned by the Queen and Dorset in the King's name. This was a lawful assembly of the magnates, summoned in accordance with the precedent of the previous minority, on the basis that there had to be some form of administration until Edward V was crowned and that the late King's councillors were best suited to assume the mantle of royal authority in the interim. Tradition decreed that this Council should meet regularly at Westminster until the coronation, when its powers would lapse and Parliament could decide on which form of government would be best. Nevertheless, many were uneasy about its convening, and were not reassured when Dorset commanded its members to gather in the Queen's presence as if she were already regent. In fact Dorset had already incurred the anger and resentment of several councillors by issuing orders himself in the name of Edward V, signing them 'Brother Uterine to the King'.

The Council met around 20th April and sat for several days. Croyland states that 'the most urgent desire of all present was that the Prince should succeed his father in all his glory'. Dorset opened proceedings by urging that the King be crowned as planned on 4th May, but some councillors raised objections, guessing the motive for such haste, and Mancini says there were those, foremost amongst them Hastings, who 'said that everything ought not thus to be hurried through; rather they should await the young King's uncle'. To this Dorset 'is said to have replied, "We are so important that even without the King's uncle we can make and enforce our decisions."' This arrogant remark provoked a heated debate over who should govern the country which lasted for several days.

'The problem of government during the royal minority,' observes Mancini, 'was referred to the consideration of the barons.' The Wydville party believed they had the Council in their pocket, but with the majority of its members recently arrived in London it soon became obvious that they did not after all have a sufficiently large majority to persuade the councillors to invest the regency in themselves. There is no evidence that the Queen herself wished to be regent; either Dorset or Rivers would have been an obvious choice. Yet even thus curbed, the Wydvilles were still a political force to be reckoned with. But they had many enemies opposing them, above all Hastings, who had insulted them in the council chamber by insisting that the base blood of the Queen's kindred unfitted them for the task of governing the realm. Already, not a fortnight after the King's death, there were rumours in the land that the Wydvilles were plotting to seize power, which only further inflamed the people's hatred towards them. The Council were aware of this, and Croyland states that 'The more prudent members were of the opinion that the guardianship of so youthful a person [as the King] ought to be utterly forbidden to his uncles and brothers of the mother's side.'

Further debate ensued and then, says Mancini, 'two opinions were propounded'. Hastings proposed that the Duke of Gloucester should govern 'because Edward, in his will, had so directed, and because by law [*sic*] the government ought to devolve upon him'. The Council considered this, discussing what powers Gloucester might enjoy as protector, a subject on which opinions were divided. Dorset envisaged Gloucester as a figurehead presiding over the Council, but other councillors argued that the King's will had conferred upon him sovereign power. If he were to be appointed protector now he would expect to have his powers extended beyond the coronation, until the King gained his majority. This might not, however, be for very long, for Edward IV had only intended the Council of the Marches to act on his son's behalf until the boy reached fourteen. Henry VI had declared himself of age at sixteen, but there were no set rules as to when a minor achieved majority, and it is probable that Edward IV confidently expected his son to attain his on his fourteenth birthday in November 1484, eighteen months hence.

The Wydvilles did not want Gloucester exercising sovereign power as protector, even for this short time, and made a second proposal. Mancini states that this 'was that the government should be carried on by many persons, among whom the Duke, far from being excluded, should be accounted the chief. By this means the Duke would be given due honour and the royal authority greater security, because it had been found that no regent ever laid down his office save reluctantly and from armed compulsion, whence civil wars had often arisen. Moreover, if the entire form were committed to one man, he might easily usurp the sovereignty. All who favoured the Queen's family voted for this proposal, as they were afraid that if Richard took unto himself the crown, or even governed alone, they, who bore the blame for Clarence's death, would suffer death or at least be ejected from their high estate.' The Wydvilles obviously feared Gloucester as much as he feared them: already it had occurred to them that he might try to usurp the throne. Contemporary writers recognised that both factions based their policies on fear of what would happen to themselves if the other party achieved power.

Whilst the Council was debating these two proposals, Gloucester's letters arrived. That to the Council was publicly circulated by his supporters, on his instructions. Mancini says, 'This letter had a great effect on the minds of the people who, as they had previously favoured the Duke in their hearts from a belief in his probity, now began to support him openly and aloud, so that it was commonly said by all that the Duke deserved the government. However, the Council voted in a majority for the alternative policy, and they fixed a day for the coronation,' 4th May. Mancini was of the opinion that by not naming Gloucester protector the Council was deliberately flouting Edward IV's wishes, but in actual fact it had acted with wisdom and moderation, curbing the ambitions of the Wydvilles whilst according Gloucester, not supreme power, but the leadership of the Council and a say in the government.

Finally, Dorset reminded the councillors that a state of war existed between England and France, and that the country should be defended from any invasion. As a result, Sir Edward Wydville was appointed Admiral of the Fleet with responsibility for assembling a navy and recruiting men, a task he began carrying out straight away, making sure that his chief officers were Wydville supporters. On 29th April he put to sea, his ostensible purpose being to move against French and Breton pirates in the English Channel.

At Ludlow, Earl Rivers had assembled the King's escort, and on 23rd April, according to Rous, 'the accustomed service of the Knights of the Garter was solemnly celebrated, concluding with a splendid banquet'. The next day, Edward V, Rivers, the King's tutor Bishop Alcock, his faithful servant Vaughan, and his relative Sir Richard Haute, set out with a 'sober company' of 2,000 men, travelling along Watling Street, the old Roman road.

Two days later, Gloucester was in Nottingham, as the city records show. Here Humphrey Persivall found him and spoke with him, says More, 'in the dead of night in his secret chamber', delivering Buckingham's message and informing the Duke that Buckingham would meet him at Northampton. Gloucester then sent Persivall back to meet up with Buckingham on the road and confirm the arrangements. Thus, says Mancini, 'the Duke allied himself with the Duke of Buckingham', and, 'having united their resources, both Dukes wrote to the young King, to ascertain from him on what day and by what route he intended to enter the capital, so they could join him, that in their company his entry to the City might be more magnificent.' The ducal messengers met up with the King's party on the road south; learning that Gloucester and Buckingham were to meet in Northampton, Mancini says Rivers agreed to do 'as they requested' and join them there. More and Rous state that he even went several miles out of his way to accommodate them, which indicates that, firstly, he did not expect anything untoward, and secondly, that he was anxious to foster good relations with Gloucester.

Gloucester was still in touch with Hastings, meanwhile, who was sending him regular reports on the Council's proceedings and events in London. When, a day or so later, the Duke left Nottingham, his plans for a coup were complete.

7

'An Innocent Lamb in the Hands of Wolves'

The King and Lord Rivers arrived at Northampton on 29th April, 1483, just as – says Croyland – Gloucester and Buckingham met up north of the town where all parties had arranged to meet. Soon after his arrival the King was joined by Sir Richard Grey, hot-foot from London and probably bearing orders from the Queen to Rivers, urging him to press on to the capital without delay. Rivers thereupon escorted King Edward fourteen miles further south, to Stony Stratford, that same day. Here, tradition says, he commandeered for his young master the Rose and Crown Inn for the night, an inn that still stands on the High Street, its ancient bricks hidden by a modern façade.

Rivers and Grey then took a small escort and prepared to ride back to Northampton. Mancini says the King asked Rivers to greet Gloucester on his behalf and pay his respects, while Croyland believed that Rivers' chief intention was to convince the Duke that the Council's plans for the minority government were in the best interests of everyone; to this end, he would adopt a conciliatory approach. Rivers ordered that the King was to continue his journey to London the next morning, with or without him. He then left for Northampton, intending, says More, 'on the morrow to follow the King and be with him at Stony Stratford early, ere he departed'.

Meanwhile Gloucester, Buckingham, and their combined escorts of 600 men, had arrived in Northampton to find the King gone. In the High Street there were three inns, side by side. Gloucester took one, which Mancini describes as 'a very strong place', and Buckingham another. When Rivers and Grey returned, Gloucester was settled in his lodging and, according to Mancini, 'graciously received' them there. Addressing Gloucester as 'my Lord Protector', a sop calculated to mollify the Duke, Rivers explained, somewhat lamely, that the reason for the King's unexpected departure had been the lack of suitable accommodation for all parties in Northampton. Gloucester appears to have accepted this with equanimity, and to have hidden any chagrin he may have felt as a result of the King having been moved for the present beyond his reach. Rivers had certainly exceeded his authority: the correct action for him to have taken would have been to wait with the King for Gloucester to arrive and then to have consulted him as to what to do. His failure to do so had been an act of gross discourtesy and inexcusable presumption. But Gloucester betrayed no trace of anger. Instead, he arranged for Rivers, Grey and their escort to occupy the third inn in the row, and then invited the Earl to take dinner with himself and Buckingham that evening at his own inn.

During the course of that meal Rivers must have acquainted the two dukes with the proceedings and rulings of the Council in London, and this, together with his awareness of the Wydvilles' deliberate with-holding of the news of his brother's death from him, indicated clearly to Gloucester precisely where he stood. Supreme power was to be denied him: he was to be a figurehead, one voice on the Council, while his dangerous enemies, the Wydvilles, controlled and dominated a king who would soon reach his majority. This was not what his brother had intended, and certainly not what he himself could tolerate. But he dissembled, showing no sign of concern, and, as More tells us, there was 'made that night much friendly cheer between these two dukes and the Lord Rivers', passing, says Mancini, 'a great part of the night in conviviality'. But, continues More, when Rivers had retired to bed in his own inn, Gloucester, Buckingham and a north country ducal councillor of Richard's called Richard Ratcliffe sat up discussing the situation until nearly dawn, deciding at length to effect a coup the next day, with the purpose of seizing the King's person and eliminating the hated Wydvilles. Vergil says: 'As is commonly believed, [Gloucester] even then discovered to [Buckingham] his intent of usurping the kingdom.' This accords with the assertions of Mancini and Croyland that Richard plotted to take the throne from the time he learned of Edward IV's death.

Gloucester and Buckingham slept not at all that night. Before dawn, they secretly ordered guards to be posted along all roads out of Northampton, to guard, says Mancini, against anyone informing the King of what was going on. Then they gathered their escort, ready to march on Stony Stratford. The doors to Rivers' inn were locked.

All sources agree that Rivers had been lulled into a sense of false security by the apparent friendliness and compliance of the two dukes. Therefore he 'marvellously disliked it' when he woke at dawn and found himself a prisoner. Mancini says that when everything was prepared for the journey, Gloucester, Buckingham and a few armed guards entered Rivers' inn and confronted him, accusing him of influencing Edward V against them and charging him with having tried to remove the King from the guardianship of the protector appointed by his father. Gloucester's men then 'seized Rivers and his companions and imprisoned them in that place', in the charge of Sir Thomas Gower.

Then, 'with a large body of soldiers and in company with the Duke of Buckingham', Gloucester, continues Mancini, 'hastened at full gallop towards the young King' at Stony Stratford, taking their joint escort with them, and Sir Richard Grey. 'Wherefore they reached the young King, ignorant of [Rivers'] arrest, and immediately saluted him as their sovereign.' Edward was already mounted alongside Vaughan, Haute and his escort, ready to leave for London, fifty miles away. Gloucester, says Croyland, 'did not omit or refuse to pay every mark of respect to the King his nephew, in the way of uncovering his head, bending the knee, or other posture required of a subject'. Buckingham also paid homage to Edward on his knees, and the boy, says More, 'received them in very joyous and amiable manner'. His joy was not to last for long.

Then, says Mancini, the two dukes 'exhibited a mournful countenance, while expressing profound grief at the death of the King's father, whose demise they imputed to his ministers, since they were accounted the servants and companions of his vices, and had ruined his health'. This extraordinary outburst to a boy just bereft of his father was a direct thrust at the Wydvilles and the first example of the moral propaganda that Gloucester came habitually to use to discredit his enemies. 'Wherefore,' the Duke continued, lest these same ministers 'should play the same old game with the son, [they] should be removed from the King's side, because such a child would be incapable of governing so great a realm by means of puny men. Gloucester himself accused them of conspiring his own death and of preparing ambushes both in the capital and on the road, which had been revealed to him by their accomplices. Indeed, he said, it was common knowledge that they had attempted to deprive him of the office of regent conferred on him by his brother. He said that he himself, whom the King's father had approved, could better discharge the duties of government, not only because of his experience of affairs, but also on account of his popularity. He would neglect nothing pertaining to the duty of a loyal subject and diligent protector.' He added that he had been forced, for his own safety's sake, to arrest Lord Rivers at Northampton.

Edward was stunned by this news and sceptical about what Gloucester had told him, as are historians today, for there is no evidence to corroborate Gloucester's allegations that the Wydvilles had actually planned attempts on his life. Mancini says the King answered 'that he merely had those ministers whom his father had given him and, relying on his father's prudence, he believed that good and faithful ones had been given him. He could see no evil in them and wished to keep them.' He went on, 'What my brother Marquess [of Dorset] has done I cannot say, but in good faith I dare well answer for my Lord Rivers, and my brother here [Grey], that they be innocent of any such matter.' But here, Gloucester interrupted, saying, 'They have the dealing of these matters far from the knowledge of your good Grace.'

Edward was not convinced. Mancini records that he answered that 'as for the government of the kingdom, he had great confidence in the peers of the realm and the Queen. On hearing the Queen's name, the Duke of Buckingham answered it was not the business of women but of men to govern kingdoms, and so if he cherished any confidence in her he had better relinquish it. Let him place all his hope in his barons, who excelled in power and nobility.'

At various points during this conversation, Grey had attempted to interrupt but had been roughly silenced by Buckingham. Now, says More, both dukes 'picked a quarrel' with him, accusing him and his kinsmen of conspiring 'to rule the King and the realm, and to set variance among the estates', and, says Croyland, 'to destroy the old nobility'. And without further ado they arrested Grey, Vaughan and

Haute in the King's presence, as all sources agree, and then, states Mancini, 'handed them over to the care of guards'.

Mancini goes on to say that thereafter Edward V, for whom this had been a most traumatic and frightening experience, 'surrendered himself to the care of his uncle, which was inevitable, for although the dukes cajoled him by moderation, yet they clearly showed that they were demanding rather than supplicating'.

Something even more ominous was now to occur. Mancini relates that Gloucester deprived the King of his escort and issued an immediate proclamation ordering that every member of it must withdraw at once 'and not approach any place to which the King might chance to come, under penalty of death'. Clearly the Duke was taking precautions against any counter-coup by Wydville sympathisers. As for the King's attendants and servants, Mancini tells us that 'nearly all were ordered home', even, says Rous, 'his special tutor and diligent mentor in goodly ways, Master John Alcock. [He] was removed like all the rest, but not, however, subjected to the rigours of imprisonment.' This is borne out by the fact that in May Alcock attended a meeting of Edward IV's executors. Separation from his personal servants and the chief officers of his household, especially the faithful Vaughan, and their replacement by men chosen by Gloucester, may well have been calculated to break the King's will. It certainly ensured that he was isolated from all Wydville influence. More says he was terribly distressed by it: 'He wept and was nothing content, but it booted not.'

Gloucester and Buckingham then returned in triumph with the King and their prisoners to Northampton, where they enjoyed a celebratory dinner, after which, says More, 'they took further counsel'. Rivers and Grey were shut up in separate rooms, and it is unlikely that the young King was allowed to see his former governor. More records that at dinner 'the Duke of Gloucester sent a dish from his own table to the Lord Rivers, praying him to be of good cheer, all should be well enough', but Rivers could not touch it and asked that it be given to Grey.

Later that day, says Mancini, Gloucester wrote to both the Council and the Lord Mayor of London, Sir Edmund Shaa, notifying them of what had taken place and assuring them that 'he had not confined his nephew the King of England, rather had he rescued him and the realm from perdition, since the young man would have fallen into the hands of those who, since they had not spared either the honour or life of the father, could not be expected to have more regard for the youthfulness of the son. No-one, save only him, had such solicitude for the welfare of King Edward and the preservation of the state. At an early date, he and the boy would come to the City so that the coronation might be more splendidly performed.' More states that Gloucester also wrote with news of his coup to Hastings.

'In this wise,' More concluded, 'the Duke took upon himself the order and governance of the young King' and successfully broke the power of the Wydvilles at a stroke, without one drop of blood being shed. To all appearances the coup had been aimed only at the Wydvilles; nevertheless, it had the effect of alienating the King, perhaps irrevocably and permanently, from Gloucester. Indeed, it may well be that Edward V saw himself, in the words of Rous, as having been 'received like an innocent lamb into the hands of wolves'. From now on his liberty would be curtailed: Mancini says that Gloucester and Buckingham decided to take turns at guarding the King, 'for they were afraid lest he should escape or be forcibly delivered from their hands'. Soon afterwards they learned that the Welsh people 'could not bear to think that their prince had been carried off'; the dukes feared that these Welsh supporters, whose existence is also attested to by Molinet, might well rise on the King's behalf. This was an added threat to the success of their plans.

Gloucester now embarked on an exercise in public relations, seeking, says Mancini, 'in every way to procure the good will of the people; hoping that if, by their support, he could be proclaimed the only ruler, he might subsequently possess himself of the sovereignty with ease, even against their wishes'. This may indeed have been just what Edward V now feared, and what others would anticipate, once news of the coup broke.

This happened just before midnight on 30th April, in London, and threw everything into a turmoil. 'The unexpectedness of the event horrified everyone,' says Mancini. The Queen was stunned by the sudden realisation that, after twenty years, her family's power and influence were at an end, and that her much-feared enemy was in control of her son, the King. She was, says More, 'in great flight and heaviness, bewailing her child's ruin, her friends' mischance and her own misfortune'. Her fear of Gloucester and what he might do to her and hers in revenge for her role in the fall of Clarence was very real indeed; she had no cause to expect any kindness or clemency from him, especially since she had done all she could to prevent him from becoming protector. Clearly she feared that her very life might be in danger.

Mancini relates that, with the aid of her son Dorset, Elizabeth Wydville at first 'began collecting an army to defend themselves and set free the young King from the clutches of the dukes. But when they had exhorted certain nobles who had come to the City, and others, to take up arms, they perceived that men's minds were not only irresolute but altogether hostile to themselves. Some even said openly that it was more just and profitable that the youthful sovereign should be with his paternal uncle than with his maternal uncles and uterine brothers.' The Queen could perceive clearly how things stood, and gathering together her younger son the Duke of York, her five daughters ranging in ages from seventeen to two, her brother Lionel, Bishop of Salisbury, and her son Dorset, she hastily withdrew in the early hours of 1st May, with as many of her personal goods as she could assemble, to the Sanctuary at Westminster Abbey, where she and her party were received in the College Hall by John Esteney, Abbot of Westminster, and, says the chronicler Edward Hall, 'registered as sanctuary persons'. Mancini states it was commonly believed that the royal treasure had some time before this been secretly removed from the Tower by Dorset and divided between himself, the Queen and Sir Edward Wydville, who was said to have taken his to sea with him. The Queen and Dorset reputedly carried theirs into the Sanctuary.

Westminster Abbey had afforded sanctuary to criminals and law-breakers since Saxon times, and the great, grim, cruciform stronghold of the Sanctuary building dated from Edward the Confessor's reign. Two storeys high, it was demolished with great difficulty in 1750. But the Queen and her relatives did not come here to mingle with debtors and common felons; they lodged in the comfort of the Abbot's house, where the Queen had given birth to Prince Edward during her previous sojourn in sanctuary in 1470. Here, she and those with her could be afforded permanent protection as fugitives.

Before dawn broke, Archbishop Rotherham of York arrived. Mancini says that 'though of humble origin, [he] had become, thanks to his talent, a man of note with King Edward'. He owed his advancement, to a great extent, to the Queen, and was stoutly loyal to her. Rotherham's London residence was York Place, by the Abbey, and having learned in the night of Gloucester's coup and the Queen's flight, he at once decided to deliver the Great Seal of England, which he held as Lord Chancellor, to the Queen, 'about whom [says More] he found much heaviness and rumble, haste and business, carriage and conveyance of her stuff into sanctuary: chests, coffers, packs, fardels, trusses, all on men's backs, some breaking down the walls to bring in the next way. The Queen sat alone, a-low on the rushes, all desolate and dismayed, whom the Archbishop comforted in the best manner he could, showing her he trusted the matter was nothing so sore as she took it for', and that he 'was put in good hope and out of fear' by a message from Lord Hastings assuring him, 'All shall be well.'

The Queen was not reassured. Hastings, she pointed out, was 'one of them that laboureth to destroy me and my blood'.

'Madam,' replied Rotherham, 'be ye of good cheer. For I assure you, if they crown any other king than your son, whom they now have with them, we shall on the morrow crown his brother, whom you have here with you.' Then he delivered up to her the Great Seal 'which, as that noble prince your husband delivered unto me, so here I deliver it unto you, to the use and behoof of your son'.

Dawn was breaking when Rotherham left. Back at York Place he looked through the window of his chamber and saw, says More, 'all the Thames full of boats of the Duke of Gloucester's servants, watching that no man should go into the Sanctuary, nor none pass unsearched'.

As the momentous news of Gloucester's coup spread, More recounts, there was 'great commotion and murmur, as well in other places as in the City, the people diversely divining upon this dealing'. Some lords, says Croyland, 'collected their forces at Westminster in the Queen's name, and others at London under the shadow of Lord Hastings'. Many citizens donned armour, says More, 'for they reckoned this demeanour attempted against the King himself, in the disturbance of his coronation'. Crowds gathered in the streets, speculating on what would happen next, and, according to Mancini, there became 'current in the capital a sinister rumour that the Duke had brought his nephew, not under his care, but into his power, so as to gain the crown for himself'.

That morning the Council met at Westminster to discuss the situation. Receiving his summons to attend, Archbishop Rotherham had second thoughts about his precipitate action in surrendering the Great Seal to the Queen, fearing, says More, 'that it would be ascribed [as it was indeed] to his overmuch lightness that he so suddenly had yielded up the Great Seal to the Queen, to whom the custody thereof nothing pertained without especial commandment of the King, [and he] secretly sent for the Seal again, and brought it with him after the customable manner'.

When the lords were assembled, Gloucester's letters were 'read aloud in the council chamber, and [says Mancini] to the populace' afterwards. More tells us that Hastings addressed the councillors, saying he was assured that Gloucester was 'fastly faithful to his prince' and that he had arrested Rivers and the rest only to ensure his own safety, for he was sure they had planned to murder him. The Duke, went on Hastings, would make sure that his prisoners received impartial justice when he arrived in London, and he implored the lords not to take up arms on Edward V's behalf. The councillors were 'somewhat appeased' by this; Mancini says they 'all praised the Duke of Gloucester for his dutifulness towards his nephews and for his intention to punish their enemies'. More believed that Hastings' reassurances did much to discredit the Wydville faction on the Council, and to allay the fears of Londoners at large as soon as they were reported in the streets. But there were those on the Council, Mancini heard, 'who realised [Gloucester's] ambition and his cunning [and] always suspected where his enterprise would lead'.

On 2nd May, Gloucester despatched his prisoners under guard from Northampton to three of his northern strongholds: Rivers was sent to Sheriff Hutton Castle, Grey to Middleham and Vaughan to Pontefract. That same day the Duke was informed, probably by Hastings, of the reaction in London to his coup and of Rotherham's rash action in surrendering the Great Seal to the Queen. Gloucester immediately sent orders to London that Rotherham was to be deprived at once of the office of Lord Chancellor, although he allowed him to retain his seat on the Council. More says the Duke 'supposed he would be faithful to Edward's heirs come what might', having learned he had been their champion at previous Council meetings. He also knew Rotherham to be a staunch friend to the Queen.

Gloucester then wrote, in the King's name, to Thomas Bourchier,

Archbishop of Canterbury, requiring him 'to see for the safeguard and sure keeping of the Great Seal of this our realm, unto our coming to our City of London, and [to] provide for the surety and safeguard of our Tower of London, and the treasure being in the same'. Gloucester had not yet found out that the royal treasure had been appropriated by the Wydvilles.

All these actions of Gloucester's were illegal, because he had no authority as protector, having been neither appointed nor confirmed in that office by the Council. The arrest and incarceration of Rivers, Grey, Vaughan and Haute, and the sacking of Rotherham were therefore, strictly speaking, acts of tyranny, and were seen as such by many at the time.

On the morning of 3rd May, Edward V, escorted by Gloucester and Buckingham, left Northampton for London. They spent the night at St Albans, and it was probably here that they passed the time in appending their signatures and mottoes to a parchment now in the British Museum:

'Edwardus Quintus'
'Loyaultié me lie. Richard Gloucestre.'
'Souvente me souvene. Harre Bokynham.'

The next morning they prepared to enter the capital.

8

The Lord Protector

On the morning of 4th May, the King, escorted by Gloucester and Buckingham, left St Albans and travelled via Barnet towards London. Mancini states that Gloucester was now ready to enter the capital, having 'ascertained the attitude of everyone, and with the help of friends' in the City 'provided against all eventualities'. Garbed in 'black cloth, like a mourner' and accompanied, says Mancini, 'by no more than 500 soldiers', he and the young King were officially welcomed to London at Hornsey Park by the Lord Mayor, aldermen and sheriffs, all mounted and clad in scarlet, followed by 410 mounted members of the great livery companies wearing new gowns of violet. Thus Edward V was escorted into his capital, 'riding in blue velvet', the two black-clad Dukes at either side. The *Great Chronicle* tells that, as they rode, Gloucester repeatedly bowed low in the saddle and presented the King to the cheering crowds, crying, 'Behold your prince and sovereign lord!' More says that his manner towards the boy was humble and reverent, the more so to convince the people of his loyalty.

Already Gloucester's propaganda machine had swung into action. Mancini says that he and Buckingham 'were seeking at every turn to arouse hatred against the Queen's kin and to estrange public opinion from her relatives'. He goes on: 'Ahead of the procession they sent four wagons loaded with weapons bearing the devices of the Queen's brothers and sons, besides criers to make generally known that these arms had been collected by the Duke's enemies and stored at convenient points outside the capital, so as to attack and slay the Duke of

Gloucester. Since many knew these charges to be false, because the arms in question had been placed there long before the late King's death, when war was being waged against the Scots, mistrust both of his accusation and designs upon the throne was exceedingly augmented.' This, and the glaring absence of the Queen, struck jarring notes upon an otherwise harmonious day.

The young King proceeded via Cheapside to St Paul's Churchyard, where the palace of the bishops of London then stood on the site of the present Chapter House. Destroyed in 1650, it was sometimes used as a royal residence during the mediaeval period, and had been chosen as a temporary lodging for Edward V. Once he was installed there, Gloucester summoned the magnates and citizens to swear fealty to their sovereign, which, 'being a most encouraging presage of future prosperity, was done by all with the greatest pleasure and delight'. Hastings, says Croyland, 'was bursting with joy at the way things were turning out'. The homage over, Gloucester retired to Baynard's Castle, where he was lodging. Here, on 7th May, Archbishop Bourchier took possession of the Great Seal.

Gloucester was clearly in complete control, not only of the King but of the Council which met on 10th May at the Bishop's Palace for a session that, according to Croyland, lasted several days. The King, says Rous, remained in residence at the palace, where 'all royal honours were paid to him', but there is no evidence that he attended any of the council meetings. Some members who had served Edward IV now found themselves dismissed by Gloucester, but others, including Hastings, Stanley, Rotherham, Stillington and John Morton, Bishop of Ely, remained, and Bishop Alcock was invited to join them.

The first item on the agenda was to decide upon a suitable, permanent residence for the King, as the Bishop's Palace was adjudged too shabby for him. Croyland says 'a discussion took place about removing the King to some place where fewer restrictions should be imposed upon him. Some mentioned the Hospital of St John', west of Smithfield, but this had Lancastrian and Wydville associations. Others suggested Westminster, but this was felt to be too close to Edward's mother in sanctuary. Then 'the Duke of Buckingham suggested the Tower'. Tradition required a monarch to reside in the royal apartments in the Tower prior to his coronation, and this suggestion 'was at last agreed to by all, even those who had been originally opposed thereto'.

This decision was reached on 10th May, and on 19th May Edward V issued a grant 'at our Tower of London'; the exact date of his removal there is not known.

At that time the Tower was an important royal residence and had not acquired the sinister reputation it earned in the Tudor period. Edward IV had held court there on many occasions, and it would have had happy associations for his son. The Tower was also a state prison, and had many offices, storerooms, the Royal Mint and a small zoo, where Londoners took their children to see the lions and leopards.

The royal apartments occupied by Edward V were truly sumptuous. They consisted of a range of mainly fourteenth-century buildings situated on the south side of the White Tower, facing the River Thames, which was wider then than it is today. There was a great banqueting hall, built by Edward I and flanked with two wings: all had castellated roofs. St Thomas's Gate (later called Traitors' Gate) adjoined the left wing, giving access from the river. The royal complex enclosed two courtyards, ringed by the White Tower, the Wakefield Tower and the Lanthorn Tower.

The Black Book of the Household, dating from the reign of Edward IV, describes the apartments of the sovereign as adjoining the Lanthorn Tower and comprising three chambers: the outer or audience chamber, the inner or privy chamber, and the bedchamber. These had stained-glass windows depicting the royal arms and the *fleur de lys*. There would have been wall-paintings similar to those discovered in the Byward Tower that had a gold and vermilion design of angels and birds, and floor tiles decorated with royal leopards and white harts, the badge of Richard II who had designed these rooms. These beautiful chambers were already falling into decay a century after Edward V occupied them, and were demolished in the 1670s, Charles II being the last monarch to use them.

Once the King's residence had been decided upon, the Council considered afresh the question of who should govern during the King's minority. This was purely a formality, as real power lay in the hands of Gloucester and everybody knew it. Mancini says that 'having entered the City, the first thing he saw to was to have himself proclaimed, by authority of the Council and all the lords, Protector of the King and realm'. Many councillors wholeheartedly supported his appointment, realising that England needed a proven, efficient, able and firm ruler at this time, when war loomed upon the horizon. Gloucester had proved himself in battle, and his record of loyalty to Edward IV and, so far, Edward V was unblemished. So long as it continued that way, the councillors, to a man, were prepared to support him, in the knowledge that, following the precedent of 1429, his office would lapse with the King's coronation, when a regency council would be convened in the King's name.

On 10th May the Duke, says Croyland, 'received the high office of Protector of the kingdom and was accordingly invested with this authority, with the consent and goodwill of the lords, with power to order and forbid in every matter, just like another king'. His official title was 'Protector and Defender of the Realm'. Unlike Duke Humphrey in 1422, Gloucester was entrusted not only with the government of the realm but also with 'the tutelage and oversight of the King's most royal person'. He was also granted sovereign power, where Humphrey had been merely a figurehead. This departure from tradition reflects not only the Council's concern for the security of the kingdom but also the extent of Gloucester's power and influence.

One man who was more than satisfied with Gloucester's appointment was, says Croyland, 'the powerful Lord Hastings, who seemed to oblige the Dukes of Gloucester and Buckingham in every way and to have earned special favour from them. [He] was overjoyed at this new world, declaring that nothing more had happened than the transfer of the rule of the kingdom from two of the Queen's blood to two noble representatives of the King's. This had been achieved without any slaughter or more spilling of blood than that produced by a cut finger.'

The lords now set a new date for the King's coronation which, says Croyland, was 'fixed as 24th June. Everyone was looking forward to the peace and prosperity of the kingdom.' According to Rous, the order was given for coins to be minted in the name of Edward V. None have survived, and the only coins remaining from this period bear Gloucester's boar's head emblem.

On 10th May, John Russell, Bishop of Lincoln and the probable author of the *Croyland Chronicle*, was appointed Lord Chancellor in place of Rotherham by Gloucester. Mancini describes Russell as 'a man of equally great learning and piety', and More says he was 'one of the best learned men undoubtedly that England had in his time'. Russell had not aligned himself with any faction and was appointed, according to Rous, much against his will, being unhappy about being promoted over Archbishop Rotherham.

This done, Gloucester, relates Mancini, 'hastened to remove the other obstacles' that stood in the way of his future security. 'He attempted to bring about the condemnation of those whom he had put in prison' – Rivers, Grey, Vaughan and Haute – 'by obtaining a decision of the Council convicting them of preparing ambushes and of being guilty of treason itself. But this he was quite unable to achieve, because there appeared no certain case as regards the ambushes, and even had the crime been manifest it would not have been treason, for at the time he was neither regent, nor did he hold any other public office.' Croyland says that 'the continued imprisonment of the Queen's relatives and servants', who had been confined 'without judgement or justice', was 'a circumstance that caused the gravest doubts' in the minds of the councillors, who felt quite strongly that all were innocent of the charges levelled against them by Gloucester. This was the first indication to the Duke that the Council were not prepared to grant his every wish, and there was worse to come, for Croyland tells us that the councillors expressed concern that 'the Protector did not, with a sufficient degree of considerateness, take fitting care for the preservation of the dignity and safety of the Queen'. Such criticism showed Gloucester that the Council did not view Elizabeth Wydville as a danger to the security of his position and that their sympathies were with her. He was deeply disturbed, but within a few days had responded to the criticism by appointing a committee of lords, headed by Buckingham and the Archbishop of Canterbury, to negotiate the Queen's voluntary withdrawal with her children from sanctuary. The committee's efforts were doomed to failure: on 23rd May, the minutes of the Corporation of London, preserved in the Guildhall, record that it had met with no success, and up to early June it was still meeting with firm refusals from an emotional and indignant Elizabeth Wydville.

It was undoubtedly in Gloucester's interests for the Queen Dowager to emerge from sanctuary into honourable retirement; her remaining there was an embarrassment and a constant reproach, its implication being that her life and her children's lives, despite all assurances to the contrary, were in danger whilst Gloucester was in power, which was damaging to his reputation. Therefore, far from preventing people from visiting the Queen in sanctuary, Gloucester now positively encouraged them to do so, and many lords called just to pay their respects.

During those three weeks, however, it became apparent that Gloucester was also seeking every opportunity to incite hatred against the Queen and to influence public opinion against the Wydvilles. Almost his first act as Protector was to seize the estates of Rivers, Grey, Dorset and other members of the family as though they had been forfeited by Act of Attainder. Such seizure was illegal, as was the redistribution of those lands amongst Gloucester's supporters. The Queen must have learned of this and it would certainly have strengthened her resolve not to leave sanctuary.

The Council's attitude to the imprisonment of the Queen's relatives and to the Queen herself, made clear to Gloucester on or soon after 10th May, brought home to him forcibly the fact that he could never enjoy complete security as Protector: there were too many Wydville sympathisers on the Council. His high office, moreover, must be surrendered in little more than a month, and while there was every expectation that he would head the regency council that would supersede it, his political, and even personal, survival would be in jeopardy once the young King attained his majority. Edward's loyalties were to his mother and his Wydville relatives and he would surely seek to restore them to power, releasing those whom Gloucester had imprisoned, whose first thought would be to exact vengeance under the benevolent eye of a young king already hostile to Gloucester. He could expect no favours at the hands of Edward V, nor mercy at the hands of the Queen: he had dealt her too many insults and injuries. Mancini says the Duke made no secret of his fears of the Wydvilles, proclaiming 'that he was harassed by the ignoble family of the Queen and the affronts of Edward [IV]'s relatives by marriage'.

Gloucester was also, says Mancini, 'actuated by ambition and lust for power'. Both Croyland and Mancini believed he had planned to take the throne himself from the time he learned of King Edward's death, and their accounts imply that after his successful coup this was what some people anticipated he would do. They also provide evidence that Gloucester's bid for the crown was carefully planned over a period of time. Mancini states that as soon as he had been confirmed as Protector, 'he set his thoughts on removing, or at least undermining, everything that might stand in the way of his mastering the throne'. Rotherham had already been neutralised, and Gloucester would hasten, in the next few weeks, 'to remove the other obstacles. Thus far, though all the evidence looked as if he coveted the crown, yet there remained some hope, because he was not yet claiming the throne, inasmuch as he still professed to do all these things as an avenger of treason and old wrongs, and because all private deeds and official documents bore the titles and name of King Edward V.'

Gloucester was well placed to make a bid for the throne. He was currently enjoying a degree of popularity with the Londoners; he had a large and influential following in the North and could command troops from there if he needed them; he was in control of the King; and he had the support of the magnates. The events of 10th May undoubtedly convinced him that he had no alternative but to seize the crown as soon as possible; if such a course had seemed desirable before, it was vitally necessary now. There can be only one interpretation of events after 10th May, and that is that Gloucester was consolidating his position in preparation for an even more dramatic coup.

On 10th May, Gloucester took the first step towards cementing his power and, says Mancini, 'turned his attention to the problem of how to remove the fleet from the control of Sir Edward Wydville, as he considered that a great part of his adversaries' strength rested on the navy'. With the authority of the Council, he denounced the commander of the navy as an enemy of the state if he did not disband his fleet, and offered great rewards to anyone taking Sir Edward alive or dead. As a result the entire fleet 'returned in a short while to port, save for two ships that had fled with Edward [Wydville] to the Breton coast of France. Now the Duke of Gloucester was freed of a great apprehension and prepared himself to face other ventures more boldly.'

For several more days the Council sat, dealing with more routine matters of government, while Edward V learned something of the business of being a king. Documents were given to him to sign, and he gathered around him in the Tower a small court peopled by loyal stalwarts such as Lord Hastings. After 10th May Council meetings would take place in the Star Chamber at Westminster, but committees of councillors gathered frequently in each other's homes and in the Tower, although there is no record of the King attending their meetings. Official documents, grants and proclamations were all issued in his name, but always 'by the advice of our dearest uncle the Duke of Gloucester, Protector and Defensor of this Our realm, during Our young age, and by the advice of the lords of Our Council'. The Protector himself signed official documents as 'brother and uncle of kings'.

On 13th May, Gloucester, in the King's name, issued writs summoning to London all the peers of the realm for a Parliament which would meet three days after the coronation. He was now urging that his protectorate be extended, and asked the Council to consider his proposal that he remain in office after the coronation and until the King attained his majority. This could only happen with the King's assent, but given Gloucester's influence it was unlikely that Edward would have opposed it. The Council prudently decided that the matter should be referred to Parliament for a decision in June.

Gloucester now took steps to reward the men who had supported him and ensure their continuing loyalty. On 10th May the Earl of Northumberland had been given various grants and offices, and on 14th May John, Lord Howard, was appointed Chief Steward of the Duchy of Lancaster. A day later Howard presented Gloucester with an expensive gold cup – a possible bribe from a man who wanted to be Duke of Norfolk, the title borne by the King's brother York in defiance of the laws of inheritance. Howard, it will be remembered, had received no compensation from Edward IV for being deprived of his hereditary rights, and probably looked to Gloucester to restore them to him.

Howard came of an old-established East Anglian family with royal connections, and was a staunch Yorkist. Aged about sixty-one in 1483, he had fought for Edward IV at Towton, Barnet and Tewkesbury, and had been rewarded with a knighthood in 1461, the Garter in 1472, a baronage in *c.* 1469–70, and several high offices including that of Treasurer of the Household. He was a violent man, whose hot temper had once landed him in prison, but he was also interested in literature, and had remained in favour with Edward IV.

Howard was a powerful man and his influence was vast, both in his native Suffolk and on the Council. He had supported Hastings in urging that Gloucester be recognised as Protector, and because of this he swiftly became, says More, 'one of the priviest of the Lord Protector's counsel'. Clearly Howard believed that Gloucester was the one man who could restore his lost inheritance, and More says that because of this he was actively involved in Gloucester's plot to seize the throne.

On 21st May, 1483, certain entries appear in Howard's domestic account book:

Item, paid to Basley, that he paid at the Tower for 6 men for a day labour:

3d a man a day	18d
Item, paid to a carpenter for making of 3 beds	8d
Item, for 100 foot of board and a quarter	2s 11d
Item, for 2 sacks lime	4d
Item, for nails for the beds	3d
Item, for his dinner	2d

Those entries probably refer to materials provided for refurbishing the rooms used by the King's servants: the beds were far too cheap to have been used by Edward V himself. Limewash was used to paint walls white, and the board may have been used as wainscot. Basley was a Colchester odd-job man who did occasional work for Lord Howard. In 1844 a writer called Payne Collier evolved a theory that this particular entry was somehow connected to the murder of the Princes in the Tower, but there is no evidence at all for this and it is inconceivable that Howard, if he was involved in such a crime, would record details relating to it in his domestic account books. No other entries in these account books relate to the Tower.

On 15th May, Buckingham was lavishly rewarded for his support by Gloucester: he was created Constable of England, Chief Justice and Lord Chamberlain of the whole of Wales for life, and constable and steward of fifty castles and lordships in the principality. He was granted power to array the King's subjects in four counties, and given control of all royal castles and manors therein. Such largesse meant that Buckingham could now exercise almost sovereign power in Wales, where he was to replace Rivers on the Council of the Marches. It also reflected not only Buckingham's rapaciousness but also Gloucester's need of his support; Rous says Buckingham's influence was vast, and Mancini records that he 'was always at hand ready to assist Gloucester with his advice and resources'. There are indications that Gloucester had already promised to restore to Buckingham the disputed share of the Bohun inheritance and had agreed to marry his son to Buckingham's daughter.

Five days later the Protector confirmed that Lord Hastings would continue to serve as Lord Chamberlain of England and Governor of Calais, and appointed him Master of the Mint. No further reward was forthcoming for the man who had been Gloucester's champion on the Council and who, by his timely intervention, had made his successful coup possible. Although the Protector 'loved him well', it was obvious that he preferred to promote Buckingham and have him as chief counsellor. The reason for this is not far to seek: Hastings had made it clear he was utterly loyal to Edward V, whom Gloucester had probably already made up his mind to supplant. Hastings therefore had received less than was his due, and may well have been resentful of the honours heaped upon Buckingham: some of them should have been his.

On 16th May, Archbishop Bourchier summoned Convocation to meet at St Paul's. Two days later the assembled clergy offered up a bidding prayer for Edward V and Elizabeth, the Queen Dowager; no reference was made to the Protector. The next day an urgent summons to attend Gloucester was sent in the King's name to the Archbishop. Such a summons could only have been issued on Gloucester's orders, and it may well be that the Protector was angry at Bourchier's omission and wished to reprimand him for it. Unfortunately, there is no record of what the summons was about.

By the end of May it was obvious to most members of the Council that their influence was diminishing beside that of Buckingham and Howard. They were becoming concerned also about Gloucester, being suspicious of his true motives and worried about the potential threat he posed to the young King. Most, however, were by now intimidated by Gloucester's treatment of the Wydvilles, and were afraid to speak out. The Protector detected their apprehension and took steps to counteract it. By the beginning of June he was sounding out the magnates and the citizens of London on a daily basis, trying to win their confidence and approval with 'largesse and liberality', saying 'always that he did not seek the sovereignty, but referred all his doings to the profit of the realm'. By this means he calmed the fears of all save those who had suspected 'from the beginning what mark he shot at'.

There was no doubt in the mind of any contemporary writer that by the end of May Gloucester had made up his mind to take the throne.

9
The Fall of Hastings

On 5th June Gloucester moved from Baynard's Castle to Crosby Place in Bishopsgate, a house he had leased in 1476 from the widow of its builder, Sir John Crosby, a prosperous grocer. The Elizabethan antiquarian John Stow describes Crosby Place as a 'great house of stone and timber, very large and beautiful, and the highest at that time in London'. It was built round a courtyard and had a solar, a great chamber, a chapel, a garden and a superb great hall with an oriel window, a marble floor, and an arched roof decorated in red and gold. This great hall survived the fire that destroyed the rest of the house in the late seventeenth century, and in 1908 was moved to Chelsea, where it stands today. Later the same day, Gloucester welcomed his wife Anne to Crosby Place; she had travelled to London from Yorkshire, leaving their son at Middleham.

By now, Gloucester was well aware that there were those on the Council who wished to prevent him from extending his power beyond the coronation. After 5th June, says Rous, he 'showed extraordinary cunning by dividing the Council'. He, and those members who supported him, including Buckingham, met in private at Crosby Place, while the rest – foremost amongst them Hastings, Rotherham, Morton and others loyal to Edward V – met at Baynard's Castle and Westminster to plan the coronation and discuss routine business. Many were convinced that Gloucester and his supporters were conspiring against the King at these secret meetings at Crosby Place, and Mancini learned that those councillors who were concerned for Edward V's safety met in private at each other's homes to discuss the situation. Lord Stanley for one was very worried about the Council being divided like this, for he had his doubts about Gloucester. But Lord Hastings hastened to reassure him, saying that his retainer, William Catesby, was a member of the Council that met at Crosby Place, and would report all its proceedings to him.

William Catesby was a lawyer from Ashby St Legers, Northamptonshire; his talents had earned him the notice of Hastings, who had made him his estate agent and procured for him a seat on the Council. In May 1483 Hastings had introduced Catesby to Gloucester, who took an instant liking to the man and was soon including him amongst his clique of preferred councillors. Before long Catesby found himself enjoying considerable influence with the Protector. But what Hastings did not know was that Catesby's first loyalty was no longer to himself: he was now playing the role of double agent, on Gloucester's behalf. Stanley may have guessed as much, for he warned Hastings to be careful.

'There is great business against the coronation,' wrote Simon Stallworthe, a servant of Bishop Russell, to Sir William Stonor on 9th June. Plans for the event were advancing steadily. On 5th June letters were sent in the King's name to fifty esquires, commanding them 'to prepare and furnish yourselves to receive the noble order of knighthood at our coronation'. Time was running short for Gloucester; his bid to remain in power after that date might fail in Parliament, and then it would be too late to make any bid for the throne, for once Edward V was consecrated it would be difficult to topple him. Hence all obstacles remaining in Gloucester's path must be removed now. 'He therefore resolved to get into his power the Duke of York,' states Mancini, 'for Gloucester foresaw that the Duke of York would by legal right succeed to the throne if his brother were removed. To carry through his plan,' he brought forward the date of the coronation by two days, to 22nd June. He must have done this before 9th June, when Stallworthe recorded that negotiations to bring the Queen out of sanctuary had broken down. Relations between Elizabeth Wydville and the councillors were by then so bad that they refused to visit her any more. Gloucester had an excellent pretext for removing York from sanctuary, for the boy's absence from his brother's coronation would have been a political embarrassment. But before Gloucester could act, events intervened.

The Council met on 9th June, but no record of its proceedings survives. Stallworthe, on that day, wrote that he had nothing to report apart from plans for the coronation. What happened next remains a mystery. Shortly before 9th June, Gloucester, says Mancini, had 'sounded out [Hastings'] loyalty through the Duke of Buckingham'. The Protector was anxious to learn how Hastings would respond to the suggestion that he, Gloucester, was the rightful King of England. Hastings, staunchly loyal to the memory of Edward IV and to his son, declared that he would accept Gloucester as protector but not as king. More says that Catesby also canvassed Hastings on Gloucester's behalf, but Hastings responded 'with terrible words', which were reported back to Gloucester.

Hastings was much alarmed by the realisation that Gloucester was indeed contemplating usurping the throne. The speculation, he now knew, had not been unfounded. Vergil states that Hastings had regretted his support of Gloucester from the day the latter had demanded the death penalty for Rivers. Then he had seen Buckingham usurp his rightful place in the Protector's counsels. Now he faced the prospect of Gloucester overthrowing Edward IV's son, the rightful King, and found it intolerable. Worse still was the knowledge that the powerful Buckingham would lend the would-be usurper his support, as would Lord Howard.

There were several people to whom Hastings could have confided his fears about what he had discovered. Chief among them was Edward V himself, whom Hastings saw regularly at the Tower: indeed, it may have been at this time that Edward gave Hastings an exquisite illuminated manuscript known as *The Hastings Hours*, now in the British Library. Hastings may have warned the King what was afoot, and Edward may have responded by urging him to do all in his power to have Gloucester dislodged from his office. Almost certainly, however, Hastings sought help and advice from fellow-councillors such as Rotherham, Stanley and Morton. Vergil says that at a meeting of his friends, probably at a private house, he discussed the possibility of seizing the King by force and even, perhaps, of deposing Gloucester from his protectorship. There was also talk of removing Buckingham from the Council. However, all these things were dismissed as being too fraught with dangers, and the meeting ended with Hastings and his friends deciding to see what transpired before taking any action, on the premise that forewarned is forearmed.

Hastings may even, in his agitation, have approached the Queen. She was the one person who should be informed if her son was in any danger. Hastings is said to have sent her a message by his mistress, Elizabeth Shore, a strange choice in the circumstances, but probably safer than visiting Westminster Abbey himself.

Then, probably on 9th June, Gloucester found out what was going on, probably through Catesby, who was in Hastings' confidence. In his anger, the Protector now chose to behave as if Hastings' activities and the meetings of councillors in each other's houses were evidence of a serious conspiracy against him, but Croyland, who was in a position to know the truth, states categorically that Hastings was not guilty of conspiring against Gloucester, a statement that is supported by Hastings' naïvety regarding the split in the Council and Catesby's loyalty to himself. Nevertheless, evidence exists to show that some people did believe that a plot had been brewing. A fragment from the commonplace book of a London merchant, dating from 1483 and discovered in 1980 in the College of Arms, states that 'divers imagined the death of the Duke of Gloucester and it was espied'. The fragment goes on to connect this with Hastings. Vergil also states that a counter-coup was being planned in June. Then there are Gloucester's own allegations, which appear below, accusing Hastings of conspiring with the Queen and her party to destroy him. We may dismiss the first two sources on the grounds that they are probably based on the propaganda later put about by the Protector.

Gloucester's allegations were probably a gross exaggeration of the truth, devised to justify the removal of a man who stood firmly in the way of his ambitions, for there is no other contemporary evidence of a conspiracy. The Wydvilles had been neutralised: the Queen, Dorset and Bishop Lionel were in sanctuary, Sir Edward had fled to Brittany, and Rivers and Grey were in prison. Hastings could have expected no help from that quarter. Nor did Gloucester take any proceedings against the Wydvilles at that time. More believed that Gloucester invented the 'conspiracy', because Elizabeth Wydville was 'too wise to go about any such folly, and if she would, yet would she of all folk least make Shore's wife of counsel, whom of all women she most hated'. What is likely is that Gloucester made Hastings' consultations with the councillors and perhaps his message to the Queen an excuse for accusing him and others of conspiracy, to suit his own purpose.

Gloucester was in no doubt that the wealthy and influential Hastings could prove a dangerous enemy whose loyalty to Edward V would ruin his carefully laid plans. Mancini says he 'considered that his prospects were not sufficiently secure without the removal or imprisonment of those who had been the closest friends of his brother and were expected to be loyal to his brother's offspring. In this class he thought to include Hastings, Rotherham and John Morton, the Bishop of Ely. Therefore the Protector rushed headlong into crime, for fear that the ability and authority of these men might be detrimental to him.' More states that Gloucester decided to eliminate Hastings because he was opposed to all his schemes, and a contemporary Welsh chronicler, Humphrey Lluyd, says that it was 'because [Hastings] would not freely have this man crowned'.

There is no doubt that Gloucester acted precipitately to deal with the problem of Hastings as soon as he learned he would not have his support; he had no time to waste. Vergil states that during the days prior to 13th June, when he was planning to act against Hastings, Gloucester suffered deep bodily feebleness and was unable to rest, eat or drink – surely signs of anger, tension and anxiety.

On 10th June Gloucester wrote to the Civic Council of York:

As ye love the weal of us, and the weal and surety of your own selves, we heartily pray you to come unto us in London, in all the diligence ye can possible after the sight hereof, with as many as ye can defensibly arrayed, there to aid and assist us against the Queen, her blood adherents and affinity, which have intended, and daily doth intend, to murder and utterly destroy us and our cousin the Duke of Buckingham and the old royal blood of this realm, and as is now openly known, by their subtle and demeanable ways forecasted the same and also the final destruction and disinheriting of you and all other inheritors and men of honour, as well of the north parts as other countries, that belongs to us; as our trusty servant, this bearer, shall more at large show to you, to whom we pray you give credence, and as ever we may do for you in time coming, fail not, but haste you to us hither.

Gloucester's real motive in summoning troops from York was the intimidation of possible opposition to his intended seizure of the throne. The concocted tale of a Wydville conspiracy was just an excuse to raise an army, and one he knew the citizens of York would respond to. Once again, he was presenting himself as the champion of the people. However, if a coup against him was as imminent as he made out, armed help from the North would not have reached him in time. Vergil believed that the troops were summoned primarily to prevent riots among the populace when 'they should see the crown bereft from Prince Edward'.

On 11th June Gloucester wrote further letters appealing for aid to the Earl of Northumberland, Lord Neville and other northern magnates. On that day or the next he despatched Richard Ratcliffe, who had been 'instructed with all my mind and intent', to the North with all the letters. Ratcliffe also carried warrants to be forwarded to Sheriff Hutton for the executions of Rivers, Grey, Vaughan and Haute, drawn up by Gloucester in defiance of the Council. Wrote Mancini: 'So as to leave no source of danger to himself from any quarter, when by means of the Council the Duke could not compass the execution of Lord Rivers and Richard [Grey], he ordered dependable officers to put them to death.' Such an action was unlawful and tyrannical, but to Gloucester it was politically vital for his future security and the guaranteed success of his bid for the throne. It was nevertheless an outrageous thing to order the execution of the King's uncle and relations, and the fact that Gloucester did it shows that he already regarded Edward V as a political nonentity whose favour he no longer needed to court. Only a man intent on seizing the throne would dare to take such a step.

On 12th June, says Croyland, 'the Protector, with extraordinary cunning, divided the Council', summoning Buckingham, Hastings, Morton, Stanley, Rotherham, Lord Howard and his son Sir Thomas Howard to a council meeting to be held in the Tower the following morning. The other councillors met on 13th June at Westminster, with orders from Gloucester to finalise plans for the coronation. This second gathering was presided over by Lord Chancellor Russell.

John Morton, Bishop of Ely, was leader of the court clerical party. He was a cultivated and learned man and a great canon lawyer, who had loyally served both Henry VI and Edward IV. Mancini calls him a man 'of great resource and caring, for he had been trained in party intrigue since King Henry's time, and enjoyed great influence'. More says that Morton would have been glad that Edward IV's son had succeeded him, for the Bishop, like several of those councillors summoned by the Protector to meet at the Tower on 13th June, had made it clear from the first that his allegiance lay with Edward V.

The fullest account of what occurred in the Tower that day comes from More, who almost certainly obtained some of his information from Morton, Rotherham and Thomas Howard, all eyewitnesses with whom he was at one time or other acquainted. We can deduce this because More gives details with a ring of authenticity that are not quoted anywhere else. Vergil also gives a comprehensive account, and internal evidence suggests that some of it came from those who had known Lord Stanley, another eyewitness.

The Council met in the morning in what Mancini calls 'the innermost quarters' of the White Tower, the King being then in the royal apartments. More states that Hastings was escorted to the Tower by 'a mean knight' whom Hall later identified as Sir Thomas Howard. More's failure to name Howard suggests that the information had come from Howard sources on condition that names be suppressed. Nor did More wish to offend his powerful friend the Duke of Norfolk, Howard's son. Later editions of More's work, published when the Howards had fallen from favour, were not so reticent. It appears that Howard was detailed by Gloucester to ensure that Hastings turned up at the council meeting. Hastings, says Croyland, having openly exulted in Gloucester's successful coup against the Wydvilles, was about to have 'this extreme joy of his supplanted by sorrow'.

Shortly before 9.00 am, the councillors were all seated, waiting, says Mancini, 'to salute the Protector, as was their custom', and believing they had been summoned to discuss the coronation. At 9.00 Gloucester entered, the embodiment of smiling amiability, an act put on, says More, to lull his victims into a sense of false security. The Duke cordially asked Morton to arrange for some strawberries to be sent to him from the Bishop's gardens at Ely Place in Holborn, which Morton hastened to do. Then, leaving the councillors to discuss routine business, Gloucester left the room.

He had laid his plans carefully and, says Humphrey Lluyd, 'maliciously'. No-one would have expected him to employ violence in the council chamber, and the element of surprise would only be to his advantage.

After one and a half hours the Protector returned, says More, 'frowning, fretting and gnawing on his lips'. He sat silent for a while, glowering, then asked Hastings, 'What do men deserve for having plotted the destruction of me, being so near of blood unto the King, and Protector of his royal person and realm?' Hastings, astonished, replied, 'Certainly, if they have done so heinously, they are worthy of a heinous punishment.' At this, Gloucester rose to his feet and snarled, 'What? Dost thou serve me with "ifs" and "ands"? I tell thee, they have done it, and that I will make good upon thy body, traitor!'

More states that Gloucester went on to accuse Hastings, Morton, Rotherham, Stanley and Oliver King, a former secretary of Edward IV, of plotting with the Queen and Elizabeth Shore against his authority and his life. Crimes against the Protector were not in fact treason, since he was not the sovereign, but Gloucester was not concerned with such niceties. More says the Duke also alleged that 'yonder witch', Elizabeth Wydville, in conjunction with Mistress Shore, 'had by their sorceries withered his arm'. As we have seen, there is no contemporary evidence that Gloucester had a withered arm. He had, however, been suffering from a bodily weakness for a few days, and probably based his accusation on this. By More's time the story had doubtless become heavily embroidered.

Mancini heard that what happened next was that Gloucester, 'as prearranged, cried out that an ambush had been prepared for him, and they [the councillors] had come with hidden arms, that they might be first to open the attack'. Whatever the exact nature of Gloucester's accusation, Hastings and the rest were given no chance to reply. Several accounts state that the Protector had secretly placed armed men either in an adjoining room or behind the arras in the council chamber. Mancini says they were under the command of Buckingham, but Vergil says that Sir Thomas Howard shared the command with two Yorkshiremen, Robert Harrington and Charles Pilkington. When Gloucester, concluding his tirade, banged on the table, the armed guard cried 'Treason!' and rushed into the room. A violent scuffle ensued which resulted in the arrests of Hastings, Stanley, Rotherham, Morton and one John Forster, a follower of Hastings and former receiver-general to the Queen. Stanley was wounded in the fracas and had blood streaming from his head. Hastings, says Mancini, was 'cut down on the false pretext of treason': he mistakenly thought that Hastings had been killed there and then by the soldiers. Then Gloucester told Hastings that he had better see a priest at once and confess his sins, 'for, by St Paul, I will not to dinner till I see thy head off!' Dinner was usually served around 11.00 am or slightly later: Hastings knew he faced imminent death.

All sources agree that Hastings was executed within minutes of his arrest, 'suddenly without judgement'. Magna Carta provided for magnates of the realm to be tried by their peers in Parliament, which was due to meet in less than a fortnight. But Gloucester could not afford to wait that long, and dared not risk an open trial since Hastings knew too much about his plot to seize the throne. The *Great Chronicle* states that the execution was done 'without any process of law or lawful examination'. It was a blatantly tyrannical act that heralded a new phase in the protectorate, that of rule by terror.

Gloucester put Buckingham in charge of the execution, who paid no heed to Hastings' pleas for mercy and protestations of innocence. A priest was summoned but, says More, no time was allowed for 'any long confession or other space of remembrance'. Then an usher led, or rather dragged, Hastings 'forth unto the green beside the chapel within the Tower, and there, on a squared piece of timber, strake off his head'. The timber, says Fabyan, 'lay there with other for the repairing of the said Tower'. Humphrey Lluyd states that Hastings 'was slain by sword', which is likely in the circumstances. It is even possible that Edward V witnessed the execution, for the west windows of the royal apartments faced Tower Green and the noise and commotion must have attracted attention. Hastings' broken body was buried soon afterwards, as he had requested in his will of 1481, near Edward IV in St George's Chapel, Windsor, where his chantry may be seen today.

'Thus fell Hastings,' wrote Mancini, 'killed not by those enemies he had always feared, but by a friend whom he had never doubted. But whom will insane lust for power spare, if it dares violate the ties of kin and friendship?' Mancini's observations support the circumstantial evidence that Hastings turned against Gloucester only days before his execution. Croyland commented that innocent blood had been shed, 'and in this way, without justice or judgement, the three strongest supporters of the new King were removed'. He was referring also to Rivers and Grey, imprisoned and condemned without trial. Hastings' contemporaries were in no doubt that his execution was a foretaste of violence to come. It proved just how ruthless Gloucester could be. At a stroke, on one day, four of his chief opponents had been silenced: one had been openly murdered. When the news of this atrocity broke it sent shock waves of horror throughout the City and the kingdom.

Vergil says that as soon as Hastings was dead Gloucester sent his men running through the streets of the City crying 'Treason! Treason!' The Londoners, hearing them, 'began to cry out likewise', becoming, says Mancini, 'panic stricken; and each one seized his weapons'. When the reason for the uproar was disclosed, the citizens were shocked and saddened, for Hastings was popular with them for his liberality and his charitable works. Vergil says 'those who favoured King Edward's children [and] had reposed their whole hope and confidence in him generally lamented' his death. Most people felt alarmed by it, for until now there had been no indication that anything was amiss in the government, and the *Great Chronicle* records how Hastings' death convinced the Londoners that Gloucester was scheming to seize the throne. In the troubled City wild rumours spread, and a wool merchant, George Cely, scribbled brief notes about what he was hearing on a spare piece of paper that still survives today: 'There is great rumour in the realm. The Scots has done great in England. Chamberlain [Hastings] is deceased in trouble. The Chancellor is disproved and not content. The Bishop of Ely is dead. If the King, God save his life, were deceased; the Duke of Gloucester were in any peril. If my lord Prince, which God defend, were troubled; if my Lord Howard were slain.' Most of these rumours were, of course, unfounded. The King was still at the Tower and would be seen there after this date.

Gloucester, meanwhile, was enjoying a celebratory dinner, after which he sent for the Lord Mayor and leading citizens of London, and informed them that Hastings had planned to murder him and Buckingham at that morning's council meeting; he had acted just in the nick of time to save himself. The Mayor then went back through the streets, telling the people of the 'plot' against the Protector. Two hours after the execution Gloucester sent a herald out to calm the populace by reading a proclamation giving details of Hastings' 'treason' and formally announcing his execution. The proclamation was so long, so detailed, and issued so swiftly that it is almost certain that it had been drawn up before the Council met. Typically, it contained an attack on Hastings' morals. It also, says Mancini, bade the people be assured. 'At first the ignorant crowd believed, although real truth was on the lips of many, namely that the plot had been feigned by the Duke to escape the odium of such a crime.' Thus, observed the *Great Chronicle*, 'was this nobleman murdered for his truth and fidelity which he bore unto his master'. Significantly, perhaps, Hastings was never retrospectively attainted of treason, unlike other enemies of Gloucester.

His death meant that the moderates on the Council now lacked a leader, which effectively deprived them of the means of opposing the Protector. Not that many were keen to now: Vergil says that 'Men began to look for nothing else than cruel slaughter, as perceived they well that Duke Richard would spare no man so that he might obtain the kingdom.' From now on many would support him 'rather for fear than any hope of benefit', for, says Croyland, all the rest of Edward V's 'faithful subjects were fearing the like treatment'. The King's supporters had been effectively intimidated.

As for those men who had been arrested with Hastings, Rotherham, according to Vergil, was committed to the temporary custody of Gloucester's trusted retainer Sir James Tyrell and, by 21st June, imprisoned in the Tower. The University of Cambridge pleaded his case and he was released on 4th July and restored to the Council. Morton was also incarcerated in the Tower, and the University of Oxford interceded for him, but Gloucester was not so merciful in his case and after a time committed him to Buckingham's custody at Brecknock Castle on the Welsh Marches. Croyland says both prelates were 'saved from capital punishment out of respect for their order', which is borne out by Mancini. Forster was briefly imprisoned, as was Stanley, but the latter was released within two weeks and restored to the Council, where he quickly ensured that he recovered the good opinion of Gloucester.

Elizabeth Shore, accused of being the go-between for her lover Hastings and the Queen, was also punished. Gloucester instructed the Bishop of London to sentence her to do public penance at St Paul's, wearing only her kirtle and carrying a lighted taper, a sight that moved many men in the watching crowds to lustful thoughts, we are told. This took place on Sunday 15th June, after which Mistress Shore was cast into prison. After her release, much to Gloucester's disgust, she married his solicitor, Thomas Lynom, and disappeared into obscurity.

She died, widowed and destitute, around 1526 and was buried in Hinxworth Church, Hertfordshire.

Around the time of Hastings' death, writes Mancini, Gloucester 'learned from his spies that the Marquess [of Dorset] had left the Sanctuary and, supposing that he was hiding in the same neighbour-hood, he surrounded with troops and dogs the already-grown crops and sought for him, after the manner of huntsmen, by a very close encirclement, but he was never found'. There can be little doubt that Dorset's flight was prompted by news of Hastings' end. In fact he fled to France, probably taking his share of Edward IV's treasure with him, as Gloucester tried, and failed, to find it. Later on Bishop Lionel Wydville left sanctuary openly and was allowed to return to his diocese.

On 15th June, Ratcliffe reached York where he delivered to the Civic Council the Protector's order for them to send an armed force to the Earl of Northumberland at Pontefract before 25th June; Northumberland would then march to London.

In the Tower, meanwhile, something very ominous had happened. Mancini tells us that 'After Hastings was removed, all the attendants who had waited upon the King were debarred access to him.' This was alarming because it meant that Gloucester was isolating his nephew and preventing others from finding out what was happening to him. He may well have feared that the King's servants might help him to escape. These servants had of course been chosen by Gloucester, but in the present situation he obviously felt he could not count on their loyalty.

Edward V could not have been anything but horrified at the death of Hastings and what it portended, the dismissal of his servants and the knowledge that he was now a virtual prisoner. The available evidence suggests that he feared he too would go the way of Hastings. Mancini says that Dr John Argentine, 'a Strasbourg doctor and the last of his attendants whose services the King enjoyed, reported that the young King, like a victim prepared for sacrifice, sought remission of his sins by daily confession and penance, because he believed that death was facing him'. The French chronicler Molinet corroborates this testimony. Forensic evidence which will be discussed later indicates that the King was suffering from a diseased jaw and perhaps toothache, which would explain why Dr Argentine had been in attendance; the pain he may have suffered can only have contributed to his depression and sense of hopelessness.

10

'This Act of Usurpation'

On Monday 16th June a wary and nervous Council met at the Tower. The date of the coronation was less than a week away and Gloucester, says Mancini, 'submitted how improper it seemed that the King should be crowned in the absence of his brother, who, on account of his nearness of kin and his station, ought to play an important part in the ceremony'. 'What a sight it shall be,' he said, according to Vergil, 'to see the King crowned if, while that the solemnity of triumphant pomp is in doing, his mother, brother and sisters remain in sanctuary.' Mancini says the Protector stated that, since the Duke of York 'was held by his mother against his will in sanctuary, he should be liberated, because the Sanctuary had been founded by their ancestors as a place of refuge, not of detention, and this boy wanted to be with his brother'. Gloucester spoke scathingly of 'the Queen's malice' and how she was trying to discredit the Council; he said it was bad for York to have no one of his own age to play with and to be 'in the company of old and ancient persons', and he proposed that Cardinal Archbishop Bourchier convey a command to the Queen to release her son. When the octagenarian prelate refused to sanction the boy's removal from sanctuary by force, fearing that reasonable persuasion might fail because of 'the mother's dread and fear', Buckingham retorted that the Queen's behaviour was not prompted by fear but by 'womanly frowardness. I never before heard of sanctuary children.' A child had no need of sanctuary, he argued, and therefore no right to it.

The Council, much intimidated and now without Hastings to voice any opposition, allowed itself to be persuaded by the Duke and agreed to Gloucester's demand. Whereupon, says Mancini, 'he surrounded the Sanctuary with troops'. Lord Howard's account books show that on that very day Howard and his son hired eight boats full of soldiers to escort Gloucester, Buckingham, Bourchier, Russell and themselves to Westminster and then form an armed chain round the Abbey.

York had been brought up at court by the Queen his mother. All we know of him comes from Molinet, who says he was 'joyous and witty, nimble, and ever ready for dances and games'. Such a lively child would probably have welcomed being released from the restrictions of life in sanctuary. But then York was only nine years old, and too young to understand what his liberation might mean.

Croyland says that Gloucester and his entourage of magnates, prelates and soldiers 'came with a great multitude to Westminster' that same day, 'armed with swords and staves'. Stallworthe testifies that there were 'great plenty of harnessed men' in the area around Westminster Abbey that day. On arrival, Gloucester, continues Croyland, 'compelled the Lord Archbishop of Canterbury, with many others, to enter the Sanctuary in order to appeal to the good feelings of the Queen and prompt her to allow her son to come forth and proceed to the Tower, that he might comfort the King his brother'.

Bourchier and Howard confronted the Queen in the Abbot's House, conveyed Gloucester's message, and informed her that the Protector desired to take her son York under his protection. They begged her to agree to this in order to avoid a scandal, and promised that her son would be safe and well looked after. The Queen expressed reservations about York's future safety, whereupon Howard asked her why her sons should be in any danger. She was at a loss for an answer, and Bourchier indicated firmly to Howard that he should 'harp no more on that string'.

Elizabeth Wydville's only hope of returning to power lay with her son the King, and while York remained with her Edward V was relatively safe and her ambitions realistically based. She did not trust Gloucester, and said so. Both More and Hall portray her as making a long speech to this effect, saying she knew there were 'deadly enemies to my blood. The desire of a kingdom knoweth no kindred; brothers have been brother's bane, and may the nephew be sure of his uncle? Both of these children are safe while they are asunder.' But Croyland, who was almost certainly an eyewitness, refers to no such speeches.

Howard now joined with Bourchier to reassure the Queen, persuading her that surrendering York was the best course. The Archbishop, who, says the *Great Chronicle*, 'thought and planned no harm' and, says Mancini, 'was suspecting no guile, persuaded the Queen to do this, seeking as much to prevent a violation of the Sanctuary as to mitigate by his good services the fierce resolve of the Duke'. No one doubted that if the Queen refused Gloucester would employ force to remove York: the soldiers outside bore testimony to that, and the House of York had its precedents for sanctuary-breaking. But Bourchier, says Croyland, assured the Queen that Gloucester 'thought or intended none harm', which was rather naïve of him, considering what had happened three days earlier.

'When the Queen saw herself besieged and preparation for violence,' says Mancini, 'she surrendered her son, trusting in the word of the Cardinal of Canterbury that the boy should be restored after the coronation.' And although Vergil writes that 'thus was the innocent child pulled out of his mother's arms', Croyland says that the Queen 'assented with many thanks to this proposal'. Later accounts describe an emotional parting, but no contemporary writer refers to any.

York was delivered, says Stallworthe in a letter to Stonor dated 21st June, to Bourchier, Russell 'and many other lords temporal', who took him to the Palace of Westminster, where 'with him met my lord of Buckingham in the midst of the hall of Westminster, my lord Protector receiving him at the Star Chamber door with many loving words'. Howard and Bourchier then conducted York by boat to the Tower, where he was reunited with his brother and, says Stallworthe, 'where he is, blessed be Jesu, merry'.

Gloucester now had both the male heirs of Edward IV in his power; he had neutralised the Wydvilles and removed nearly all those who had opposed him. 'From this day,' says Croyland, 'the Duke openly revealed his plans.' Now that those plans were being finalised, Gloucester apparently decided that the royal apartments should be vacated by the King and his brother in preparation for his own coronation. Vergil states that Gloucester was in fact lodging in the Tower from 16th June, and shortly after that date, says Mancini, Edward V and York 'were withdrawn to the inner apartments of the

Tower proper, and day by day began to be seen more rarely behind the bars and windows'. Mancini's reference to bars indicates that the boys were Gloucester's prisoners, which is borne out by the *Great Chronicle*, which states that they were 'holden more straight, and then was privy talk in London that the Lord Protector should be king'.

The Tower was a very public place to which the citizens were admitted to view the menagerie or for administrative purposes; therefore it is quite credible that the Princes (as we shall refer to them) were seen on several occasions. To begin with they were allowed outdoors for exercise. The *Great Chronicle* records that 'During this Mayor's year, the children of King Edward were seen shooting and playing in the garden of the Tower by sundry times.' The Mayor referred to was Sir Edmund Shaa, who held office from October 1482 to October 1483. However, the reference to the boys playing must relate to the period immediately after 16th June and before the second week in July, when Mancini says the boys had ceased to appear at the windows altogether; it may also refer to Edward V before he had been joined by York. Mancini makes it clear that these outdoor games occurred less frequently as the days went by.

No source is specific in naming exactly which part of the Tower the Princes were withdrawn to after 16th June. Tradition has it that they were held in what is now known as the Bloody Tower. In 1483 it was called the Garden Tower because the left side of it adjoined the garden of the Lieutenant's (now the Queen's) House. Because the Princes were seen playing 'in the garden of the Tower' it has long been assumed that they were lodged in the Garden Tower, once a means of access to the old royal apartments. This assumption has been given credence by the high standard of accommodation in the Garden Tower and its proximity to the Lieutenant's House, vital for security purposes. But there is no other evidence that the Princes were ever there, nor was the Garden Tower re-named the Bloody Tower until 1597. In 1532 it was still being referred to as the Garden Tower, which argues a contemporary lack of association with the Princes.

The garden of the Lieutenant's House was also in close proximity to the massive White Tower, the old Norman keep with its 9-foot-thick walls. Here were the original royal apartments, still occasionally used, and here too, on the upper floors, important state prisoners had been housed since the twelfth century. This was the most secure part of the

Tower, 'the Tower proper', as Mancini says, and the place most likely to have been chosen as the Princes' abode by Gloucester. Here they could be lodged in relative comfort in any one of the turret chambers or rooms in the upper regions. Here, too, was later found forensic evidence to indicate their presence, which will be discussed later. In the White Tower the Princes were out of the way, and no-one could gain access to them without Gloucester's authority.

The Protector now turned his attention to another possible obstacle to his schemes, the eight-year-old Earl of Warwick who, since the flight of Dorset, was without a legal guardian. Mancini says that 'about this time Gloucester gave orders that the son of the Duke of Clarence should come to the City, and commanded that the lad should be kept in confinement in the household of his wife, the child's maternal aunt. For he feared that if the entire progeny of King Edward became extinct, yet this child, who was also of royal blood, would still embarrass him.' What Mancini is here implying is that Gloucester had already contemplated the extinction of Edward IV's sons.

Gloucester was now apparently in a very strong position: he had all the Yorkist male heirs to the throne in his power, he had rid himself of his enemies, and armed support was on its way to him from York. But his position was still under threat. Firstly, both the Wydvilles and the King were now permanently alienated from him: More says Gloucester told Buckingham that Edward V had been so offended by their actions that there was no chance of a reconciliation. When the King attained his majority, both dukes could expect the worst for, according to Gloucester, he would never forget what was done to him in his youth. Secondly, the execution of Hastings had alienated a number of Gloucester's supporters on the Council, further reducing his minority and the likelihood that the Council would support an extension of his powers after the coronation. Thirdly, that coronation was only days away, and many lords had already arrived in London to attend it and the Parliament that was to follow. The King could not open Parliament until he was crowned, and that event could not be deferred any longer because the business of the kingdom was being held up. Gloucester therefore had to act quickly if his plan was to succeed, and there can be no doubt that his ambition, his fear of what the future would otherwise hold, and his chronic sense of insecurity all gave added impetus to this necessity.

Croyland states that, with the strongest supporters of the King having been removed 'and all the rest of his faithful subjects fearing the like treatment, the two dukes did henceforth just as they pleased'. Buckingham had been involved in Gloucester's plans from the beginning: More refers to his 'guilty foreknowledge', saying that 'when the Protector had both the children in his hands he opened himself more boldly to the Duke of Buckingham, although I know that many thought that this Duke was privy to all the Protector's counsel'. What Gloucester opened himself about was almost certainly the exact details of his scheme to seize the throne.

The plan was to declare Edward V and Richard of York unfit to inherit the crown; therefore, as Warwick was supposedly barred from the succession by his father's attainder, Gloucester would be next in line to the throne and would demand to be acknowledged as the rightful king. But, given that the act of recognition by the magnates at his crowning would have the effect of erasing any doubts about Edward V's title to the throne, Gloucester knew he had to make public his claim before 22nd June, the date set for the coronation.

In what Croyland refers to as his 'haughty mind', Gloucester was already king. He began acting like one, according to Mancini, who says that 'when Richard felt secure from all those dangers that at first he feared, he took off the mourning clothes that he had worn since his brother's death and, putting on a purple robe, he then rode through the capital, surrounded by a thousand attendants. He publicly showed himself so as to receive the attention and applause of the people, as yet under the name of Protector; but each day he entertained to dinner at his private dwellings an increasingly large number of men,' doubtless with a view to winning their support. 'When he exhibited himself through the streets of the City, he was scarcely watched by anybody, rather did they curse him with a fate worthy of his crimes, since no-one now doubted at what he was aiming.'

Undaunted at the loss of his early popularity, Gloucester pressed on with his plans. By 17th June he had decided to cancel the Parliament called for 25th June, and on that day issued writs rescinding the official summonses sent to the members and magnates. Lord Chancellor Russell's draft speech for the state opening of that Parliament, composed at this time, still survives; ironically, after urging unity amongst the opposing factions in government and praising the good qualities in the King, Russell recommended the continuance of Gloucester's protectorate until Edward V attained his majority, when 'ripeness of years and personal rule be concurrent together'. He envisaged Edward V having cause 'to rejoice himself and say, "Uncle, I am glad to have you confirmed in this place, you to be my Protector in all my business"' with powers encompassing 'the defence of the realm and the tutele [education] and oversight of the King's most royal person during his years of tenderness, to be his tutor and protector'. Gloucester, even had he known of Russell's recommendation, may nevertheless have felt that he lacked sufficient support to push the motion through in Parliament.

Between 17th and 21st June, Gloucester postponed the coronation indefinitely; on what grounds, we do not know. The Tudor chronicler, Richard Grafton, says a new date was set, 2nd November, but there is no contemporary evidence for this, and the magnates who gathered in London on 25th June, speculating as to when the ceremony would in fact take place, certainly did not know about it. What was more, preparations for a coronation were still going ahead. The accounts of Piers Curteys, Keeper of the Royal Wardrobe, show that Edward V's coronation robes were ready: a short gown of crimson cloth of gold and black velvet and long gowns of crimson cloth of gold lined with green damask, blue velvet and purple velvet, as well as a doublet of black satin and a bonnet of purple velvet. Dishes had already been prepared for the coronation banquet, and animals slaughtered in readiness. By Saturday, 21st June, London was a-buzz with rumour and speculation.

Two days earlier the Civic Council in York had called up the troops required by the Protector; Mancini says they numbered 6,000 and were mainly from the estates of both Gloucester and Buckingham. News that a large armed force had been summoned from the North reached London on that Saturday, causing much alarm and concern, especially since there was already a considerable military presence, wearing Gloucester's livery, in the City. 'With us is much trouble, and every man doubts other,' wrote Stallworthe to Stonor that day, mentioning that all Hastings' men 'are switching allegiance to the Duke of Buckingham'. The mood of the capital was so tense and hostile that the Lord Mayor, a supporter of the Protector, organised a watch in the interests of keeping the peace.

Gloucester now, says Mancini, 'took special opportunity of publicly showing his hand'. Sunday, 22nd June, should have been Edward V's coronation day. Instead, Londoners attending a sermon at Paul's Cross in London heard for the first time Edward's claim to the throne impugned. The preacher was Dr Ralph Shaa, the Mayor's brother, a Cambridge-educated doctor of theology. Like his brother he supported Gloucester, and the latter saw in him the perfect instrument for making public some astonishing revelations concerning the royal succession. Indeed, both the Shaa brothers had exerted themselves to win over the Londoners to Gloucester's party, and there were a few cheers for Dr Ralph from several strategically placed retainers of the Protector as he entered the open-air pulpit before the cathedral. There he delivered his sermon, taking as his text a quotation from the Apocrypha: 'But the multiplying brood of the ungodly shall not thrive, nor take deep rooting from bastard slips, nor lay any fast foundations.'

Gloucester, avers Mancini, had 'so corrupted' Dr Shaa and other 'preachers of the divine Word that in their sermons' – that at Paul's Cross was not the only one of its kind delivered that day – 'they did not blush to say, in the face of decency and all religion, that the progeny of King Edward should be instantly eradicated, for neither had he been a legitimate king, nor could his issue be so. Edward IV, said they, was conceived in adultery, and in every way was unlike the late Duke of York; but Richard, Duke of Gloucester, who altogether resembled his father, was to come to the throne as the legitimate successor.' At this point Gloucester was meant to appear with Buckingham and other lords in a nearby gallery but he mis-timed his entrance and the dramatic gesture fell flat. Dr Shaa resolutely continued, ignoring his silent audience, praising the Duke's virtues and stressing that by character and descent he was legally entitled to the throne. But his speech, and those of other preachers in London, met with scant approval from the citizens, whose initial liking for Gloucester had dissolved in the wake of Hastings' execution, the cancelled coronation – which boded no good – and what they viewed as an armed threat from the North. Dr Shaa, they felt, was little better than a traitor. Indeed, his sermon wrecked his good reputation as a preacher, and his death in 1484 was attributed by the *London Chronicles* and More to shame and remorse.

Nevertheless, both he and other preachers had called for the disinheriting of Edward IV's children on the grounds of that King's alleged bastardy. In making this allegation, Gloucester was well aware that he was defaming the venerable reputation of his aged mother the Duchess of York, who had become a Benedictine nun in 1480 and lived in pious retirement at Berkhamsted Castle. To make matters worse, the Duchess had just arrived in London for her grandson's coronation.

Allegations of bastardy were common propaganda tools in the fifteenth century. This was not the first time they had been levelled at Edward IV. Mancini's tale that the Duchess, angry in 1464 at her son's marriage to Elizabeth Wydville, had offered to declare him a bastard, dates from 1483 and probably reflects rumours current at that time: it is not supported by contemporary evidence. Both Warwick and Clarence had called Edward IV a bastard for their own political purposes, but without substantiating their claims by evidence. No-one, in 1483, believed the allegations of Dr Shaa and others, but this was scant comfort to the Duchess who, according to Vergil, 'being falsely accused of adultery, complained afterwards in sundry places to right many noble men, whereof some yet live, of that great injury which her son Richard had done her'. It may be that her complaints carried some weight, for the allegations were suddenly dropped and not followed through. We know very little of Gloucester's subsequent relations with his mother; only one letter from him survives, expressing conventional filial devotion. But there is no escaping the fact that he had, to further his own ambitions, publicly insulted and slandered her, an appallingly unfilial act; and in 1484, when the Act 'Titulus Regius' was passed, setting out Richard's title to the throne, he insisted on the allegations of bastardy being indirectly levelled again, having himself described as 'the undoubted son' of York.

It was obvious in June 1483, however, that this particular horse was not going to run, and necessary therefore that Edward V's unfitness to wear a crown be established by other means. Shortly after the fiasco of Shaa's sermon, Gloucester had it put about that Edward IV's marriage to Elizabeth Wydville was invalid because he had at the time been contracted to another lady, and that their children were bastards and incapable of inheriting the throne. It was this that was the eventual basis of Gloucester's claim to sovereignty.

Although the supposed facts of this matter were recorded in 1484 in the Act 'Titulus Regius', the fullest contemporary account of the 'precontract story' was written by Philippe de Commines more than ten years later. According to this, Robert Stillington, Bishop of Bath and Wells, had presented himself before the Council on 8th June and disclosed some astonishing information. He 'discovered to the Duke of Gloucester that his brother King Edward had been formerly very enamoured of a certain English lady and had promised her marriage upon the condition he might lie with her. The lady consented and, as the Bishop affirmed, he married them when nobody was present but they two and himself. His fortune depending on the court, he did not discover it, and persuaded the lady likewise to conceal it, which she did, and the matter remained a secret.' Commines says the Bishop produced 'instruments, authentic doctors, proctors and notaries of the law with depositions of divers witnesses' to prove his story.

The lady in question was a gentlewoman called Lady Eleanor Butler. Lady Eleanor, whose name first appears linked to Edward IV's in 'Titulus Regius', was described in that Act as the daughter of John Talbot, Earl of Shrewsbury (1388?–1453), although Commines casts doubt on this; an unidentified Sir John Talbot is described in other sources as Eleanor's brother. Her date of birth is recorded as 1435, but this cannot be verified. Around 1449–50 she married Sir Thomas Butler (or Boteler), the son and heir of Ralph, Lord Sudeley, and went to live at Sudeley Castle near Winchcombe, Gloucestershire. Sir Thomas died in 1460–61, leaving Eleanor a childless widow with a legal dispute on her hands. Lord Sudeley had transferred two manors in Warwickshire to his son on his marriage, but had failed to obtain the King's licence to do so beforehand; as a result these manors were confiscated. Shortly after being widowed Eleanor is said to have petitioned Edward IV for their restoration, which was granted her in 1461. This is the only contemporary record of any dealings between her and the King, and if a precontract ever existed between them then it would have dated from the period between Eleanor's widowhood in 1461 and Edward IV's marriage to Elizabeth Wydville in 1464.

Lady Eleanor died shortly before 30th June, 1468, the day on which she was buried in the conventual church of the Carmelites in Norwich. Buck states that she had retired there shortly after giving birth to a child by the King, but there is no contemporary evidence for this. The child, said to have been known at first as Giles Gurney and later on as Edward de Wigmore, was supposed to have been the great-grandfather of Richard Wigmore, secretary to Elizabeth I's chief minister, Lord

Burleigh. Buck also says that Lady Eleanor's family persuaded Stillington to go to Gloucester with the truth.

But was it the truth? The answer to that question is crucial, and for centuries writers have argued the pros and cons of the matter, and still cannot reach agreement. The overwhelming consideration must be that public acceptance of the invalidity of Edward V's claim to the throne was highly advantageous to Gloucester, who had everything to gain from it. Furthermore, these revelations of Stillington's, if they were made at all, were made at a most convenient time. Indeed, as several writers have pointed out, their very timeliness undermines their credibility. And if we examine the facts of the story, several flaws immediately become apparent.

Commines was the only contemporary writer to state that the precontract story came from Stillington; English writers do not mention him. The Bishop's allegations are unsubstantiated by any other evidence or source, and none of the proofs he allegedly produced are referred to elsewhere. Commines believed that 'this bad, wicked bishop' had 'kept thoughts of revenge in his heart' because Edward IV had had him imprisoned in 1478, and that this had prompted him to take his story before the Council; he had fallen from favour and hoped to regain it when a grateful Protector became king. Stillington's imprisonment was brief, however, and he had regained some of his former influence. Moreover, Gloucester at no time in the future showed him any mark of favour nor rewarded him as he did his other supporters.

There is no record of Stillington appearing before the Council on 8th June or any other date, nor is there any evidence for him being examined in connection with his allegations. On 9th June Stallworthe, referring to the Council's meeting on that day, had nothing to report, which would hardly have been the case if such sensational revelations had been produced the day before.

A precontract, in that period, was a promise before witnesses to marry followed by sexual intercourse. Many couples lived together on the strength of this and did not have their unions blessed in church. A precontract was as binding as a marriage and could only be dissolved by the ecclesiastical authorities. By 1330 the law recognised that an existing precontract with one partner was a bar to marriage with another and sufficient to bastardise any children of a subsequent marriage. Edward IV is said to have promised marriage to Lady Eleanor in return for sex, which may well have constituted a valid precontract. Stillington is then supposed to have married them without any witnesses being present, which is inconceivable considering his reputation as a canon lawyer and theologian. A marriage without witnesses was automatically invalid, and therefore – taking the story at face value – the King could only be said to be precontracted to the lady, not married to her. It is also inconceivable that neither Stillington nor Lady Eleanor disclosed the matter when Edward IV married Elizabeth Wydville, given that both would have known the royal marriage to be bigamous and invalid, and the succession at stake. At the time the marriage was unpopular and created a furore as it was, and the Bishop at least would not have lacked supporters had he spoken out. Lady Eleanor's pedigree was no poorer than Elizabeth Wydville's, so the disclosure of her precontract could hardly have made matters worse.

Nevertheless the precontract story was well-conceived and plausible, giving Edward IV's reputation with women and the notorious circumstances of his marriage to Elizabeth Wydville, though no proof to substantiate it was forthcoming at the time, nor has been since. Edward IV had lived with his wife for nineteen years, united in the eyes of Church and State, and no-one had ever suggested in the slightest way that their marriage was invalid because of a previous precontract. In the normal way, Gloucester should have had the allegations laid before a properly constituted ecclesiastical court, which would conduct a searching investigation into the validity of the late King's marriage in order to prove beyond any doubt that it was unlawful and its issue illegitimate. Only then could the children of the marriage be legally declared bastards and unfit to inherit, and that by Parliament itself, which had the power to rule on questions affecting inheritance. But Gloucester, probably realising that his allegations would never stand up in an ecclesiastical court, did not submit them for examination, a most telling omission that is evidence enough that he had insufficient proof to support them.

No contemporary writer believed the precontract story. The well-informed Croyland, the only contemporary chronicler to give an accurate account of it, knowing how crucial it was, dismissed the tale as false, calling it 'the colour for this act of usurpation'. Mancini did not believe the tale either.

It appears, then, that there is no truth in the precontract story and Commines' account of Stillington's role in it. 'That fable,' wrote Bacon, 'was ever exploded.' What is likely is that it was invented by Gloucester to suit his own ambitions and justify what he was about to do with or without the connivance of others, as soon as he realised that the public would not accept the allegations of Edward IV's bastardy as the pretext for his claiming the throne.

Nevertheless, in our own time there are still writers who insist that there had been a precontract, that Stillington had confided as much to Clarence, and that Edward IV had Clarence executed to silence him. Clarence, of course, had much to gain from the possession of such information: he was next in line to the throne. It is strange, therefore, that Clarence, who was always so ready to slander his brother, never made use of what he allegedly knew, and stranger still that Gloucester, who was at court at the time and in the King's confidence, never learned of the allegations, or, if he did, never made use of them until June, 1483. There is no evidence at all that Stillington told Clarence of a precontract, and no reason to believe that Clarence's removal was due to anything other than the specific, blatant crimes with which he was charged. Nor is it conceivable that Edward IV would have released Stillington from prison after Clarence's death, knowing he was the possessor of such dangerous knowledge.

While London seethed with gossip, at Sheriff Hutton Castle on 23rd June, Anthony Wydville, Earl Rivers, was informed that he was to be taken to Pontefract Castle on the morrow to be executed. Before leaving, he made his will, and the following day was taken under guard – as were Grey and Haute – to Pontefract, where Vaughan was held; there, all four were told they were to die the next day. That night, says Rous, Rivers 'wrote a ballad in English', in which he said he was 'willing to die'.

On that same day in London, Buckingham went to the Guildhall to address the Mayor, aldermen and chief citizens on behalf of Gloucester, who did not appear. The Duke spoke for half an hour, deploying all his considerable powers of eloquence and persuasion, so that all who heard him marvelled. The gist of his speech was recorded by all the London chroniclers, Vergil, and More, whose father, being a London judge, was probably present in the Guildhall that day. Buckingham's main objective was to persuade the people that Gloucester was their rightful king. He said he would not venture to go further into the matter of the bastardy of Gloucester's brothers since the Protector bore 'a filial reverence for the Duchess his mother', and enlarged instead upon the precontract story. Gloucester, he said, was reluctant to accept the crown for he knew 'it was no child's office', but he might do so if the citizens pressed him to it. The Duke ended by appealing to them to do so.

There was a deathly silence. It was obvious that very few believed there had ever been a precontract between Edward IV and Eleanor Butler, much less that Gloucester was the rightful king. A few, at length, murmured their approval, but this was mainly due to fear of reprisals from Gloucester rather than loyalty to him or conviction, whereupon Buckingham's men attempted to redeem the situation by throwing their caps into the air and shouting 'King Richard!' But the execution of Hastings had alienated many of Gloucester's former supporters and it was becoming obvious that he was not going to be swept on to the throne on a tide of public opinion.

Nor would the public's confidence have been restored by knowledge of what occurred on the following day, 25th June, at Pontefract. Evidence in York Civic Records shows that Sir Richard Ratcliffe had arrived at the castle with the troops from York a day or so previously and conveyed the Protector's order for the executions of the four prisoners to the Earl of Northumberland, who was awaiting him there with an army of his own. Rous says that 'the said lords were condemned to death by the Earl on the false charge that they had in fact plotted the death of Richard, Duke of Gloucester and, for a thing they had never contemplated, the innocent humbly and peaceably submitted to a cruel fate.' Croyland confirms that the executions took place 'by command of Richard Ratcliffe, and without any form of trial being observed'. Rous, in a later passage, describes Northumberland as the men's 'chief judge', implying that some sort of formal condemnation had taken place, but Rous was a less reliable commentator than Croyland, and Rivers had been informed of his imminent death two days previously at Sheriff Hutton. As a nobleman he had the right to be tried by his peers in Parliament, but this had been denied him, as it had been denied Hastings.

Rivers, Grey, Vaughan and Haute were beheaded in the presence of Northumberland, Ratcliffe – who supervised the proceedings – the assembled northern forces, and some of the public. None of the men were allowed to make a speech. Rous says that afterwards, when the bodies were stripped for burial, Rivers was found to be wearing a 'consecrated hair shirt' which was long after displayed in the church of the Carmelite friars in Doncaster. Rivers, Grey and Haute were buried naked in a common grave in a monastery at Pontefract, while Vaughan, whom Croyland calls 'an aged knight', was eventually laid to rest in Westminster Abbey under a Latin epitaph which translates as 'To love and wait upon', an allusion to his devoted service to Edward V.

All contemporary writers agree that Rivers and his associates had committed no crime. No evidence against them was ever produced. Rous says they 'were unjustly and cruelly put to death, being lamented by everyone, and innocent of the deed for which they were charged'. More states that their only fault was in being 'good men, too true to the King', and Vergil avers that their true offence was to stand in the way of Gloucester's ambitions. Croyland observes that this was the 'second innocent blood which was shed on the occasion of this sudden change'. In all, their executions constituted yet more blatant acts of tyranny committed by Gloucester.

By now a great number of lords and commoners had arrived in London for the coronation, and on 25th June all were summoned to Westminster. Mancini says they 'supposed they were called both to hear the reason for Hastings' execution and to decide again upon the coronation of Edward, for it seemed after such an unprecedented alarm that the coronation must be deferred. When the Duke [of Gloucester] saw that all was ready, as though he knew nothing of the affair, he secretly despatched the Duke of Buckingham to the lords with orders to submit to their decision the disposal of the throne.' Buckingham brought with him, says Croyland, 'a supplication' or petition, 'in an address in a certain roll of parchment', which was to be approved by the assembly before being laid before Gloucester. This petition had almost certainly been drawn up by Gloucester and Buckingham. Some historians infer that the magnates were its authors, but while it was written in their name, this is implausible. The only magnates involved were likely to have been the two Dukes and perhaps Lord Howard:

Rous says Gloucester 'feigned a title to the crown for his own advancement', and Croyland relates 'how it was at the time rumoured that this address had been got up in the north, whence such vast numbers were flocking to London, although at the same time there was not a person but what very well knew who was the sole mover at London of such seditious and disgraceful proceedings'.

This petition no longer survives but its text was incorporated, seemingly word for word, into the Act of Settlement called 'Titulus Regius', passed in 1484, which set forth Gloucester's title to the throne, and its gist was recorded by several contemporary writers. It was couched in lofty, indignant, moral tones, typical of the propaganda used before it and later on by Gloucester, and its purpose was not only to justify the deposition of the lawful sovereign, but to present the Duke to the people as he saw himself, an upright and strong ruler who could offer stable government in place of the uncertainties of a minority.

Buckingham's address opened with an attack on the government of Edward IV, who had let himself be ruled by the Wydvilles. This time there were no allegations that Edward IV had been illegitimate. Instead, says Croyland, 'it was set forth that the sons of King Edward were bastards, on the ground that he had contracted a marriage with the Lady Eleanor Butler before his marriage to Queen Elizabeth'. In fact the petition, and the subsequent Act, asserted that the King's marriage to Elizabeth Wydville was invalid on three counts: firstly, because it had been made without the assent of the lords of the land and as a result of sorcery practised by Elizabeth and her mother (no evidence was produced to substantiate these allegations); secondly, because it had been 'made privily and secretly, without edition of banns, in private chamber, a profane place, and not openly in the face of the Church, after the law of God's Church, but contrary to the laudable custom of the Church of England'; and thirdly, because 'at the time of contract of the said pretenced marriage, and before and long time after, King Edward was married and troth-plight to one Dame Eleanor Butler. Which premises being true, as in very truth they been true, it appeareth and followeth evidently that King Edward and Elizabeth lived together sinfully and damnably in adultery against the laws of God and His Church, and all the issues and children of the said King Edward been bastards and unable to claim anything by inheritance, by the law and custom of England.'

According to the petition, next in line after Edward IV would have been Clarence's son, the young Earl of Warwick, but for Clarence's attainder, which, says Mancini, rendered Warwick 'ineligible for the crown, since his father, after conviction for treason, had forfeited not only his own but his son's right of succession'. This was not strictly correct. Gloucester was well aware that Warwick had a strong claim to the throne, better than his own. However, there was little danger of anyone claiming it on his behalf at present because Warwick was only eight. As time went by he would pose a greater threat. Attainders were reversible: over 80 per cent of the attainders passed during the period 1453–1509 were later reversed. Henry IV, Henry VI and Edward IV had all succeeded to the throne after being previously attainted. And Clarence's attainder deprived his children of inheriting only 'the honours, estate, dignity and name of duke'; it did not exclude them from the succession. However, as far as Gloucester was concerned, the time for legal niceties was long past.

Warwick's exclusion meant, concluded Buckingham, according to Croyland, that 'at the present time no certain and incorrupt blood of the lineage of Richard, Duke of York was to be found, except in the person of Richard, Duke of Gloucester', his undoubted son and heir, who had been born in England, unlike Edward IV, who had been born in France. Mancini quotes Buckingham as saying that Gloucester was 'legally entitled to the crown and could bear its responsibility, thanks to his proficiency. His previous career and blameless morals would be a sure guarantee of his good government.' He spoke of Gloucester's 'great wit, prudence, justice, princely courage and memorable and laudable acts, and also the great noblesse and excellence of [his] birth and blood'. 'For which reasons,' says Croyland, 'he was entreated at the end of the said roll to assume his lawful rights' and asked if he would accept and take upon himself the crown and royal dignity.

Mancini says that, according to Buckingham, there was a problem over this, for it was likely that Gloucester 'would refuse such a burden'. He might, however, 'change his mind if he were asked by the peers'. Buckingham then left the assembled lords and commons to examine Gloucester's claim. Many certainly had reservations about it, and it would become clear in time to come that few Englishmen ever found the allegations on which it was based plausible. Nor had any proofs been offered to substantiate them. Croyland, who was on the Council, believed them to be fraudulent; he was not alone. But the lords, says Mancini, 'consulted their own safety, warned by the example of Hastings and perceiving the alliance of the two Dukes, whose power, supported by a multitude of troops, would be difficult and hazardous to resist; and therefore they determined to declare Richard their king and ask him to undertake the burden of office'. They were 'seduced', states Vergil, 'rather for fear than hope of benefit'. In fact, their decision was unanimous, dictated by the desire for self-preservation, realisation that every minority brought with it more problems than were desirable in an unstable political climate, especially now when the young King's title had been publicly impugned, and the knowledge that Gloucester was certainly capable of providing strong government.

The assembly that convened on 25th June was undoubtedly constitutional, even though it did not meet in Parliament, but it now went beyond the law and declared Edward IV's marriage to Elizabeth Wydville invalid and their children illegitimate, then agreed that Edward V had been formally deposed. In fact, he and his siblings were not formally disinherited until 'Titulus Regius' was passed in 1484, and therefore his deposition on 25th June, 1483, was illegal. Nevertheless the assembled magnates declared him a 'proved' imposter, and the contemporary Harleian MS. 433 in the British Library states that, their oath to Edward V notwithstanding, 'now every good, true Englishman is bound upon knowledge had of the said very true title [of Gloucester] to depart from the first oath so ignorantly given to him to whom it appertained not.'

On the following day, says Mancini, 'All the lords foregathered at the house of Richard's mother [Baynard's Castle], whither he had purposefully betaken himself, that these events might not take place in the Tower where the young King was confined. There the whole business was transacted.' The Protector was also determined to emulate his brother Edward IV, whose accession ceremonies had taken place at Baynard's Castle.

Again, the proceedings were constitutionally correct. Buckingham rode at the head of the deputation, which comprised the lords, commons, knights, Lord Mayor of London, aldermen and chief citizens, all anxious to win the favour of their future monarch and so avoid his terrible displeasure.

Buckingham presented the petition, beseeching Gloucester most eloquently that he should accept the crown, so that the country might escape the dangers of a minority and a disputed succession and enjoy peace through stable, firm government. He told the Duke that the people would not have the sons of Edward IV to reign over them, and that if he refused their request they would have no choice but to choose someone else. Gloucester displayed initial reluctance but at length agreed to accept the crown. Thus, says Croyland, 'having summoned armed men in fearful and unheard of numbers from the north, the Protector assumed the government of the kingdom, with the title of king'. Mancini says he usurped or occupied ('*occuparit*') the kingdom.

The reign of Richard III, for so the new King was styled, was dated from that day, 26th June, 1483, as he himself confirmed in a letter of 12th October, 1484, referring to it as the date 'when we entered into our just title'. He had ascended the throne with very little blood being spilt, yet his usurpation would lead in a short time to a second outbreak of the War of the Roses and the ultimate destruction of his own House.

I I

Richard III

Following the precedent set by Edward IV, Richard III left Baynard's Castle on the day of his accession and rode to Westminster Hall where, according to Croyland, 'he obtruded himself into the marble chair' called the King's Bench. Thus enthroned, he took the sovereign's oath in the presence of a vast gathering that included his magnates, justices and serjeants-at-law, exhorting the latter most sternly to 'justly and duly minister his laws without delay or favour', dispensing justice 'indifferently to every person, as well as to poor as to rich'. He then rode back to Baynard's Castle, saluting and bowing to the people lining the roads: 'A mind that knoweth itself guilty is in a manner dejected to a servile flattery,' commented More. In the evening the new King rode to St Paul's to hear the heralds proclaim his title. On this occasion he received an enthusiastic reception 'with great congratulation and acclamation of all the people in every place', according to a letter of Lord Dynham, Captain of Calais. How much of this was dictated by fear, how much was flattery and self-seeking, and how much the momentum of the occasion it is impossible to tell, but since the beginning of June the Londoners had been distinctly cool towards their former protector.

The manner of Richard III's usurpation of the throne revealed traits in his character hitherto suspected only by a few. Many had praised him for his courage, his blameless private life and his loyalty to his brother. Now that much-vaunted loyalty had been proved to be merely skin-deep: Edward IV had not been dead three months yet Richard had already branded him a bastard and a bigamist, attacked his government, and disinherited his children. Croyland and other contemporary observers all make much of Richard's duplicity, and Croyland in particular constantly implies that Richard's public image of an upright, principled monarch was a sham which concealed his innate dishonesty and deceitfulness. More also stresses the contradictions between what Richard said and what he actually did. Mancini states he was renowned for concealing his real faults, and his tone suggests he believed the King to be a crafty villain. He was, says More, 'close and secret'. Rous accuses Richard III of being 'excessively cruel' and even likens him to the antiChrist, and Commines records that Louis XI of France, who was not the nicest of men, condemned Richard as 'extremely cruel and evil'. More calls him 'malicious, wrathful, envious and ever froward'.

Nevertheless, Richard III did possess great abilities and potential as a ruler. Croyland says he carried out all his enterprises 'swiftly and with the utmost vigilance', but even this had its darker side, according to Vergil, who asserts that the King was 'a man much feared for his circumspection and celerity'.

There were still those who found much to praise in him. Two men who met him in 1484 were decidedly impressed: Nicholas von Poppelau spoke of him having 'a great heart', and Archibald Whitelaw, the Scots envoy, declared he had 'so much spirit and great virtue'. Undoubtedly Richard had a charismatic charm that he could exert when he wished to; there are many still in thrall to it today. More praise came from Pietro Carmeliano who, in his introduction to his *Life of St Catherine* (1484), eulogised Richard in the conventional manner then adopted in such works:

> For justice, who can we reckon above him throughout the world? If we contemplate the prudence of his service, both in peace and in waging war, who shall we judge his equal? If we look for truth of soul, for wisdom, for loftiness of mind united with modesty, who stands before our King Richard? What emperor or prince can be compared with him in good works or munificence?

Undoubtedly this was the persona that Richard meant the world to perceive; it should be remembered, however, that the book was dedicated to Sir Robert Brackenbury, one of Richard's most devoted supporters, and was hardly likely to contain anything less than flattering to Brackenbury's patron.

The high moral tone of Richard's propaganda was in glaring contrast to his private life. Early in his reign he declared to his bishops that 'his principal intent and fervent desire is to see virtue and cleanness of living to be advanced, and vices provoking the high indignation and fearful displeasure of God to be repressed. And this put in execution by persons of high estate,' who would show 'persons of low degree to take thereof example'. Less high-minded were his attacks on the morality of his opponents. No king before him had used the propaganda of character assassination to discredit his enemies, and Richard's preoccupation with other people's sinfulness seems on the face of it almost to have bordered on the obsessive or prurient. One proclamation offering rewards for the capture of certain traitors was titled 'Proclamation for the reform of morals', and reads more like an attack on illicit sexuality than a condemnation of treason. Elizabeth Shore's humiliating penance at Paul's Cross was another example. Nevertheless, it is unlikely that Richard felt any real concern for public morality beyond affecting an interest to enhance his own reputation and using accusations of immorality as a propaganda weapon to destroy the reputations of his enemies.

Mancini speaks of Gloucester's 'blameless morals', referring to his private life, of which little is known but enough to prove him a hypocrite. He had bastards, born probably before his marriage, and it is true that there are no references to him keeping a mistress for many years after it. But there is evidence that Richard's morals were not all they were vaunted to be. In September 1483 Bishop Thomas Langton, who had a good opinion of the King, wrote a letter in English praising him to the Prior of Christ Church, Canterbury. Yet in that same letter is a Latin postscript, so written because it refers to a subject of some delicacy. Unfortunately this part of the letter is damaged by damp and barely decipherable now, but what it appears to say, in translation, is: 'I do not take exception to the fact that his sensuality [*voluptas*] appears to be increasing.' And there is other evidence, which will be discussed in Chapter Seventeen, that Richard was not faithful to his wife after his accession.

But if the new King was a hypocrite in his private life, he appeared to be no such thing in his spiritual life. 'Which of our princes shows a more genuine piety?' asked Carmeliano. Certainly Richard III professed a deep and genuine religious faith in the conventional Catholic form: he conscientiously attended to his devotions, went on pilgrimages to religious shrines, was a most generous benefactor to many religious houses, such as Durham Cathedral, and founded eighteen chantries. He also cherished an ambition to go on a crusade against the Turks. The Convocation of Canterbury commended him for having a 'most noble and blessed disposition' towards the Church.

Richard also owned a number of devotional books, all of which he acquired second-hand and all, save one, in English, which indicates that they were for private reading and of significance to him. They included a copy of the first version (c.1390) of John Wycliffe's English translation of the New Testament, which had been banned in England as heretical – it bears Richard's signature, '*A vo me ly Gloucestre*', and is now in the New York Public Library. There was also an account of *The Visions of St Matilda*, inscribed 'Anne Warrewyk' and 'R. Gloucestre'. Most interesting of all is Richard's illuminated *Book of Hours*, his only Latin work, which may have been passed on to him by his wife. After Richard's death it became the property of the Lady Margaret Beaufort, one of his greatest enemies, who was almost certainly responsible for deleting his name from the text and the end page. It is now in Lambeth Palace Library.

This *Book of Hours* contains an interesting private prayer, written in English by or for Richard III and dedicated to St Julian, an almost certainly fictitious nobleman who, through mistaken identity, killed his own parents. As penance, he and his wife founded a refuge for the poor, where one day a mysterious traveller appeared and informed Julian that Christ had accepted his penance. The cult of St Julian was a popular one in western Europe in Richard's time, and many religious foundations were dedicated to him. It appears that Richard's prayer to St Julian was inserted into his *Book of Hours* by a scribe with indifferent handwriting some time after his accession, and while the sentiments expressed in it were by no means uncommon at the time, they must have held a special significance for the King, for this was, after all, a prayer used in private devotions:

Deign to release me from the affliction, temptation, grief, infirmity, poverty and peril in which I am held, and give me aid. Show to me and pour out all the glory of Thy Grace. Deign to assuage, turn aside and bring to nothing the hatred they bear towards me. Deign to free me from all the distresses and griefs by which I find myself troubled.

There is more in the same vein, with the King pleading for aid against his enemies and detractors and, presumably, the threat of invasion from abroad. Then there is a passage that may be especially significant.

You made me from nothing, and have redeemed me by Thy most wonderful love and mercy from eternal damnation to everlasting life. Because of this I ask You, O most gentle Jesus, to save me from all perils of body and soul and, after the course of this life, deign to bring me to You, the living and true God.

The references to griefs, enemies and possible invasion date this prayer almost certainly to the year 1485. Richard praises Christ with heartfelt gratitude for having redeemed him from eternal damnation: what, one is tempted to wonder, had he done to merit such damnation? Was it his usurpation of the throne and disinheriting of his brother's progeny? Or was it something far worse? His tyrannical rule had led to the deaths of several innocent men; yet, ask the revisionists, how could such a pious man, with an obvious leaning towards the religious mysticism popular in his day, be capable of acts of tyranny and violence? The fact is that he was indeed capable of them. There are many historical examples of men of genuine faith acting with appalling savagery and tyranny, which they themselves believed were justified. Richard III's own contemporaries, Ferdinand of Aragon, Louis XI and Cesare Borgia, took a pragmatic approach to such matters, as he himself did. They lived in a violent, opportunist age, but that did not preclude them professing a sincere devotion to God and the Church.

Besides being a benefactor of that Church, Richard III was also a generous patron of the arts and learning. His court exceeded his brother's in magnificence, for he was well aware of the political value of impressive ceremonial. He lived in ostentatious luxury and dressed himself in sumptuous imported Italian velvets, cloth of gold, silks and satins, many embroidered and furred with ermine. His preferred colours were crimson, purple and dark blue. Foreign visitors to his court were awed by the splendour. Not only was it an exquisitely dressed court, but also an impressively housed one. Rous praises Richard's achievements as a builder, and there is evidence that the King was interested in architecture. As well as beautifying his own castles at Middleham, Barnard Castle, and Sudeley, after it was confiscated from the Butler family, he made improvements to many royal residences, including Warwick Castle and Nottingham Castle. He also had a great interest in heraldry: in 1484 he founded the College of Arms in London; earlier, Caxton had dedicated his book, *The Order of Chivalry*, to Richard.

Musicians from all over Europe came to Richard III in search of preferment, for his cultural and musical interests were well known. The court of Edward IV had been famed for its music, and Richard now built on that reputation, patronising the composers William Pasche and Gilbert Banastre, and taking a special interest in the choir of the Chapel Royal. Queen Anne had her own minstrels as well.

Scholars, too, sought the King's patronage. He was a notable patron of the Universities of Oxford and Cambridge and of King's College, Cambridge. He was interested in the study of politics, and employed as his personal chaplain the humanist John Droget. As well as devotional books, Richard also owned volumes on heraldry, war, the art of government, and the works of Chaucer.

For all his high-minded interests, his piety and his obvious abilities, Richard III was not popular. His usurpation of the throne had been achieved at the cost of his popularity in the South, where his subjects did not approve of the manner in which he had mounted the throne; nor did they believe his claim to it to be lawful. His actions during the weeks leading up to his accession had incurred public opprobrium and dismay, and there is every reason to suppose that many people in England, like the chroniclers of the time, viewed Richard III as an usurper, tyrant and hypocrite. While the Londoners reeled, shocked and stunned by the murder of Hastings and paralysed by fear of the northern troops summoned by their Protector, Richard had seized his advantage and pressed home his claim.

But now he would have to hold on to what he had taken, and to do that he would need the support of his chief magnates, those men who had helped him rise to his present eminence; men such as Buckingham, Howard and Northumberland, who might all be kept loyal with lavish rewards and the promise of future preferment. The rest of the magnates, moderates and older nobility, who had supported Richard through fear of the consequences to them if they didn't, must now be won over by the example of good government that the King intended to set in order to justify the satisfaction of his ambitions. On these magnates his continuance in his regal office depended, and at the present time they, like his common subjects, resented, feared and distrusted him. Nor was their antipathy solely the result of the disinheriting of Edward IV's children by an uncle who had always professed his profound loyalty to them and their father. It was also a reaction to the insidious promotion by Richard of northerners, a process which had already begun by the time of his accession.

In the South of England northerners were regarded then as uncouth, brutish, undisciplined savages, a view cemented by the appalling behaviour of Margaret of Anjou's rampaging northern troops who accompanied her south in 1461. Londoners in particular retained horrified memories of them. Fifteenth-century society was insular and localised and therefore northerners were regarded as another race, and a hostile one at that. Yet, from the time of his appointment as Protector, Richard, who had good reason to favour the northerners for their love and loyalty towards him, began appointing them to prestigious court and administrative posts, much to the fury of the southern magnates and the Londoners. On his accession he promoted three of his northern retainers to high office: Sir Francis Lovell became chamberlain of the royal household, Sir Robert Percy became comptroller, and John Kendal of York became Richard's secretary. For a time the King retained the services of Edward IV's household officials, but then he began replacing them with northerners loyal to himself, which gave rise to many complaints and much resentment. He also preferred several northerners to the Council itself, and during his reign over 80 per cent of those made Knights of the Garter were northerners. Richard was seen as almost a northerner himself because he had identified himself so much with northern interests, and this, as much as anything else, was at the root of his unpopularity. It also accounts for much of the hostility of contemporary chroniclers, most of whom came from the South.

On the day that Richard ascended the throne, says More, the deposed King Edward V, still in the Tower, 'had it showed to him that he should not reign, but his uncle should have the crown. At which word the Prince, sore abashed, began to sigh, and said, "Alas, I would my uncle would let me have my life yet, though I lose my kingdom."' The boy, continues More, was comforted by the unnamed messenger, who was probably a person of rank and standing, perhaps Lord Howard. More, as we shall shortly see, had good reason to know what was happening in the Tower at that time, and that Edward went in fear of his life, which is independently corroborated by Mancini.

On 27th June, the King confirmed that Bishop Russell would continue as chancellor. He then proceeded to reward those who had supported him, meaning to retain their loyalty by his munificence. On 28th June Lord Howard was created Duke of Norfolk and hereditary Earl Marshal of England, and was given half the Mowbray estates. On that same day, Lord Berkeley was given the other half and created Earl of Nottingham. Howard's son Thomas was created Earl of Surrey.

The dukedom of Norfolk and the earldom of Nottingham had until that day been vested in Richard, Duke of York, the younger of the Princes in the Tower, by Acts of Parliament passed in 1478 and 1483. These Acts had not been repealed because Parliament had not yet convened, nor had any legislation depriving York of his legitimate status or his honours been passed. The titles, however, had come to him through marriage and not by hereditary right, and thus would not be affected by any Acts disabling York from inheriting the throne. Certainly Howard and Berkeley, as coheirs of Anne Mowbray, had the better claim to the titles, but York's claim, irregular as it was, was enshrined in a law which still stood unchallenged by Parliament.

Richard III, as we have seen, had no time for legal niceties. He had had his nephews declared illegitimate and probably felt that this was sufficient justification for depriving them of all their other titles and honours. His subjects had not opposed Edward V's deposition and were not likely to protest much about York losing his dukedom to Howard. Some writers have suggested that Richard had murdered York before 28th June, but there is good evidence that he was alive after that date, which will be discussed in due course.

Buckingham also received the first of his rewards on 28th June: he was appointed Great Chamberlain of England and given many lands and castles. Two days later the double-agent William Catesby was appointed Chancellor of the Exchequer and an Esquire of the Body to the King. Catesby acted as Speaker in Parliament in 1484 and was one of Richard III's foremost councillors.

The King's coronation was set for 6th July. Five days before that the army he had summoned from the North arrived at the gates of London and camped outside. Mancini says it numbered 6,000 men. Although this presence was no longer needed to put down any rebellion against Richard's accession, the King decided to retain its services until after his coronation because 'he was afraid lest any uproar should be fomented against him at his coronation. He himself went out to meet the soldiers before they entered the City.'

'There was hasty provision made for his coronation,' records the *Great Chronicle*. On 4th July the King and Queen went in the royal barge along the river from Westminster to the Tower of London, where Richard formally released Archbishop Rotherham and appointed Lord Stanley steward of his household. He and Queen Anne then took up residence in the royal apartments.

Security for the coronation was tight. On that same day a proclamation ordered the imposing of a 10.00 pm curfew for the next three nights and forbade the citizens of London to carry arms. Visitors to the City had to stay in officially approved lodgings. Mancini states that the northern soldiers were 'stationed at suitable points' along the streets, and that they stayed there until after the coronation.

On 5th July the King donned a gown of blue cloth of gold and a mantle of purple trimmed with ermine. The Queen put on 'a kirtle of white cloth of gold and a mantle with a train of the same', bordered with ermine. Then, he on horseback, she in a litter, they 'left the Tower, passing through the midst of the City, attended by the entire nobility and a display of royal honours', and so came to Westminster, where they would spend the night. 4,000 'gentlemen of the north' followed in the procession. As he rode, the King, says Mancini, 'with bared head greeted all onlookers, and himself received their acclamations'. But the evidence in most contemporary accounts of the period show that the mood of the public was resentful, even hostile, for all that many were carried away by the holiday mood of the occasion.

Nevertheless this was to be one of the most splendid of all mediaeval coronations in England, and the best attended, as almost the entire

English peerage had come to London for the Parliament which had been postponed. In the morning of 6th July Queen Anne gave her husband a long embroidered mantle of purple cloth of gold, made to her order by the Keeper of the Wardrobe, Piers Curteys. She herself wore purple robes made from 56 yards of velvet, which must have been uncomfortably hot on a July day. Thus attired, Richard and Anne made their way through the White Hall to Westminster Hall, where they sat enthroned on the King's Bench. Then, the procession having formed, they walked barefoot upon striped cloth to St Edward's shrine within Westminster Abbey, preceded by the nobility of England. Norfolk officiated as Earl Marshal and High Steward and carried the King's crown. Buckingham, who had the 'chief rule and devising' of the ceremonial, carried the King's train. The Duke of Suffolk carried the sceptre, his son the Earl of Lincoln the orb, and the Earl of Surrey the sword of state. Richard himself was supported by Bishop Stillington. The Queen's train was carried by Lady Stanley, the former Margaret Beaufort, and her attendants were led by the Duchesses of Suffolk and Norfolk. Significantly, perhaps, the King's mother, the Duchess of York, did not attend the coronation. The Duchess of Buckingham was also absent, by order of her husband, who made it plain he was not parading his Wydville wife for all to see.

For the anointing, Richard and Anne, according to the account preserved in the Harleian MSS. in the British Library, 'put off their robes and stood all naked from their waists upwards, till the Bishop had anointed them'. Then 'Te Deum' was sung 'with great royalty', after which, says Mancini, Archbishop Bourchier, 'albeit unwillingly, anointed and crowned [Richard] King of England'.

After the peers had paid homage to their new sovereign and Richard and Anne had received Holy Communion, the procession re-formed and left the Abbey, the King preceding the Queen back to Westminster Hall, where the coronation banquet lasted five and a half hours. It was noticed that the Archbishop did not attend, and his place at the King's right at the high table on the dais was taken by the Bishop of London. The day ended with the King and Queen retiring to a fanfare of trumpets.

A day or so after the coronation Richard and Anne went to Greenwich Palace and thence to Windsor. The northern troops were sent home, the tension in London having dissipated, and the King gave his attention to organising his Council and planning a progress through his kingdom. The progress was to be a well-planned exercise in public relations and self-promotion, with the King exerting himself to charm and win over his new subjects with liberality and accessible justice.

After the coronation, the Princes in the Tower were never seen alive again.

12
Conspiracies

Dominic Mancini left England during the week after the coronation, and his account, sadly for us, ends there. He says that, before his departure, the Princes had 'ceased to appear altogether', and this is corroborated by every other source. Already, people were thinking and fearing the worst. Mancini writes: 'I have seen many men burst forth into tears and lamentations when mention was made of [Edward V] after his removal from men's sight; and already there was a suspicion that he had been done away with. Whether, however, he has been done away with, and by what manner of death, so far I have not at all discovered.'

Mancini's account is the earliest evidence of rumours that the Princes were dead. Given the fate of earlier deposed kings – Edward II, Richard II and Henry VI had all been secretly murdered – it is hardly surprising that people should suspect that the same fate had overtaken Edward V and his brother. The people with whom Mancini associated would have been intelligent men of standing in business and courtly circles; the fact that they believed the Princes to be already dead is proof that these rumours were not mere speculative gossip but the product of serious concern on the part of informed men who were not so hard-headed that they could fail to be deeply distressed when contemplating the possible murder of two children.

It is clear, nevertheless, as we shall see from the *Croyland Chronicle* – whose author was well-placed to know the truth – that the Princes were not yet dead. Fabyan states simply that they were now 'under sure keeping. They never came abroad after,' but More, who had reliable sources close to the Tower, gives more details of the Princes' imprisonment. They were, he says, 'both shut up, and all others removed from them, only one called Black Will or Will Slaughter except, set to serve them and see them sure. After which time the Prince never tied his points [i.e. did up his hose] nor aught wrought of himself, but with that young babe his brother lingered in thought and heaviness and wretchedness.' More's account is substantiated by the details of Edward's captivity passed from Dr Argentine to Mancini, and almost certainly describes Edward's mental condition a few weeks after Argentine last saw him. By that time the boy was so sunk in misery and fear that he was unable to perform even basic tasks, such as dressing himself properly.

William Slaughter, whose nickname 'Black Will' may have derived from his appearance or, more ominously, his character, was both gaoler and servant to the Princes. More, in a later passage, reveals that the number of attendants was soon increased to four, and that 'one of the four that kept them' was Miles Forrest, 'a fellow fleshed in murder before his time'. No record exists of Forrest's crime(s), but it is thought that he was a northerner; a Miles Forrest had been keeper of the wardrobe at Barnard Castle in Yorkshire, a residence owned by Richard III since his marriage. This was almost certainly the same man, and he was undoubtedly known to the King. It is typical of Richard that he should entrust such a task to one of his loyal northerners.

Meanwhile the King, taking no chances, was still heaping rewards on Buckingham, who was given even more honours and wider powers to ensure his support. On 13th July Richard issued a provisional grant naming the Duke rightful heir to the disputed Bohun inheritance, this grant to be confirmed by Parliament, which would reverse a former grant giving some of the Bohun estates to Elizabeth Wydville. On 15th July Buckingham was appointed Lord High Constable of England, an office which made him chief commander of the army and gave him jurisdiction over military offences, control of all matters relating to heraldry and chivalry, and responsibility for fortifications and defence. In this latter capacity the Tower of London, the chief military stronghold of the capital, came under his jurisdiction. However, contrary to what several writers have asserted, his office did not give him the right to demand entry to the fortress without the permission of its Lieutenant or Constable, who, although they were subordinate officers, were not empowered to obey orders from the Lord High Constable unless they came direct from the King, under his seal.

The Tower records for the beginning of Richard III's reign are no longer extant, and therefore we do not know who occupied the offices of Lieutenant and Constable. The Lieutenant was the officer with overall charge of and responsibility for the Tower, and had a lodging there. There are indications that Lord Howard may have acted as Lieutenant for a time: the entries in his account books, already referred to, and the fact that it was he and his son who obtained barges and escorted York to the Tower.

The Constable was subordinate to the Lieutenant and had charge of any prisoners and the day to day running of the Tower. In July 1483 the office of Constable was held, nominally, by John, Lord Dudley, an old man; after him, Lord Dacre had the reversion, and after him John Howard, Duke of Norfolk. There is no evidence to show that either Dudley or Dacre took an active part in the affairs of the Tower. Rivers had been deputy constable but that appointment had lapsed when he was arrested.

Obviously this state of affairs could not be allowed to continue, especially since the Tower now housed the Princes, two state prisoners of the utmost importance. Hence on 17th July the King appointed another northerner, Sir Robert Brackenbury, as Constable of the Tower, with special responsibility for the safe-keeping of the Princes. Brackenbury came from Selaby, County Durham. He had entered Gloucester's service some years previously and risen to the rank of treasurer of his household in the North. In those years he had conceived great respect, devotion and loyalty for his master, and had accordingly been taken into Richard's confidence, becoming one of his most trusted servants. Brackenbury himself was a well-intentioned if naïve man of kindly disposition, who was popular at court. The *Chronicle of Calais* calls him 'gentle Brackenbury' and Polydore Vergil stresses his integrity. As far as Richard was concerned Brackenbury was the ideal man for the job of Constable. He was utterly loyal, could see no wrong in his master, could be fully trusted with state secrets, and was known and respected as a man of honour. No-one would suspect Brackenbury of ill-treating or harming his prisoners. He was also well aware of the high-security risk posed by the presence of the Princes in the Tower, for they were a potential focus for rebellion and the King's enemies might try to spirit them away. But no-one would get past the staunch Brackenbury without a King's warrant. Thus, says Croyland, 'the two sons of King Edward remained in the Tower of London in the custody of certain persons appointed for that purpose' – a reference to Brackenbury and the four attendant-gaolers, Slaughter, Forrest and two unnamed others, referred to by More.

On the day after Brackenbury was appointed Constable, a royal warrant was issued authorising payment of wages to thirteen men for their services to 'Edward, bastard, late called King Edward V'. These were the servants whose dismissal after the death of Hastings was recorded by Mancini.

Preparations for the royal progress were completed that July. On the day before he was due to set out, Richard appointed his seven-year-old son, Edward of Middleham, Lord Lieutenant of Ireland, a title customarily borne by Yorkist heirs to the throne. Then, on 20th July, the King left Windsor, leaving Queen Anne behind, for it had been arranged that she should join him later. He went to London, and two days later rode out westwards at the head of a great procession, accompanied by his nephew the Earl of Lincoln and probably by Buckingham. Both Vergil and More say that Buckingham rode with the King as far as Gloucester, where they parted. Rous gives a detailed description of the royal retinue but fails to mention Buckingham: this is probably accounted for by the fact that Rous lived at Warwick, which Richard visited after Buckingham had left his train. It may seem strange that Buckingham's name had earlier been omitted from a list of those present at a dinner given in the King's honour by Magdalen College, Oxford, but it is not necessarily proof that the Duke remained in London, as some have alleged.

Richard spent this first night of his progress at Reading. There, on 23rd July, he issued a grant pardoning Lord Hastings' 'offences' and promising 'to be a good and gracious lord' to Hastings' widow, Katherine, who was granted the wardship and marriage of her son Edward, possession of her late husband's moveable property, and custody of his estates during her son's minority. Hastings' high offices had been shared between Buckingham, Catesby and Lovell. Richard displayed similar generosity to the widow of Lord Rivers. He was anxious to convince his subjects that he was not the tyrant they believed him to be, that he only punished traitors when he had to, and that his vengeance did not extend to their families.

On 24th July the King reached Oxford, where he dined at Magdalen College, stayed the night, and spent much of the following day. Then he rode to Woodstock Palace nearby where he piled further honours upon Norfolk, appointing him Lord Admiral of England, Surveyor of Array in thirteen counties, Steward of the Duchy of Lancaster, and a member of the Council. He also granted him forty-six manors in East Anglia and the rents from twenty-five others, all the former property of Lord Rivers. Three days later Norfolk received twenty more of Rivers' manors. Next to Buckingham, he was now the most wealthy and powerful subject in the kingdom.

Richard spent another day at Oxford on 26th July, inspecting the colleges, then stayed for a few days as the guest of Lord Lovell at his nearby house, Minster Lovell. But while he was there the tranquillity and apparent success of the progress so far was disturbed by the arrival of alarming news that would have a direct bearing on the fate of his nephews in the Tower.

For all the magnificence of his coronation, his cultivated display of majesty and his attempts to buy the loyalty of his magnates, Richard III knew his position to be insecure. Many of his subjects, particularly the gentry in the South and West, felt nothing but odium for the way in which this near northerner had set aside the rightful King and usurped the throne. His blatant acts of tyranny had alienated many of those who might have supported him, and there was a hard core of gentlefolk who were ready and willing to take action to restore Edward V to the throne. The popular view seems to have been that Richard's claim was based on a tissue of lies and that Edward ought never to have been deposed.

The only informed account of what happened next comes from Croyland, who says that while the coronation and progress 'were taking place, King Edward IV's two sons were in the Tower of London under special guard. In order to release them from such captivity, the people from the South and the West of the kingdom began to murmur greatly and to form assemblies and confederacies, many of which worked in secret, others openly, with this aim.' The conspirators appear to have been disaffected Yorkists, loyal to the line of Edward IV but not to Richard III, as well as Lancastrian dissidents and the Wydville faction: the Queen's three brothers, Lionel, Edward and Richard, were all involved. Some of the plotters appealed to Buckingham to join them, but he rejected the offer out of hand.

Very few details of these conspiracies are known. The Elizabethan antiquarian John Stow wrote in 1580 of a plot in July 1483 to secure the release of Edward V from the Tower by diverting his gaolers with a blaze. This may indeed have been the object of one of the conspiracies, but there is no other evidence for it. What we do know is that a plot was hatched in the Sanctuary, not to rescue Edward V – which the intriguers must have realised was impossible, but to spirit his sisters overseas. This plot seems to have originated, according to Croyland, with 'those men who had taken refuge in the sanctuaries', a possible reference to the Queen's brothers. There can be little doubt that Elizabeth Wydville herself was involved: her co-operation would be vital in such a plan. Like many people, she feared for her sons' safety, and when it was put to her 'that some of the King's daughters should leave Westminster and go in disguise to parts beyond the sea', she perceived that this would guarantee some measure of safety to all her children. If anything happened to Edward and Richard, the Lady Elizabeth would in the eyes of many be the rightful Queen of England; abroad, she would be free to make a strategic marriage with one of a number of foreign princes who would be willing and eager to take up arms to restore her to her inheritance and so gain a crown. Wrote Croyland: 'If any fatal mishap should befall the male children of the late King in the Tower, the kingdom might still, in consequence of the safety of the daughters, some day fall again into the hands of the rightful heirs.' And the fact that Edward IV's daughters were abroad and able to challenge Richard's title might make the usurper think twice about doing away with his nephews, which is what people feared he would do. In agreeing to participate in this conspiracy, the Queen was not only attempting to safeguard the legitimate Yorkist succession but seeking to preserve her own political influence.

The King, however, had his spies, who discovered what was going on and reported it to him at Minster Lovell in late July. He may also

Richard: Rex tertius

1 *above* Richard III: early 17th century (?) copy of a portrait by an anonymous artist of *c*.1518-23 in the Royal Collection. When this picture was painted the legend of the villainous 'crookbacked king' with one shoulder higher than the other was firmly established.

2 *above right* The earliest surviving portrait of Richard, dating from *c*.1516-22 and almost certainly a copy of a lost original painted from life, shows no apparent deformity.

3 *right* The 'Broken Sword' portrait by an unknown artist, *c*.1533-43. X-rays show that drastic alterations were made later on, when Richard's reputation was rehabilitated, to give the deformed-looking king a more normal appearance.

4 Edward IV: his son Edward, the elder of the two Princes, was 'his greatest joy'.

5 Elizabeth Wydville: 'everyone, as he was nearest of kin unto the Queen, was so planted next about the Prince, whereby her blood might of youth be rooted in the Prince's favour' (Sir Thomas More).

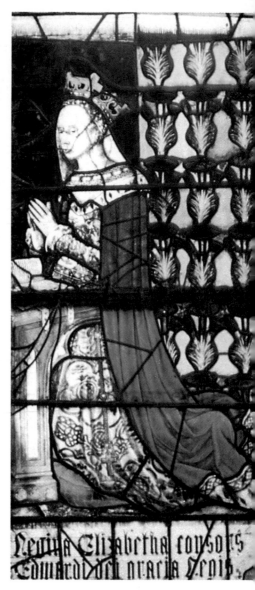

6 *opposite page* Illustration from The York Roll: at the top is Richard Neville, Earl of Warwick, 'the Kingmaker', and his wife, Anne Beauchamp, the mother-in-law whom Richard III treated so callously. To the left is Warwick's daughter Anne Neville with her two husbands, Edward of Lancaster and Richard III, with Edward of Middleham, Prince of Wales, her son by Richard, below. To the right is Anne's sister Isabella Neville with her husband, George, Duke of Clarence, and their children Edward, Earl of Warwick, and Margaret, later Countess of Salisbury.

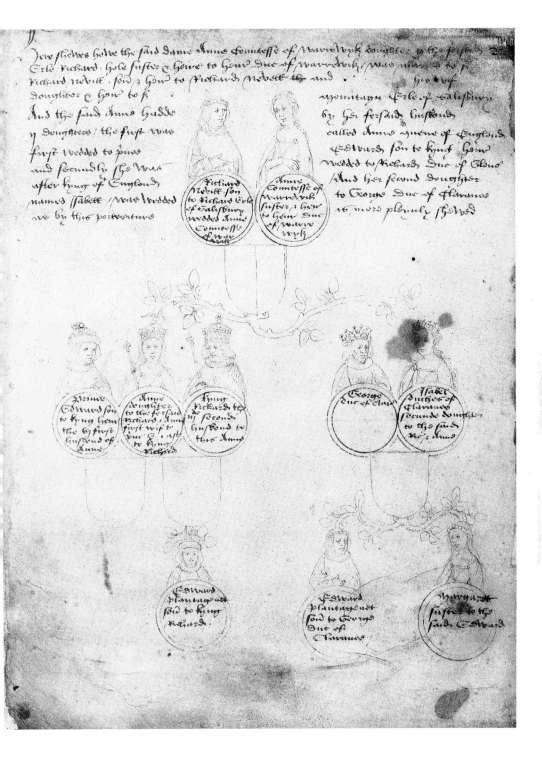

Here shewes howe the said dame Anne Countesse of Warwyck doughter to the forsaid
Erle Richard. hole suster & heire to Henr Duc of Warwyck. was maried to the forsaid
Richard Nevell. son & heir to Richard Nevell &c and ...

Doughter & heir to ...
And the said Anne hadde
ij doughters / the first was
first wedded to prins
and secondly she was
after kyng of England
named Isabell / were wedded
&c by this portrature

... montagu Erle of Salisbury
by her first husband
called Anne quene of England
& Edward son to kyng Henr
wedded to Richard Duc of Glou...
And her second doughter
to George Duc of Clarence
is more pleynly shewed

7   The Tower of London: contemporary sources indicate that the Princes were imprisoned in the White Tower. The forebuilding housing the staircase beneath which the bones of two children were found in 1674 may clearly be seen in front of the White Tower, facing the River Thames.

8   *above left* Henry Tudor: this obscure scion of the royal house, whom Richard III referred to as 'an unknown Welshman', claimed to be 'the very heir of the House of Lancaster'.

9   *above* Elizabeth of York and her sisters: Elizabeth claimed that Richard III 'was her only joy and maker in this world, and she was his in heart, in thought, in body and in all'.

10   *left* Margaret Beaufort, Countess of Richmond: a wise but dangerous woman who 'imagined the destruction of the King' (The Rolls of Parliament)

Ricardus dux Eboraci secundus
filius Edwardi quarti

Edwardus Princeps Walli...
primus filius Edwardi quarti

'Tho: Moor L. Chancelour'

11 *opposite page* The Princes in the Tower: Lord Chancellor Russell wrote that Edward (*right*) had a 'gentle wit and ripe understanding, far passing the nature of his youth'. The French chronicler Jean Molinet describes York (*left*) as 'joyous and witty, and ever ready for dances or games'.

12 *above* Sir Thomas More: 'I shall rehearse you the dolorous end of these babes, not after every way that I have heard, but after that way that I have heard by such men and such means as me thinketh it were hard but it should be true'.

13 *above right* The burial of the Princes: More says they were buried 'at the stair foot, meetly deep under the ground, under a great heap of stones'.

14 *right* Ruins of the minoresses' convent at Aldgate after the fire of 1797: here, in 'the great house within the close', lodged four ladies who may well have known the truth about the Princes' fate.

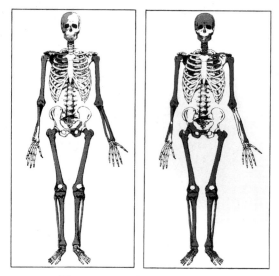

15 The remains found in 1674: 'They were small bones of lads in their teens, fully recognised to be the bones of those two Princes' (Eye-witness report, 1674; *Archaeologia*).

16 The urn in which the bones repose in Westminster Abbey: 'a curious altar of black and white marble', designed by Sir Christopher Wren in 1678.

17 The skull of Anne Mowbray: York's child-bride and the Princes' cousin, exhumed in 1964. Dental evidence indicates a familial relationship between her bones and those in the urn.

have learned from Buckingham of the conspirators' bid to gain his support. He certainly had intelligence of the embryonic conspiracies in the South and West, but it was the Sanctuary plot in Westminster that took Richard by surprise and caused him the deepest concern and anxiety. These conspiracies were incontrovertible evidence that, while the Princes lived, he would never be secure on his throne. Nor, it seemed, would the Wydvilles ever stop plotting against him and stirring up rebellion.

On 29th July, the King issued a warrant under his privy seal to Lord Chancellor Russell in London:

> Right reverend Father in God, right trusty and well-beloved, we greet you well. And whereas we understand that certain persons of such as of late had taken upon them the fact of an enterprise, as we doubt not ye have heard, be attached, and in ward, we desire and will you that ye do make our letters of commission to such persons as by you and our Council shall be advised for to sit upon them, and to proceed to the due execution of our laws in that behalf. Fail ye not hereof, as our perfect trust is in you.

Because this warrant is referring to a matter on which Richard expected Russell to be well informed, much has been left unsaid. The enterprise undertaken by certain persons now 'in ward' must refer to the Sanctuary conspiracy. Croyland states that after this conspiracy was uncovered 'the noble church of the monks at Westminster and all the neighbouring parts assumed the appearance of a castle and fortress, while men of the greatest austerity were appointed by King Richard to act as the keepers thereof. The captain and head of these was one John Nesfield, Esquire, who set a watch upon all the inlets and outlets of the monastery, so that not one of the persons shut up could go forth, and no-one could enter without his permission.' Thus the inmates of the Sanctuary could be truly said to be 'in ward'.

The latter part of the warrant implies that the King wished the conspirators to be questioned by the Council and afterwards prosecuted. But there is no record of any such proceedings, and it may be that the councillors were prevented from carrying out their master's orders because some conspirators had gone to ground or even fled abroad, and some, such as the Queen, were beyond their reach in sanctuary. But whatever the case, this conspiracy had failed. The daughters of Edward IV remained in sanctuary and his sons remained in the Tower.

Ironically, by seeking to ensure the boys' safety, the conspirators – including their own mother – had sealed their fate.

13

The Princes in the Tower

Richard III learned of the Sanctuary plot before 29th July. On that day, or shortly afterwards, he arrived with his train at Gloucester. More says that 'on his way' there he 'devised as he rode to fulfil that thing which he before had intended. For his mind gave him that, his nephews living, men would not reckon that he could have right to the realm; he thought, therefore, without delay to rid them, as though the killing of his kinsmen could amend his cause and make him a kindly king.' It was an opportune time to act: the magnates had left London, he himself was nowhere near the City and hopefully beyond suspicion, and the initial alarm over his usurpation seemed to have died down.

More and Vergil say that when Richard arrived at Gloucester he sent for a man called John Green, 'whom he specially trusted'. John Green can be traced; he had been employed, in various capacities, by Richard when he was Duke of Gloucester, and by Sir James Tyrell, Richard's faithful retainer. He may well have been the same John Green who is recorded in the *Calendar of Patent Rolls* for 1474–5 as working in Edward IV's household. On 30th July, 1483, John Green signed a warrant appointing one John Gregory to take hay, oats, horsebread, beans, peas and litter for all the expenses of the King's horses and litters for a period of six months.

The King, says More, sent Green 'unto Sir Robert Brackenbury, Constable of the Tower, with a letter and credence that the same Sir Robert should in any wise put the two children to death'. It has been argued that Richard III would never have committed such an order to

147

paper, but it is nevertheless plausible that he did so. His letter, like the one he sent from Minster Lovell, is likely to have been discreetly worded so as not to compromise himself. Green was to supply the 'credence', the unwritten, explicit details, to Brackenbury, and both were men trusted implicitly by Richard.

Continues More: 'This John Green did his errand unto Brackenbury.' But Brackenbury was not of the stuff of which murderers are made. Vergil says he feared the consequences to his own reputation and safety should his complicity in what More calls 'so mean and bestial a deed' ever be made public. In Green's presence, he knelt 'before Our Lady in the Tower' and 'plainly answered that he would never put [the Princes] to death, though he should die therefor'.

Believing that his orders would be carried out within a few days, the King rested at Gloucester until 2nd August. The Duke of Buckingham was with him but this would be the last time they saw each other, for before 2nd August Richard had managed somehow to alienate Buckingham. What caused this has been a matter for some speculation. Vergil says 'dissension sprang between the King and the Duke' because Richard would not grant Buckingham the Bohun inheritance. But Richard had already made a provisional grant of it on 13th July, so this cannot have been the reason for Buckingham's sudden disaffection. More was probably nearer the truth when he conjectured that although Buckingham had supported Richard's plan to usurp the throne, when the King revealed to him at Gloucester that he had given the order for the killing of the Princes, Buckingham realised that things had gone too far and wanted to dissociate himself. There is no other logical reason for his alienation, only something as cataclysmic as this could have provoked it. Buckingham owed all his vast wealth and political influence to Richard, and if he defected he would be placing all that, as well as his own life, at risk.

Buckingham left the progress at Gloucester, pleading pressing business on his Brecon estates, and the King, suspecting nothing, bade him farewell and rode to Tewkesbury. For some time afterwards he would continue to write to Buckingham as though their alliance was as strong as ever. But, says More, the Duke, on his way home, considered how best to remove this 'unnatural uncle and bloody butcher from his royal seat and princely dignity'.

Many revisionists still adhere to the theory that it was Buckingham who murdered the Princes. This theory rests on the evidence of four slightly later sources. Commines states that the Duke 'caused the death of the two children', and later that he had acted on Richard's orders. The manuscript fragment in the College of Arms says the Princes were 'murdered on the vise [advice]' of the Duke of Buckingham, and another in Ashmole MS. 1448.60, dating from c.1490, states that Richard III killed his nephews 'at the prompting of the Duke of Buckingham, it is said'. There is no contemporary evidence for the Duke's involvement in the plot to kill the Princes. The sources quoted above appear to have reported the gossip then circulating both in England and abroad, gossip which perpetrated many far-fetched theories as to what had happened to Edward V and his brother.

Molinet, an untrustworthy source, says that 'on the day that Edward's sons were assassinated there came to the Tower of London the Duke of Buckingham, who was believed, mistakenly, to have murdered the children in order to forward his pretensions to the throne'. Molinet states elsewhere that the Princes were murdered in late July, but according to Croyland they were alive until the first week in September, and Croyland was in a position to state that as a fact. On 2nd August Buckingham went to Brecon where he stayed until October.

Buckingham, alone, could not have murdered the Princes for several reasons: he was not in the right place at the right time; he had no authority to gain access to them; Brackenbury would not have admitted him to their prison without a royal warrant signed by the King; and if these obstacles had somehow been overcome Richard III would have speedily found out about it and publicly accused Buckingham, in tones of moral outrage, of the murder. But Richard did no such thing, not even later when Buckingham was charged with other kinds of treason and it would have been politically advantageous to have laid the deaths of the Princes at his door, thus diverting suspicion from Richard himself. This in itself is strong evidence that the Duke had no hand in the murder. Even more convincing is Buckingham's own behaviour after he left Gloucester. According to More, Buckingham himself later declared to Bishop Morton: 'God be my judge, I never agreed or condescended to it.'

Richard arrived at Warwick Castle on 8th August. There he received further details of the conspiracies in the South and West, which can only have hardened his resolve to do away with the Princes. In the meantime Queen Anne had arrived with the Earl of Warwick, and she was with Richard when ambassadors from Ferdinand and Isabella of Spain came to propose a marriage between Edward of Middleham and a Spanish infanta.

The King remained at Warwick until 15th August, when he went to Coventry. More states that John Green, returning from the Tower, recounted Brackenbury's refusal to comply with the order to kill the Princes 'to King Richard at Warwick'. Richard was annoyed, but his anger was probably superficial, for no open breach occurred with Brackenbury. Not only did Richard know Brackenbury to be an honest man with scruples, qualities that could only reflect upon and benefit the master who had appointed him, but he also could not afford publicly to censure the man or remove him from office because questions would be asked, and Richard did not at that point want public attention focused upon the Tower and its inmates. Before long he had resolved that Brackenbury should be left out of his plans.

For the present, however, Richard vented his displeasure – according to More, who relished scatalogical details – whilst sitting on the close stool, grumbling to 'a secret page of his', who was certainly in Richard's confidence and probably therefore a spy whose function was to assess the loyalties of members of the royal household.

'Ah, whom shall a man trust?' sighed the King. 'Those that I have brought up myself fail me, and at my commandment will do nothing for me.'

'Sir,' replied his page, 'there lieth one on your pallet without that I dare well say to do your Grace pleasure the thing were right hard that he would refuse.' He meant by this Sir James Tyrell who, says More, 'was a man of right goodly personage and for Nature's gifts worthy to have served a much better prince. The man had an high heart, and sore longed upward, not rising yet so fast as he had hoped, which thing this page well had marked and known.'

Tyrell had acted as Richard's confidential servant for at least ten years. His family hailed from Gipping in Suffolk, and it has been remarked upon that he bore the same name as Walter Tirel who had supposedly murdered King William Rufus in 1100, though no connection can be traced. James was knighted in 1471 after the Battle of Tewkesbury, and in 1473 had escorted Richard's mother-in-law, the

Countess of Warwick, from sanctuary to Middleham Castle, which proves he had already established himself as trustworthy. Thereafter he served his master well in the West and in the North, as constable of Cardiff Castle, and on campaign in Scotland where he was made Knight Banneret. In June 1483 he had briefly acted as gaoler to Archbishop Rotherham, and early in Richard III's reign had been appointed Master of the King's Henchmen. In late July he had travelled on the King's business from London to York and thence to Warwick, where his duties were to serve Richard as a Knight of the Body, which was why he was sleeping on a pallet outside the door to the royal bedchamber, his function being to guard his sovereign and guarantee him a peaceful night's sleep. More implies that Tyrell had hoped for better rewards for his devoted service, but that Ratcliffe and Catesby stood in his way. The page told the King that Tyrell was so desperate to rise in the world and have his revenge on his rivals that he would agree to do anything, however unpleasant.

Richard had apparently been unaware of how desperate Tyrell was for advancement, and he decided there and then that he would entrust him with arranging the murder of the Princes. He rose from the privy, pulled up his breeches, 'and came out into the pallet chamber where he found in bed Sir James. The King, calling up Sir James, broke to him secretly his mind in this mischievous matter, in which he found him nothing strange.'

While Richard plotted with Tyrell, Buckingham was still travelling to Brecon, which he reached by the middle of August. Vergil says he now deplored his failure to resist 'King Richard's evil enterprise'. At Brecknock Castle, his prisoner, John Morton, Bishop of Ely, awaited him. Morton loathed Richard III and regarded him as a usurper who should be eliminated without scruple. He had made no secret of his views and it was therefore natural that Buckingham should confide in him.

More's book ends with an account of the conversations between Morton and Buckingham which may have come direct from Morton himself, as no other source gives similar details. The Duke told Morton that after hearing of the King's resolve to murder the Princes, he 'abhorred the sight and much more the company' of Richard. More says Buckingham told Morton he was considering pressing his own claim to the throne, and that Morton told him he had 'excellent virtues meet for the rule of the realm'. Unfortunately More's unfinished narrative ends at this point.

Morton was a shrewd man and his political instincts were sound. He must have been appalled to learn that Richard had ordered the murder of the Princes and probably predicted that the usurper would not reign for long after the deed was done. It is likely that he warned Buckingham of what would happen to him if Richard's enemies succeeded in deposing him: none as yet knew of Buckingham's disaffection, and he would be dealt with as befitted the tyrant's chief supporter.

More states that Buckingham's conversation with Morton was what persuaded him actively to rebel against the King. It is clear from the attainder later passed on Buckingham that this was to be a separate conspiracy from those in the South and West – one lead by Buckingham and the clever Morton, whose situation was already precarious and who was later attainted with the Duke for plotting treason.

Buckingham is said by the Tudor chronicler Edward Hall to have not long afterwards met Margaret Beaufort, Countess of Richmond by virtue of her first marriage to Edmund Tudor and now the wife of Lord Stanley, on the road between Bridgenorth and Worcester. She, thinking Buckingham to be still close to the King, begged him to intercede with Richard on behalf of her son, Henry Tudor, an exile in Brittany for many years, telling the Duke she longed to have him home. Henry Tudor was the Lancastrian claimant to the throne, but he was virtually unknown in England and few people took him seriously, except for his mother, who, the evidence suggests, had been involved in the conspiracies against the King. Buckingham may have suspected or known as much and realised that here was a potential ally. He told the Countess what was in his mind and confided that he was considering making a bid for the crown himself, but she, with great firmness, reminded him that both she and her son stood as 'both bulwark and portcullis' between him and the throne. Only if he supported Henry Tudor's claim would she lend him her support. Buckingham, whose chief motive in rebelling was probably self-preservation, and who had probably always been a Lancastrian at heart, began then to consider abandoning his regal pretensions and offering his allegiance to Henry Tudor instead. The Countess, he knew, would be a valuable ally.

Margaret Beaufort was a fervent Lancastrian. For all her small stature she was a formidable woman: highly intelligent, literate, strong-minded, devout and austere in her religious observances. She was the sole heiress of the Beaufort descendants of John of Gaunt and Katherine Swynford. In 1455, at the age of twelve, she had been given in marriage by Henry VI to Edmund Tudor. He was one of the sons of Katherine of Valois, widow of Henry V, and her Welsh clerk of the wardrobe, Owen Tudor, who may have been her husband, although there is no evidence to prove it. In 1452, however, Parliament had declared Edmund and his brother Jasper legitimate, and Henry VI had created them earls of Richmond and Pembroke respectively. Edmund's marriage to Margaret Beaufort was highly advantageous to him, but in 1456 he was captured and imprisoned by the Yorkists in Carmarthen Castle, where he died later that year. Twelve weeks later, in January 1457, his widow, aged only thirteen, bore a son, Henry Tudor, at Pembroke Castle. He was to be her only child, her 'own sweet and most dear son', and would all his life excite in her the deepest maternal sentiments and ambitions.

Henry was Earl of Richmond from his birth. His early years were spent at Pembroke in the care of his mother and his uncle Jasper. Between 1459 and 1464 Margaret married the Lancastrian Sir Henry Stafford, who later switched his allegiance to Edward IV, thus allying his staunchly Lancastrian wife with her enemies. In 1461 Jasper fought for the Lancastrians against Edward, and when the latter became king that year Jasper was forced to flee abroad. The new King made Henry the ward of Lord Herbert, a loyal Yorkist to whom had been granted the ownership of Pembroke Castle, and in whose custody the boy spent his formative years. King Edward undoubtedly hoped that being brought up in a good Yorkist family would preclude Henry from having any ideas about pressing his somewhat tenuous claim to the throne or developing strong Lancastrian sympathies. Certainly he did not see his mother after 1461, and before 1462 he was deprived of the earldom of Richmond, which was given to Clarence.

During the brief restoration of Henry VI in 1470–71 Jasper Tudor returned from exile and presented his nephew at court, on which occasion Henry VI is said to have predicted that Henry Tudor was 'he unto whom both we and our adversaries must yield and give over the dominion'. Henry and Jasper then returned to Wales. After the deaths of Henry VI and his son the House of Lancaster's claim to the throne became vested in Henry Tudor, the only viable claimant. However, he was only fourteen at the time, unknown and penniless, and, since he was unlikely to be more than an irritation to Edward IV for some years to come, few took him seriously as a pretender. The King, nevertheless, would dearly have loved to get his hands on him, and therefore Henry and Jasper were obliged to flee in 1471 to Brittany, where they remained for the next thirteen years. Francis II, Duke of Brittany, offered them a refuge, refusing to surrender them to Edward IV, despite the latter's demands, but promising instead not to let them leave the duchy. In the end Edward was paying Francis II to keep them there and Henry chafed against his lack of freedom, complaining to Commines that 'since the age of five he had been guarded like a fugitive and kept in prison', though Commines adds that Duke Francis treated him 'reasonably well'.

Margaret Beaufort, meanwhile, had married a third husband, Lord Stanley, a prominent Yorkist, and had become a frequent visitor to the court of Edward IV. Before the King died she had almost managed to persuade him to agree to a reconciliation with her son, which indicates that Edward no longer considered Henry a serious political threat, but the King's death put an end to the Countess's hopes. At least now Henry was allowed more freedom by Duke Francis, even if he was desperately short of money.

From 1471 onwards the only people who supported Henry Tudor's claim to the throne were his mother, his immediate kinsmen, and his friends in exile, of whom the most prominent were Jasper Tudor and the Earl of Oxford. Henry's claim derived from his mother, to whom he always deferred as the lawful heiress to the House of Lancaster. There was nothing in law to prevent Margaret Beaufort from claiming the crown herself, but in the political climate of the late fifteenth century she would have found very few supporters because of her sex. However, the crown had passed by descent through a woman on several occasions: King Stephen, Henry II and the Yorkist kings were notable examples of monarchs whose claim to the throne came via a female line.

There were, in fact, descendants of the House of Lancaster with a better claim to the throne than Henry Tudor, namely the King of Portugal and the Queen of Castile, both descended from John of Gaunt by the lawfully-born daughters of his first and second wives. The Beaufort descendants of Gaunt, as we have seen, were barred from the succession, although it was widely felt that this had no basis in law. In any case the House of York had by far the best claim to the throne. On the face of it Henry Tudor's prospects of wearing a crown seemed quite remote.

Richard III was not to begin with troubled by Henry Tudor's pretensions. He was still on progress, and had travelled from Coventry, via Leicester, Nottingham and Doncaster, to Pontefract Castle, which he reached on 27th August. Here he was greeted by his small son Edward, who had been created Prince of Wales the day before and had just travelled over by chariot from Middleham. It was probably at Pontefract that Richard issued orders for the appointment of commissioners to deal with those arrested in connection with the conspiracies to restore Edward V.

Crowds were out in force to see the King and Queen make their ceremonial entry into York on 30th August. This was not entirely spontaneous because a week beforehand the King's secretary, John Kendal, had sent, on Richard's command, a letter to the City fathers commanding them 'to receive his Highness and the Queen as laudably as your wisdom can imagine'. They should be 'worshipfully received with pageants' and other celebrations – guaranteed crowd-pullers. 'Many southern lords and men of worship are with them and will greatly remark you receiving their Graces.' The civic authorities had risen magnificently to the occasion, determined to impress the southerners, and Kendal's assurance that the King intended to have 'his lords and judges in every place sitting, determining the complaints of poor folks with due punishment of offenders [against] his laws' brought many hopeful people to the streets to see the King welcomed by the Mayor and aldermen outside the Micklegate Bar and entertained inside the city walls with three spectacular pageants. If Richard was popular anywhere it was in York, and there were cheers for him that day.

Shortly afterwards Thomas Langton, who had the King to thank for his promotion to the See of St David's and would soon receive an even richer see, that of Salisbury, when Lionel Wydville fled into exile, wrote of Richard:

He contents the people where he goes best that ever did prince, for many a poor man that hath suffered wrong many days have been relieved and helped by him and his commands in his progress. And in many great cities and towns were great sums of money given him which he hath refused. On my truth, I liked never the conditions of any prince so well as his; God hath sent him to us for the weal of us all.

For all the sycophancy implicit in this letter, it is clear that Richard was doing his best to win the support and approval of his subjects by demonstrating his resolve to restore law and order and firm government to the benefit of even the poorest members of society. A cynic might say that this was an overt bid for popularity that was ultimately for Richard's benefit, but it was also a placatory and conciliatory measure meant to restore the public's confidence in him.

Yet at the same time the King had other, darker deeds on his mind. More states that on or before 15th August, 1483, Richard III despatched Tyrell from Warwick 'to Brackenbury'. Vergil, however, implies that Tyrell was actually sent from York, and the Wardrobe Accounts corroborate this with evidence that Sir James left York for London on 30th–31st August 1483 with orders to collect robes and wall-hangings for use at the investiture of the Prince of Wales, due to be held in York on 8th September. These accounts also show that Tyrell obtained cloth for himself and the King's henchmen at this time. This provided perfect cover for Tyrell's more important business in London.

Back in June, Richard Ratcliffe, on urgent business, had ridden from London to York in four days. Tyrell, who needed to be back by 8th September for the investiture, probably took the same length of time, arriving in London around 3rd September. More portrays Tyrell as keen to carry out his sovereign's orders, but Vergil says he felt he had been 'forced to do the King's commandment' and 'rode sorrowfully to London, very unwillingly'. Maybe Tyrell, desperate for promotion, was now wishing it could be achieved through any task other than this. It is perhaps significant that he would not be in the room when the murder was carried out.

With Tyrell rode a man whom More describes as Sir James' 'own horsekeeper, a big, broad, square, strong knave' called John Dighton. As a groom he may well have known John Green, who helped look after the royal horses. All we know of his background is that he may have been the John Dighton who was bailiff of the manor of Ayton in North Yorkshire, which was owned by the Earl of Northumberland, Richard's ally.

More states that Tyrell carried a letter from the King to Brackenbury, 'by which he was commanded to deliver Sir James all the keys of the Tower for one night, to the end he might there accomplish the King's pleasure'. It is probable that Richard's mandate was worded in such a way as to absolve Brackenbury from all responsibility in the matter. Giving up the keys of the Tower to Tyrell did not in itself constitute mortal sin: Brackenbury may have accepted that it was necessary for the Princes to be eliminated, though he did not want to be the man to do it, or he may have believed the knight had come to take the Princes away, either abroad or into hiding in England, to foil any future conspiracies. On the other hand the mandate might equally well have contained a warning to Brackenbury not to oppose his sovereign's wishes. Brackenbury had now had leisure to ponder his earlier refusal, knowing whence he had derived his good fortune, and his loyalty to Richard III was never thereafter in doubt. The fact that he had had to be so delicately cozened in the matter is proof that no-one without a warrant from the King would have been able to gain access to the Princes.

Croyland states authoritatively that the Princes remained in the Tower while the coronation, the royal progress and the investiture of Prince Edward on 8th September were taking place. After that he does not say what happened to them, and his silence is most eloquent, for a man in his position must have known or guessed something about their fate. In fact the Princes must have been murdered before 8th September, for Tyrell would have had to leave London on 4th September at the latest to get the Wardrobe materials back to York in time for the investiture. If he left York on 30th August and the journey took four days, the likeliest date he was in London was 3rd September, and that was the night on which the murders almost certainly took place.

More's account of the killing of the Princes is unique: no other writer offers as much detail, and it is its very detail that argues its authenticity. It is true that More asserted that the killings took place on 15th August, but this could have been due to the faulty memories of those who gave him his information: while people remember events with clarity, they often have trouble recalling dates accurately.

More says that after the King's letter had been handed by Tyrell to Brackenbury at the Tower 'and the keys received, Sir James appointed the night next ensuing [i.e. that night] to destroy [the Princes], devising before and preparing the means'. The plan was 'that they should be murdered in their beds. To the execution whereof he appointed Miles Forrest [and] John Dighton.' Next, he removed the Princes' three other attendants, including William Slaughter, of whom no more is recorded. It may be that these men were dismissed on the pretext that the Princes were being removed elsewhere. Slaughter, in any case, may have become too attached to his charges: it is significant that of the four attendants only Forrest was chosen to assist in the murder, and it may have been he who warned Tyrell that Slaughter was not to be trusted.

At midnight that night, 'the silly [i.e. innocent] children lying in their beds', Tyrell positioned himself outside their bedchamber, while Forrest and Dighton 'came into the chamber and suddenly lapped them up among the clothes, so bewrapped them and entangled them, keeping down by force the feather bed and pillows hard into their mouths, that within a while smothered and stifled; their breath failing, they gave up to God their innocent souls into the joys of Heaven, leaving to the tormentors their bodies dead in the bed. Which after that the wretches perceived, first by the struggling with the pains of death, and after long lying still, to be thoroughly dead, they laid their bodies naked out upon the bed' – an authentic detail, for most people slept naked – 'and fetched Sir James to see them. This traitorous death,' concluded More, 'delivered them of their wretchedness.'

Vergil records none of these details: despite his intensive research he had to admit that, although he knew that Tyrell 'murdered those babes, with what kind of death these children were executed is not certainly known'. Of course, he had not had access to More's sources. He did, however, point out that Tyrell could, that night, 'without danger to his life, have spared the boys, rescued them from death, and carried them to safety, for without doubt all the people would have risen in arms to save them'. But Tyrell had done no such thing. He wanted preferment without further risk to himself.

John Rous states it was 'afterwards known to very few by what manner of death [the princes] had suffered', and other writers gave different versions of the murders which doubtless derived from rumour. André says the Princes were put to the sword, while *The Song of the Lady Bessy* alleges they were drowned in wine, echoing a rumour recorded in the *Great Chronicle of London* for the year 1484, when people were surmising that the boys suffered the same fate as their uncle Clarence. Molinet says they were walled up in a chamber in the Tower and left to starve to death. Finally John Rastell, More's brother-in-law, writing in *The Pastime of People*, published in 1529, gives two versions of the Princes' fate; firstly he says that a grave was dug and the children, in response to a cry of 'Treason!', were coerced into a large chest, in which they were buried alive. Here Rastell appears to be reporting a rumour which may have been circulating for more than forty years, while his second version of what might have happened is drawn in part from More's *Richard III*, with added detail – again, probably derived from popular rumours – for dramatic effect:

> But of the manner of the death of this young king and his brother there were divers opinions; but the most common opinion was that they were smothered between two feather beds, and that in doing the young brother escaped from under the feather beds and crept under the bedstead, and there lay naked awhile till that they had smothered the young King so that he was surely dead. And after that one of them took his brother from under the bedstead and held his face down to the ground with his one hand, and with the other hand cut his throat-bole with a dagger.

After the murder, More says, Tyrell, 'upon the sight of [the bodies], caused those murderers to bury them at the stair foot, meetly deep under the ground, under a great heap of stones'. Dighton, a strong, brawny man, would have been capable of this heavy work and we may assume that Forrest was similarly strong and tough. Forensic evidence which will be discussed in depth later on confirms More's account of the Princes' burial. Rastell, however, says their bodies were put in a chest and loaded on to a ship bound for Flanders. When the ship reached the Black Deeps at the mouth of the Thames the chest was thrown into the sea. Rastell thought this story must have been true because 'the bones of the said children could never be found buried, neither in the Tower nor in none other place'.

With the Princes murdered and buried in the space of one night, Tyrell relinquished the Tower keys to Brackenbury and rode to York where he saw the King, 'who gave him thanks and, some say, made him a knight'. In fact, Tyrell had been knighted in 1471. What Richard did by way of reward was to ensure Tyrell's rise to prominence by appointing him to a succession of lucrative offices over the next two years, thus guaranteeing that he would enjoy the status at court he had so avidly sought. Tyrell also amassed considerable wealth, so that his annual income rapidly became equal to that of some barons. In 1483 he became Master of the King's Horse and between November 1483 and April 1484 was given prominent posts formerly occupied by convicted traitors, whose estates he was commissioned to administer. He received a number of stewardships and was made Sheriff of Wenlock in 1484 and Chamberlain of the Exchequer. In 1485 he was sent on a secret mission concerning 'the King's weal' to Flanders, and then appointed Captain of Guisnes Castle, which guarded the Pale of Calais, the last English possession remaining in France.

As for those others who assisted Tyrell with the murder of the Princes, Forrest and Green both received grants from the King late in 1483, and Green was appointed to several offices: Receiver of the Isle of Wight and overseer of the Port of Southampton on 14th December 1483, and Escheator of Southampton in December 1484. On 20th September 1483 he was granted a general pardon for all offences by the King, and in order to avoid questions being asked about his activities, his neighbours in Warwickshire were all granted one too. Such pardons were not unusual during the aftermath of conspiracies. Forrest was rewarded with a post at Baynard's Castle, but did not fare so well. It seems he was overcome by the enormity of what he had done for, says More, he sought sanctuary at St Martin le Grand in London, where he 'piecemeal rotted away' and died before September 1484, when the King granted his widow a pension of five marks, which was quite usual in such cases. As for Dighton, he was given a pension but seems to have taken to a life of crime, of which we shall hear more in due course. Slaughter, perhaps tellingly, received no reward.

Brackenbury was rewarded by the King for his co-operation, being given several grants and appointments later that year, some of which were lucrative offices once occupied by Hastings. The Constable was also granted some of the forfeited estates of Lord Rivers and others.

More, and other later writers, all claimed that the Princes' bodies were afterwards dug up and reburied. There is no evidence to support the allegations made by Rastell, Hall, Grafton and Hardying that they were reburied at sea in the Black Deeps. Grafton and Hall say that King Richard ordered one man, a priest, to disinter the chest from its burial place under several feet of rubble, remove the corpses and place them in a lead coffin punctured with many holes, and cast them into the sea. The priest is supposed to have died soon afterwards 'and disclosed it never to any person that would utter it'. But then how did the chroniclers know of it? In any case it is hardly likely that a solitary priest could have successfully undertaken such a task.

More, whose sources were much sounder, states that Richard III, after learning how the Princes' bodies had been disposed of, 'allowed not, as I have heard, the burying in so vile a corner, saying he would have them buried in a better place, because they were a king's sons. Lo! The honourable heart of a king, for he would recompense a detestable murder with a solemn obloquy! Whereupon, they say that a priest of Sir Robert Brackenbury took up the bodies again and secretly interred them in such place as, by the occasion of his death, which only knew it, could never since have come to life.'

Once again, we have a tale of a solitary priest disinterring bodies that had been buried deep under rubble by two brawny men, though of course he may have had help from Brackenbury, who employed him. It is characteristic of Richard III that he should contemplate the reburial of his nephews. As a youth he had witnessed the reinterment at Fotheringhay of his father and brother Edmund, and in 1484 he himself ordered the reburial of Henry VI, whose bones were moved from Chertsey to Windsor. It was therefore plausible that he had ordered the reburial of the Princes, but it is unlikely in view of the forensic evidence discovered two centuries later in the Tower.

What is possible is that one of More's sources deliberately gave him the wrong information in order to avoid a search being made for the bodies and the uncovering of incriminating evidence. Or More may have simply reported what people had supposed had taken place, in view of the fact that no bodies had been found up to that time, despite several searches. It may even be that Richard III ordered a priest to perform obsequies over the grave, and that More and others assumed, in view of the mystery surrounding the bodies' whereabouts, that he had also ordered the Princes' reburial.

From Richard III's point of view, if it was necessary that the Princes should die, it was also necessary that people should know they were dead, in order to put an end to speculation and confound those who might plot to restore Edward V. According to Vergil, 'King Richard kept the slaughter not long secret, who within few days after permitted the rumour of their deaths to go abroad to the intent that, after the people understood no male issue of King Edward to be now left alive, they might with better mind and goodwill bear to sustain his government.' It is unlikely that these rumours spoke of the Princes being murdered – just that they had died. As it was widely accepted by the beginning of October that they lived no more, and the rumours would have had to be in circulation for at least a fortnight to be this effective, it is quite likely that it was indeed Richard himself who instigated them. When, on 8th September, he walked hand in hand with his son and his wife into York Minster for young Edward's investiture as Prince of Wales, the King did so in the belief that he had removed the last dynastic threat to his throne and put an end once and for all to the conspiracies that had overshadowed his reign.

14
The Wicked Uncle

It has been stated many times, in many books, that there is no proof that Richard III murdered the Princes in the Tower, and very little likelihood that the full facts about their disappearance from the pages of history will ever be known. That it is impossible, 500 years after the event, to prove beyond reasonable doubt who murdered them or, indeed, that they were murdered at all.

But is it? Most of the facts of the matter are recorded in the surviving contemporary sources, and beyond this there is a vast amount of compelling circumstantial evidence that substantiates the known facts and leaves no room for any alternative theories.

It has often been said that the evidence available to us would not be sufficient to secure the King's conviction in a modern court of law, and this claim appeared to have been vindicated by the 'Not Guilty' verdict that resulted from Channel 4 Television's 'The Trial of Richard III' in 1984. However, the fact is that some of the most pertinent evidence was not offered at that 'trial'. Historians, moreover, are not, and should not, be bound by the same rules as juries. The historian will be more familiar with the bias of contemporary material and is able to take far more evidence into account than would be allowed a jury. A jury must be satisfied beyond reasonable doubt that a person is guilty of a crime; a historian constructs his theory on a balance of probabilities. In this case there are facts and the testimony of witnesses as well as probabilities, and the historian is perhaps therefore in a better position than a modern jury to arrive at the truth.

So what is the case against Richard III? The most damning evidence is the simple fact that the Princes disappeared for good whilst they were being securely held in the Tower under the King's protection, as prisoners, and that Richard gave no explanation of what had happened to them nor made any reference to their continuing existence after this time. Nor did he produce them alive to counteract rumours deeply damaging to his reputation as king, or, later, to confound once and for all the treasonous designs of a Lancastrian pretender. Not to have produced the Princes when it was to his distinct advantage to do so is strong evidence that he was guilty of having had them assassinated.

It is highly unlikely that any third party could have gained access to the Tower to carry out the murder without the King's knowledge. We have already seen how securely the Princes were confined and how loyal to Richard was Constable Brackenbury, who had charge of them. Even had these stringent security precautions been breached and another person succeeded in killing the boys, Richard III would have found out about it almost at once, and it would have been in his interests to name and prosecute the culprit, since the children, although declared bastards, were still his nephews and the sons of a king; people had an interest in them. But Richard did no such thing. The fact remains that he himself was the only person with the authority and obvious opportunity to dispose of the Princes. He also had several powerful and compelling motives for wanting them out of the way.

He was insecure on his throne. He was not popular, and the basis of his title to that throne was precarious, since few believed in the precontract story. His future security depended largely on him retaining the loyalties of his magnates, and there were many of them who resented him because of his northern affiliations. While Edward V lived he remained a focus for rebellion; Richard had seen alarming proof of that in the recent conspiracies on Edward's behalf. He had also seen enough treachery during the Wars of the Roses to convince him that self-seeking, power-hungry nobles would readily espouse the cause of a would-be king if there was hope of rewards for themselves, and he was well aware that any legislation bastardising the Princes could always be reversed by Parliament in the event of a successful coup on their behalf. Then would follow the triumphant return to power of the Wydvilles, who would not hesitate to destroy the man who had executed Rivers, Grey, Haute and Vaughan, insulted the Queen, and deposed and disinherited her children. The revisionists have often argued that, once the Princes had been declared illegitimate, they posed no further threat to Richard, and that he had no motive for killing them. This argument does not take account of the realities of fifteenth-century politics, the fact that Richard himself viewed the Princes as a danger (otherwise he would never have kept them in such strict confinement), and the fact that there had already been several plots to restore Edward V. It was these, undoubtedly, that spurred the King to the realisation that the former King and his brother must be removed beyond the reach of any conspirators as soon as possible.

There were several historical precedents for the murder of a deposed monarch or of persons whose existence threatened the security of a reigning king. Every deposed monarch so far – Edward II, Richard II and Henry VI – had been assassinated on the orders of the men who had overthrown and succeeded them. Arthur of Brittany, Thomas of Woodstock, Humphrey of Gloucester and George of Clarence had all posed a threat to the crown at one time or another, and had all been eliminated. Richard III himself had early on learned a lesson in ruthless pragmatism from the deaths of Henry VI and Clarence, and he had excellent reasons for following precedent.

The House of York had a history of employing violence for political ends. Richard's previous acts of tyranny, such as the executions of Hastings and Rivers, prove that he was a ruthless man who did not shirk from using violence as a means to an end. He was no respecter of the law and was undoubtedly capable of cold-blooded murder. Nothing we know of his early-life experiences and character is at variance with this conclusion. Given that the victims in this case were two children aged twelve and ten, his own nephews, we may assume he felt he had no alternative but to get rid of them; he may even have been reluctant to take such a step, but his reasons for doing so were sufficiently compelling for him to risk both his popularity and his future security as king, should the truth ever come to light.

Thus the murder had to be carried out in the strictest secrecy. The King took only a select few, who were unlikely to talk, into his confidence. Afterwards he adopted a policy of 'least said, soonest mended'. Even high-ranking courtiers did not know what had happened. But the disappearance of two royal children, one a former sovereign, raised questions in many people's minds, questions that many must have been too scared to voice. It was only later, when the threat of reprisals had been removed, that people began to ask those questions openly, or to speak of what they knew.

After the murder, Richard III may have remained officially silent on the subject of the Princes, but his behaviour is indicative of a man with a guilty conscience. His personal prayer in his *Book of Hours*, dedicated to St Julian who murdered his parents and then obtained God's forgiveness, perhaps held a special significance for Richard. He also planned to found a chantry at York served by no less than 100 priests who would offer masses for the salvation of his soul; enlisting the prayers of so many priests, unprecedented in England, is a strong indication that Richard felt he had some serious sins to expiate.

Sir Thomas More says he 'heard by credible report by such as were secret with [Richard's] chamberers' that the King 'never had quiet in his mind; he never thought himself sure. He took ill rest at night, lay long waking and musing, sore wearied with care and watch, rather slumbered than slept, troubled with fearful dreams. His restless heart continually tossed and tumbled with the stormy remembrance of his abominable deed.' Croyland also refers to Richard having bad dreams on the night before the Battle of Bosworth in 1485, while Vergil states that the King's conscience began to trouble him after the death of the Princes.

This evidence is, of course, all circumstantial, but even without the further evidence in contemporary sources it is the basis of a formidable case against Richard III. There is plenty of evidence that Richard's contemporaries believed him guilty of murdering the Princes, and that the 'Black Legend', alleged by the revisionists to have originated with later Tudor chroniclers, was already established in Richard's own lifetime. It was only elaborated upon after his death because men felt able to speak more freely about him. Evidence for this is to be found in nearly every source.

Mancini, writing in December 1483, refers to 'the Duke of Gloucester, who shortly after suppressed Edward's children'. The verb used is '*oppressis*', which has sometimes been incorrectly translated as 'destroyed', but it is likely that Mancini was implying the same thing because rumours that Richard had murdered his nephews had reached France by the time Mancini was writing. Even before the coronation, he records, men had feared the worst. Mancini would not have been surprised to learn that it was widely believed to have happened.

Croyland, astonishingly, is silent on the fate of the Princes, and yet he, of all people, must have had some knowledge or suspicion of the truth. Quoting 'a certain poet' on the three King Richards of England, he refers to 'the third, [who] after exhausting the ample store of Edward's wealth, was not content until he suppressed his brother's progeny'. Again, this ambiguous word 'suppressed', which could refer either to disinheritance or to murder, or even imprisonment. Croyland wrote his chronicle after Richard's death and therefore his reticence on the subject argues either that, not being favoured with the King's confidence, he really did not know what had happened to the Princes and considered it frivolous to speculate, or he wished to cover up his own complacency in the matter, or even that he felt he ought to be discreet until Henry VII's policy on the subject became clear, or until new and conclusive evidence came to light.

Two contemporary manuscript fragments, one in the Ashmolean Museum, Oxford, and one in the College of Arms, London, accuse Richard III of the murder of his nephews, and on 1st March, 1486, a Spanish envoy, Diego de Valera, who obtained much of his information from 'trusty merchants who were in England at the time of the battle' (of Bosworth, in August, 1485), observed in a letter to King Ferdinand and Queen Isabella of Spain:

It is sufficiently well known to your Royal Majesties that this Richard killed two innocent nephews of his, to whom the realm belonged after his brother's life. It is alleged that he had them murdered with poison.

Dafydd Llywd ap Llywelyn ap Gruffydd, a Welsh bard of Marthar-fan, wrote in c.1485–6 an 'Ode to King Richard, who destroyed his two nephews', calling him 'a servile boar [who] without penance' murdered 'Edward's sons in his prison. He slew without favour of the Bench his two young nephews. He caused disgrace, the bravery of cruel Herod.'

More contemporary evidence is to be found in some Flemish wall paintings in Eton College Chapel. They were begun before 1479–80 and were complete before the end of 1487, but were covered up in the Reformation and only rediscovered in 1847. They portray, in allegorical guise, the usurpation of Richard III, who is represented as the evil brother of an emperor. This villain is shown wearing a collar with the Yorkist emblem of the Sun in Splendour and a crescent similar to a crescent pendant found near Middleham Castle and linked to Richard III and Anne Neville by the engraved initials 'R' and 'A'. The paintings show that the emperor entrusted his family to his brother, who betrayed that trust and murdered his nephew, then accused the empress of the deed. She is shown retiring to a convent, as did Elizabeth Wydville in 1487. The parallels with Richard III are obvious, as they were intended to be. This work could not have been merely Tudor propaganda. It was in a public place within a royal foundation, and what it portrayed had to be entirely credible to onlookers.

We come now to what the Tudor chroniclers had to say about the fate of the Princes. John de Giglis, papal collector in England, and Pietro Carmeliano, both writing in 1486 under the patronage of Henry VII, predictably portray Richard III as a tyrant who murdered his nephews. And Rous, writing in 1490, states firmly that Richard 'killed Edward V, together with his brother'. William Parron, court astrologer to Henry VII, makes the same accusation in his work *De Astrorum vi fatale*, written in 1499. Bernard André, a few years later, says that Richard III ordered the Princes to be put to death secretly. Not surprisingly, *The Song of the Lady Bessy* alleges much the same thing.

These works were naturally biased in favour of the régime that had replaced Richard, yet they were circulated amongst men who had known him well and would instantly recognise any jarring inconsistencies. They also refer to the murder of the Princes in such a way as to imply that they are not informing their readers of some sensational piece of news but stating a well-known fact.

One striking piece of evidence comes from Philippe de Commines, who in his memoirs states that the 'wicked' and 'cruel' King Richard 'arranged the death of his two nephews'. He then tells us that Louis XI of France, a crafty and unscrupulous monarch known as the 'Universal Spider' because of his intrigues, believed that Richard III was responsible for having 'the two sons of his brother King Edward put to death', and would have nothing to do with him because, he said, he was 'extremely cruel and evil'. Louis XI died of the effects of a stroke on 30th August, 1483. For a week beforehand he had been unable to speak. Yet at the beginning of July he had written a most courteous letter to

Richard III, congratulating him on his accession and offering to do him any service, 'for I desire to have your friendship'. Within six weeks Louis' attitude had changed dramatically, and it is likely that his spies in England had heard the same kind of speculative rumours that Mancini had heard in early July. It is worth noting that every contemporary European chronicler believed in Richard's guilt.

In the early 1500s, in England, Robert Fabyan wrote, 'It was common fame that King Richard had within the Tower put unto secret death the two sons of his brother Edward IV.' The *London Chronicles* all make similar accusations and some date the event to 1483.

All of this evidence is circumstantial, but it reflects the weight of public opinion at the time. For the best evidence, that of actual witnesses, we must turn to Sir Thomas More's biography of Richard III, spurned by most revisionists and some serious historians but now, in the light of recent discoveries and study, beginning to be respected once more as a key source for the death of the Princes, and with good reason. More's book contains the earliest account of the murder. He supplies numerous details that are nowhere else recorded, saying: 'I shall rehearse you the dolorous end of these babes, not after every way that I have heard, but after that way that I have heard by such men and such means as me thinketh it were hard but it should be true.' He tells us he got his information from 'them that knew much and had little cause to lie'.

It seems highly likely that More's account came very near to the truth. He himself believed it to be true, and he had plenty of means of searching out and verifying the facts, having been moved to do so by the realisation that the deaths of the Princes had 'so far come into question that some remain yet in doubt whether they were in Richard III's time destroyed or no'.

We should now pause to consider why the account of the murder given by Sir Thomas More, on which the reconstruction of the events in the previous chapter is based, should be accepted as an authentic record of the facts. More himself claims to have relied greatly upon the confession said to have been made in 1502 by Sir James Tyrell, the man allegedly chosen by Richard III to arrange the murders. This confession was never published but there are good grounds for believing it to be genuine, which will be discussed in Chapter Twenty. More, however, almost certainly used other, equally important sources. One was John

Dighton, an associate of Tyrell's and, according to Francis Bacon, 'the principle means of divulging the tradition'. More knew of Dighton's whereabouts at the time he was writing because he states he was still alive and 'in good possibility to be hanged', and we may therefore suppose that he had contacted him and obtained information from him. But More had other, perhaps better, links with those who were in a position to know about the Princes' fate.

At New Year 1505, More dedicated his first book, his *Life of John Picus*, to his 'right entirely beloved sister in Christ', Joyeuce Lee or Leigh, a Poor Clare nun and the sister of his friend Edward Lee. More had been friendly with the Lee family, prosperous London grocers, for some years, and often visited Joyeuce after she became a nun at the Minoresses' convent in Aldgate, which stood outside the City wall and opposite the Tower of London. Here she lived in 'the great house within the close' with a group of well-born ladies who, for reasons of their own, had chosen to retire behind convent walls. Between them, these ladies could have imparted a great deal of information about the Princes in the Tower.

One was Elizabeth, daughter of Sir Robert Brackenbury, Constable of the Tower at the time of the Princes' disappearance. Sir Robert had been killed at the Battle of Bosworth in 1485, and in 1504–5 Elizabeth was living in penury at the Minories. With her lodged Mary Tyrell, a sister or cousin of Sir James Tyrell, and Mary's aunt, Anne Montgomery, whose husband Thomas had been an executor of Edward IV's will and an adherent of Richard III. Finally there was Elizabeth Mowbray (née Talbot), Dowager Duchess of Norfolk, a relative of Eleanor Butler, and mother-in-law of Richard, Duke of York, the younger of the Princes; she had retired to this house at the beginning of Henry VII's reign and later invited the other ladies to join her. She, above all, would have had a keen curiosity about the fate of her son-in-law. It is inconceivable that the Princes' disappearance would not have been discussed by this group of ladies, who all had good reason to know something about it, and even more inconceivable that More, on his visits, did not obtain information from them. Indeed, the possession of such unique information may have been what inspired him to write his book and so put an end to the rumours then in circulation.

Sir Thomas did more than any other writer, except Shakespeare, to publicise the 'Black Legend' of Richard III. Erasmus tells us that More particularly loathed tyranny, and it may be that he wrote his biography primarily as a moral tale to illustrate the nature and consequences of tyranny. Certainly he himself believed Richard to be guilty of many crimes, though he did try to be fair to him, praising his courage and his qualities as a military leader. And while his descriptions of Richard's deformities are exaggerated, they were drawn from earlier sources and used by More, in the fashion of his time, as outward manifestations of villainy to underline the moral thrust of his work.

As has been demonstrated to striking effect, More's account fits in almost perfectly with the known facts of the Princes' disappearance and the events of late summer 1483. Croyland informs us that the sons of Edward IV remained in the Tower under guard while events such as the coronation, the progress and Edward of Middleham's investiture as Prince of Wales on 8th September were taking place. He does not refer to them being alive after this date, which is probably significant. Croyland speaks with the authority of one who knows what is going on; as an historian he was a man of caution, and therefore it is likely that his information is trustworthy.

John Rous, however, implies that the Princes were already dead by the time of Richard's usurpation, saying 'he ascended the throne of the slaughtered children, whose protector he was himself'. Elsewhere, he says of Richard that, as Duke of Gloucester, he 'received his lord, Edward V, with embraces and kisses, yet within about three months he killed him, together with his brother'. This would place the murder before the end of July, and neither date ties in with the evidence of Croyland, More and Vergil. Nor, by the same token can we trust the evidence of Molinet, who states that the Princes were murdered five weeks after they entered the Tower. As York joined his brother there on 16th June, this would argue a date in late July, which is not borne out by the other evidence.

We do not know when Richard III first conceived the idea of murdering his nephews. There is no evidence that his decision to do so was made before Edward V's accession. The idea was probably born after Richard realised that his power might not last beyond the coronation, which was in May 1483. He had probably made up his mind by the time he was plotting against Hastings, for it is known that he had already decided to move York from sanctuary to the

Tower. The transfer of both princes to high-security quarters, and the removal of their servants, were arguably the first premeditated steps towards actually carrying out the deed, an event that must have, of necessity, to await a propitious moment. This would preferably be when the furore over Richard's accession had died a natural death and he himself was away on progress.

What probably spurred Richard III into actually committing the murder was news of the conspiracies to restore Edward V, proof enough that the deposed king posed the deadliest of all the threats to Richard's security. Fortunately for Richard, that former king, a helpless child, was in his power.

It has often been suggested that either Buckingham or Norfolk were somehow involved in the murder of the Princes. The case against Buckingham will be examined in the next chapter, where it will be shown to be unsubstantiated. Norfolk, meanwhile, stood to lose his dukedom if ever Edward V was restored to power, but there is, however, no evidence to support the theory that Norfolk was Richard's accomplice.

Nor is there any evidence to substantiate the claim, made by Sir George Buck and based on information in 'an old manuscript book which I have seen', that 'Dr Morton and a certain Countess, contriving the death of Edward V and others, resolved it by poison'. This countess was presumably Morton's friend and confidante, Margaret Beaufort, Countess of Richmond, but she would not have been able to gain access to the Tower. Morton himself was a prisoner of the Duke of Buckingham at Brecknock Castle at the relevant time. Apart from the practical difficulties involved, there is no contemporary evidence of any such plot.

Some revisionists, among them Mr Jack Leslau and the late Audrey Williamson, have claimed that the Princes were not murdered in the Tower in 1483 but were secretly moved by the King to a safe haven in the country in order to confound future conspirators. Rumours that they were still alive were current for years after their disappearance, and Vergil records a popular theory that they had been spirited abroad. Such theories are easily understood, given that the alternative was too dreadful to contemplate: even in that violent age, child murder attracted the deepest revulsion, and still, today, we look for evidence that would reassure us it never took place. Alas, there is none. When the

Princes were alive people knew of their existence and referred to it. After the late summer of 1483 – silence. Had they survived they would have left traces. There are none anywhere.

Some revisionists, notably Sir Clements Markham and Jeremy Potter, have asserted that, when Richard III established a household at Sheriff Hutton Castle, Yorkshire, in 1484 for his nephew John de la Pole, Earl of Lincoln and newly-appointed President of the Council of the North, the Princes were still alive and were secretly moved there. This assertion rests on the evidence of two warrants in Harleian MS. 433 in the British Library. One, dated 23rd July, 1484, refers to Lincoln and Lord Morley being at breakfast with each other and 'the children together' at another breakfast. The second, dated 9th March, 1485, is a warrant to Henry Davy to deliver two doublets of silk, one jacket of silk, one gown, two shirts and two bonnets to 'the Lord Bastard', a title used for the deposed Edward V in the *Wardrobe Accounts*. Elsewhere in official documents the former King is called 'Edward Bastard'.

There were royal children at Sheriff Hutton: the King had sent young Warwick there and probably his sister Margaret also. It is possible that the four younger daughters of Edward IV were at some time in residence too, as well as the King's bastard son, John of Gloucester – to whom the second warrant most probably refers. John was not a lord in the official sense, but as the King's natural son he was styled as such out of courtesy. There is nothing to suggest that the Princes were ever at Sheriff Hutton. If they had been, many people would have known about it.

An intriguing theory about the Princes' survival has been put forward by Mr Jack Leslau, an amateur historian from London. He contends that the Princes were given new identities in 1485 after a secret agreement between Henry VII and Elizabeth Wydville, Henry agreeing to spare them and marry their sister in return for Elizabeth's consent to their 'disappearance'. Mr Leslau contends that Edward V is to be identified with Sir Edward Guildford, son of Sir Richard Guildford, Comptroller of the Royal Household and, later, Marshal of Calais; Sir Edward's only child Jane became the wife of John Dudley, Duke of Northumberland and Lord Protector of England during the minority of Edward VI. Sir Richard Guildford was a prominent courtier, whose father had been comptroller of Edward IV's household. His first wife was Anne, daughter and heiress of John Pimpe of Kent, and by her he had two sons and four daughters, of whom Edward was not the eldest. Sir Richard married secondly, in the reign of Henry VII, Joan, sister of Sir Nicholas Vaux, who bore him another son Henry between 1478 and 1489. The sheer practical difficulties of Mr Leslau's theory defy belief: Sir Richard was well-known at court. How he managed to explain the sudden acquisition in 1485–6 of a teenaged 'son' to his friends and acquaintances is baffling. More to the point, in 1485–6 there would have been many in Guildford's circle who would have recognised Edward V. He could not have 'disappeared' by this route.

Mr Leslau has also claimed to have identified Richard, Duke of York, in one Dr John Clement, who was a notable scholar and protégé of Sir Thomas More. He became President of the Royal College of Physicians and died in 1571. Clement probably came from a Yorkshire family and, according to Nicholas Harpsfield, More's mid sixteenth-century biographer, was 'brought up in Sir Thomas's house. The said Clement was taken by More from Paul's School in London and hath since proved a very excellent, good physician, and is singularly seen [i.e. proficient] in the Greek tongue.' Harpsfield tells how More wrote of him, 'being yet a child', to Erasmus, the great Dutch humanist, saying: 'My wife greets you, and also Clement, who makes such daily progress in Latin and Greek that I entertain no small hope that he will be an ornament to his country and to letters.' Harpsfield also refers to 'this young Clement'. More himself calls Clement 'my pupil servant', and a woodcut by Ambrosius Holbein, dated 1518, shows Clement as a youth coming to serve More and two of his friends with wine. In 1526 Clement married Margaret Gigs, More's foster daughter, who was born around 1508. Clement had been her tutor before their marriage, and she too became a noted Greek scholar and evinced a keen interest in medicine.

However, Mr Leslau claims that John Clement was actually Richard, Duke of York, who was older than More by some four or five years. Thus, although Clement was still a schoolboy when More took him into his household, we are asked to believe that More wrote as he did to Erasmus of a man over forty. All the evidence offered above shows that Clement was considerably younger than his patron and was born much later than 1473. It is of course possible that he was fifty-three when he married Margaret Gigs, and ninety-eight when he died, but it is unlikely, and it is impossible to reconcile the chronology of his early life with that of York.

Mr Leslau appears to rest his case on two apparently significant pieces of evidence. The first is that there is no documentation extant for the early lives of Guildford and Clement. Mr Leslau sees this as ominous, but in fact it is unusual to find detailed evidence of the early lives of even royal persons of this period. Many children died young; in aristocratic pedigrees birthdates for eldest sons are more often than not calculated from the date of their parents' marriage (if known), because their actual birthdates are rarely recorded. That of Sir Edward Guildford, a younger son, would be very difficult to determine today with exactitude. And Clement, who was of comparatively lowly birth, would have spent his early years in virtual obscurity.

The second piece of evidence is supposedly in Rowland Lockey's painting of the family of Sir Thomas More. This group portrait, executed c.1593 and now at Nostell Priory near Wakefield, is a copy of a similar painting of 1527–8 by Hans Holbein, now lost. The Lockey painting is one of two commissioned for More's grandson, and shows Sir Thomas surrounded by his family and members of his household at Chelsea. John Clement stands in the doorway carrying a scroll, behind Lady Alice More and two of her daughters.

Mr Leslau believes it is significant that Clement's head is supposedly higher than anyone else's – though in fact, it is not – and that above him the doorway is adorned with carved *fleurs-de-lys*, emblems of the French royal house which were then quartered with the leopards of England on the English royal arms in token of the claim of the kings of England to be rulers of France by ancient right. Also above Clement is a Latin inscription: 'John, the rightful heir'.

We are fortunate that Holbein's original sketch for his painting survives; this does not portray Clement, but it does show the doorway with the *fleur-de-lys* carvings, part of the architectural design of the room and therefore hardly significant. As for Lockey's inscription, this probably refers to the fact that John Clement, a staunch Catholic and outstanding scholar, was the man most suited to be More's rightful spiritual heir.

Mr Leslau has devoted many years to developing his theory, and recently his claims have attracted considerable publicity because he is hoping to have the remains of both Guildford and Clement genetically tested to see if they are blood relations. If this proves the case, he hopes to have the same test carried out on Edward IV's remains, in the hope of establishing a link. Mr Leslau's theory is intriguing, but there is no contemporary evidence to support it and much against it.

Audrey Williamson, in her book *The Mystery of the Princes*, published in 1978, asserts that, according to a tale handed down in the Tyrell family, the Princes were taken from the Tower to Gipping in Suffolk, a manor much favoured by Sir James Tyrell. Unfortunately this theory rests mainly on conjecture and on a record of Elizabeth Wydville visiting Gipping with her eldest son, which must date to before 1483. There is no evidence that the Princes ever left the Tower alive.

Finally, there is the mysterious Richard Plantagenet of Eastwell, Kent, whom some have claimed was really Richard, Duke of York. Eastwell Church, near Ashford, which dates from the thirteenth century, is now derelict, having been badly damaged by a V2 rocket during the Second World War. A plain tomb still stands in the ruins of the church, and the parish registers record that its occupant, 'Richard Plantagenet, was buried the 22nd day of November, 1550'. Beyond this nothing more would have been known of him but for the publication in 1779 of a book called *Desiderata Curiosa* by one F. Peck, which recounts an oral tradition handed down in the family of the earls of Winchelsea, descendants of a Kentish landowner called Sir Thomas Moyle, who owned Eastwell Park in the sixteenth century. Around 1530 Moyle had the manor house rebuilt, and one day he noticed an old man, one of the bricklayers, reading a book in Latin. It was an unheard-of thing for a labouring man to be reading such a book, or even reading at all, and an intrigued Moyle quizzed the man forthwith. In the course of their talk, an astonishing tale was revealed to him.

The bricklayer said he had been born in 1469 and that his name was Richard Plantagenet. As a child, he had known nothing of his parents, having been brought up in the house of his nurse, whom he at first believed was his mother. When he was eleven he had been sent to the house of a tutor in London. The tutor looked after him well and taught him reading, writing and Latin. He did not know who paid the fees for his education, but whoever it was sent a gentleman to pay his board and bring provisions and clothing every quarter. Once he was taken to a magnificent house where a richly dressed man, wearing a 'star and garter', questioned him kindly and gave him ten gold pieces.

When he was sixteen, in 1485, he had been taken to an army camp; he later realised it was Bosworth Field. He was brought to the royal pavilion where the same man embraced him. He realised then that he had been greeted by King Richard III. The King told Richard that he was his natural son and promised to acknowledge him publicly as such. 'But, child,' he went on, 'if I should be so unfortunate as to lose the battle, take care to let nobody know that I am your father, for no mercy will be shown to anyone so nearly related.' He gave the boy a purse of gold and bade him farewell.

After the battle, Richard rode to London, sold his horse and clothes, and used his gold to apprentice himself to a bricklayer. That was how he had come to be at Eastwell Park. Moyle believed his story and kindly offered the old man accommodation in his new manor house, but Richard declined. He asked only to be able to build a one-roomed cottage on the estate, where he could live out his days in peace. Moyle agreed, and settled a pension on him. For twenty years Richard Plantagenet lived in that cottage, with his beloved books, until his death in 1550 at the age of eighty-one years. His story only came to light when the eighteenth-century Earl of Winchelsea found the entry in the parish registers and realised that the story handed down in his family might after all be true.

Although there is no contemporary evidence to substantiate this tale, some of the details are plausible, but why Richard III should have delayed acknowledging this son when he had acknowledged two other bastards is not explained. Perhaps he had no wish to compromise the honour of Richard's mother. What is implausible is the modern theory that Richard Plantagenet of Eastwell was in fact Richard, Duke of York. There is nothing whatsoever to suggest that he was anything other than Richard III's bastard, and even that cannot now be stated with any certainty. Indeed, all the evidence for the alleged survival of the Princes rests on elaborate, if well thought-out, theories that have little or no foundation in fact and cannot be substantiated by the available source material.

Of course it is possible that the Princes died natural deaths, as some have suggested. Forensic evidence which will be discussed in Chapter Twenty-One shows that Edward V may have suffered from osteomyelitis, an infection of the bone, a condition that could in those days prove fatal. It may have been this that Dr Argentine was treating him for in June 1483. Thomas More states that when Archbishop Bourchier came to remove York from the Sanctuary, Elizabeth Wydville told him that the child was 'so sore diseased with sickness that she dared not trust him to another's care'. No other source mentions this illness. It could be that the Queen had hoped to delay York's departure by claiming that he was ill. But had he really been so sick, at least one eyewitness would surely have commented on the fact.

It seems too fortuitous and too coincidental for both Princes to die conveniently so soon after Richard III's accession. But if this had been the case, there was no reason for him to hide their deaths; in fact, it would have been to his advantage to put an end to the conspiracies by producing their bodies and giving them decent burial, playing the role of grieving uncle. But Richard did no such thing.

In conclusion, then, we may say that the evidence overwhelmingly suggests the Princes were murdered by Richard III in 1483, that this was what Richard's contemporaries and later generations believed had happened, and that Sir Thomas More's account is very near to the truth. It would be comforting to present the revisionist theory as fact, but there is just not the evidence to substantiate it.

15
Rebellion

By the time the Princes were murdered, Buckingham was considering treason against his sovereign. Margaret Beaufort and Bishop Morton had been working assiduously to enlist Buckingham to her son's cause. At Morton's request the Countess appointed her steward, Reginald Bray, a cousin of Lady Hastings and a man described by Morton as 'sober, secret and well-witted', to act as her secret emissary to Brecknock, his chief objective being to overcome any scruples Buckingham may have had about breaking his oath of allegiance to the King and convince him that he should support Henry Tudor. Bray was also exerting his powers of persuasion on such lesser nobility and gentry as seemed hostile to Richard III.

Buckingham deliberated for the best part of a month before he finally decided to support a rebellion. What prompted his decision was probably confirmation from the King that the Princes were dead. The researches of Carol Rawcliffe for her unpublished thesis 'Henry, 2nd Duke of Buckingham: Political Background' (1972–3), cited by Pamela Tudor-Craig, show that Richard, unsuspecting, wrote on several occasions to Buckingham at Brecknock. It is logical to assume that he may well have sent the Duke a discreetly worded letter indicating that the deed was done. Only this would have made Buckingham so sure that the Princes were dead. More depicts the Duke saying to Morton that 'when he was credibly informed of the death of the two young innocents, O Lord, how my veins panted, how my body trembled and my heart inwardly grudged!' The chronology may be incorrect but the sentiment sounds plausible enough, being corroborated by Vergil who says that Buckingham was mortified when he learned of the murder. There is no doubt that Buckingham passed on what he knew to Morton, Margaret Beaufort, Henry Tudor and, later, the Wydvilles. No-one else was in a position to do so Moreover, the Princes' disappearance and the rumours put about by the King only served to confirm his story. But there was one thing Buckingham obviously did not know – and Richard would never have disclosed this in a letter – and that was how the Princes had died and how their bodies had been disposed of. Had Buckingham learned these details he would certainly have later on communicated them to Henry Tudor, who would have made use of the knowledge when he came to the throne. But Henry did no such thing: he was, it seems, as much in the dark about these details as Buckingham.

The Duke sent Bray to communicate his decision to join the rebels, and also the news of the murder of the Princes to Margaret Beaufort, who was just on the point of sending a courier to Brittany. The conspirators now began to plan actively, using Bray and the Countess's young confessor, Christopher Urswick, as go-betweens. Their ultimate objective was the overthrow of Richard III and the establishment of Henry Tudor on the throne of England, which would benefit all concerned, except perhaps Buckingham, who could hardly have expected to receive more from Henry than he had from Richard III, which lends weight to the argument that his disaffection from the latter was prompted by revulsion at the murder of the Princes. Buckingham may have seen himself as a latter-day kingmaker, and his later attainder states he was involved in treasonable communication with Henry and Jasper Tudor 'many times before and after' 24th September, 1483. Both the Countess and Morton could certainly hope for great things from Henry, who would be most anxious to reward those who had helped him gain a crown.

The conspirators realised that, on the death of the Princes, Elizabeth of York had become *de jure* Queen of England. It was probably Margaret Beaufort who first saw the advantages of a marriage between Elizabeth and Henry Tudor, 'the very heir of the House of Lancaster'. Such a union would resolve most of the differences and long-standing divisions between the Lancastrian and Yorkist factions, and would also validate the rather tenuous Tudor claim to the throne: as Elizabeth's husband Henry would be the rightful king. Vergil says that Margaret Beaufort, 'being a wise woman, after the slaughter of King Edward's children was known, began to hope well of her son's fortune, supposing that the deed would without doubt prove for the profit of the common weal, if it might chance the blood of Henry VI and King Edward to be mingled by affinity, and so two most pernicious factions should at once be taken away'. It appears that the plan was hers from the first and that she did all in her power to promote it. Vergil claims she plotted the marriage with Elizabeth Wydville before Buckingham lent his support to the conspiracy, but this does not accord with the chronology of events in other accounts and, moreover, the Queen could only have received confirmation of the death of the Princes through Buckingham. It is clear that neither of these plans – the rebellion, and the marriage in particular – would have been proposed or implemented had the conspirators been in any doubt that the Princes were dead. This is further evidence that they died before 24th September, the day recorded by the *Rolls of Parliament* as that on which the rebels launched their enterprise.

Urswick was despatched to Brittany to lay details of the proposed marriage before Henry Tudor, while the Countess went to London to break the news of the Princes' death to their mother. For this thankless task she used the services of a Dr Lewis, an experienced physician of grave demeanour who attended both the Countess and Elizabeth Wydville. The Countess would have looked too conspicuous visiting the Sanctuary but Dr Lewis could come and go with impunity.

Both Vergil and More have left accounts of how Elizabeth Wydville reacted to the awful news. Vergil says she 'fell into a swoon and lay lifeless a good while; after coming to herself, she wept, she cried aloud, and with lamentable shrieks made all the house ring. She struck her breast, tore and cut her hair, and prayed also for her own death, calling by name her most dear children and condemning herself for a madwoman for that, being deceived by false promises, she had delivered her younger son out of sanctuary to be murdered by his enemy.' More repeats all these details, adding that 'after long lamentations she kneeled down and cried to God to take vengeance'. Both these accounts have the ring of authenticity and convey vividly the bereft mother's agony.

Later, or perhaps on another, subsequent occasion, Dr Lewis gently broached the subject of the proposed marriage, saying that although her sons were dead she could still become the mother of kings if she agreed to the union of her daughter Elizabeth with Henry Tudor. If this went ahead, he said, 'no doubt the usurper should be shortly deposed and your heir again to her right restored'. Above all, the rival factions of York and Lancaster would be united.

Uppermost in the Queen's mind was the burning desire to take revenge on her sons' murderer, and she agreed to the marriage with alacrity, which she would not have done had she not been convinced that the Princes were dead. Henry Tudor had been her late husband's enemy, and it is hardly likely that she would have supported his claim to the throne if she had not had sufficient proof of her sons' deaths. Moreover, this marriage now made good political sense, and she could once more foresee a future in which she was restored, as mother of the Queen Regnant, to something approaching her former power and influence. She therefore sent Dr Lewis back to Margaret Beaufort to tell her that 'she would do her endeavour to procure all her husband King Edward's friends to take part with Henry, her son, so that he might be sworn to take in marriage Elizabeth, her daughter'. If he agreed to do this, and overthrew the usurper, she would recognise him as king.

Thus the Wydvilles joined Buckingham and others of their former enemies in a coalition to bring down Richard III, and plans for the rebellion, co-ordinated probably by Bishop Morton and communi-cated by Lewis, Bray and Urswick, were laid down during the next two to three weeks. Margaret Beaufort sent her chaplain Richard Fox to Brittany with the news that Elizabeth Wydville had agreed to acknowledge Henry as king if he married her daughter.

The time was indeed ripe for rebellion. In the first week or so of September, says Croyland, 'the people living in the regions of the City of London and several other southern counties embarked upon aveng-ing their grievances against Richard III'. The chief causes of their disaffection were Richard's indiscriminate 'plantation of northerners in the south' and the desire to bring about the restoration of Edward V, who was then still thought by a considerable number of people to be alive. 'When at last the people began considering vengeance, it was publicly proclaimed that Henry, Duke of Buckingham, had repented of his former conduct and would be the chief mover in this enterprise against the King.' One of the *London Chronicles* states that 'Many knights and gentlemen gathered together to the Duke of Buckingham, which intended to have subdued King Richard, as the said King Richard had put to death the Lord Chamberlain and other gentlemen, and thereupon many gentlemen intended his destruction.' The fact that several small but influential groups of conspirators were now uniting under so powerful a magnate as Buckingham posed a serious threat to the King. And the rumours of the murder of the Princes, spread initially by Richard with the intention of removing the occasion for rebellion, gave it instead a new impetus.

Later that September, says Croyland, 'a rumour was spread that the sons of King Edward had died a violent death, but it was uncertain how'. Croyland makes it clear that this was not the rumour initiated by the King, and implies that Buckingham and his accomplices were responsible for it. This rumour – disseminated over a wide area by agents working for Buckingham and Margaret Beaufort – spread fast and soon infiltrated the court itself. Within a short while it was the talk of the courts of Europe. This was what the conspirators wanted, for they meant to heap such opprobrium on Richard III that his people would be ready to rise up and join them when the time came. What was to their advantage was that there was no point in spreading a rumour that the King could so easily have disproved by producing the Princes alive; the story was entirely credible and people believed it. Within weeks of their deaths it was widely accepted that the Princes had been murdered in the Tower on the King's command. This is hardly surprising since no-one had seen the boys since early July at the latest and the life expectancy of a deposed monarch was notoriously short. Evidence of how strongly the rumours were believed is to be found in the commonplace book of Richard Arnold, a London merchant, for the year 1482–3: 'This year the sons of King Edward were put to silence.' Fabyan says it was soon 'the common fame' that King Richard had killed his nephews.

The late fifteenth century was a violent age not noted for sentimentality. It was accepted that men often died horribly in battle or on the scaffold. Yet the murder of children provoked appalled shock and indignation. The Tudor chronicler Hall spoke for the majority when he wrote:

To murder a man is much odious, to kill a woman is in a manner unnatural, but to slay and destroy innocent babes and young infants the whole world abhorreth, and the blood from the earth cries for vengeance to Almighty God. Alas, whom will he save when he slayeth the poor lambs committed to him in trust?

Vergil says that 'when the fame of this notable foul fact was dispersed through the realm, so great grief struck literally to the heart of all men that the same, subduing all fear, wept everywhere, and when they could weep no more, they cried out, "Is there truly any man who would not have abhorred so foul a murder?"' Mancini also, it will be remembered, had referred to men weeping, and that was back in July when the Princes were still alive but people had begun to fear for their safety. King Richard, it was now felt, had committed an atrocious crime, and should pay for it.

The fact that people believed so implicitly in Richard's guilt was of greater significance historically than whether or not he had actually committed the crime. It damaged irrevocably his already tarnished reputation, and it cost him the brief popularity fuelled by the progress. It also lost him much support among the Yorkist old guard who had served Edward IV, and it prompted many more people to join those who were already conspiring against him. Alive, the Princes had represented a potential threat to Richard's security; dead, they were a very real danger.

This public belief in the death of the Princes had an immediate effect. There had been some conspirators, mainly in the South, who maintained the belief that Edward V still lived in the Tower, and whose chief motive in rebelling was his restoration. But now, faced with compelling rumours which were doubtless confirmed by links with Buckingham and Margaret Beaufort, these men also switched their allegiance to Henry Tudor and co-ordinated their plans with those of the other plotters, so that the planned rebellion became one cohesive movement to overthrow Richard III and establish a Tudor dynasty; this amounted, in effect, to a fresh outbreak of the Wars of the Roses. This time, however, the House of York would be opposing that of Tudor in a conflict which – in the final analysis – was the direct result of Richard III's murder of the Princes.

Margaret Beaufort was now sending frequent messages and letters to her son in Brittany, urging him to come to Wales and join Buckingham in this righteous war against the usurper. Legally, as her attainder later stated, she was a traitor, 'imagining the destruction of the King and assisting Henry, Duke of Buckingham, in treason'. The Countess, of course, would not have viewed her activities in that light. The triumph of her son might be only weeks away, and she would not contemplate failure since she must have known that it would herald the ruin of all the conspirators.

After his successful visit to York, Richard III travelled on 20th September to Gainsborough in Lincolnshire. Queen Anne had left for Middleham with the Prince of Wales and Warwick. By 24th September the rebel plans were complete and co-ordinated uprisings were scheduled to take place, according to the Rolls of Parliament, on 18th October.

There were to be five separate uprisings. In Kent, the Hautes, close kin to the Wydvilles, were to march from The Mote near Maidstone and Ightham Mote. Exeter was to be roused by Dorset, Sir Thomas St Leger, the husband of Richard III's sister Anne, and members of the Lancastrian Courtenay family, earls of Devon. Lionel Wydville was to organise a rising in Salisbury. Buckingham would have an army standing at battle alert in Wales.

On 24th September, Buckingham, on behalf of both the Yorkist and Lancastrian factions, wrote to Henry Tudor, inviting him to invade England on 18th October, to deliver the realm from tyranny. Vergil says this invitation was conditional upon Henry swearing a solemn oath that once England was his he would marry Elizabeth of York and, says Croyland, 'together with her take possession of the throne'.

Henry Tudor had until now made no effort to promote his claim to the English crown. He owed this new and unexpected opportunity to do so entirely to the murder of the Princes and its effect on Richard III's reputation. He now found himself transformed from a penniless fugitive to king-elect in the eyes of many, and he lost no time in taking advantage of Buckingham's invitation. While the conspirators were busy enlisting support among the gentry in the south of England, Henry and his uncle Jasper Tudor persuaded Duke Francis of Brittany to loan him 10,000 crowns, enough to employ 5,000 mercenaries and fit out some ships. It appears that some of the royal treasure appropriated by the Wydvilles went to finance the venture. By 2nd October Henry Tudor was ready to invade England.

The rebels were aware, even now, that King Richard could command awesome support. He could still count upon the loyalty of great magnates such as Norfolk and Northumberland and many northern nobles and gentlemen. However, the rumours concerning the Princes were now so widespread, and so damning to him, that his position had been considerably weakened. By the beginning of October Richard must have been aware of the malicious rumours put about by his enemies and of their devastating effect upon public opinion. Croyland says he was aware that many of his subjects saw him as 'the wretched, bloody and usurping boar', the White Boar being his personal emblem.

He knew now that the Princes posed a greater threat in death than they had in life. An innocent man would have countered this threat by exhibiting the Princes alive or making a statement disclaiming all responsibility for their deaths, for which he could have offered a plausible explanation, and he would have produced their bodies for honourable public burial. But Richard kept silent and ignored the rumours. He neither denied them, nor made any statement about the fate or whereabouts of the Princes, nor accused anyone else of murdering them. His policy on the subject was complete silence, a silence he maintained to the end of his life: a silence that has condemned him in the eyes of most historians, and which probably confirmed his contemporaries' worst suspicions.

On 3rd October, 1483, Henry Tudor's fleet sailed from Brittany but a storm drove his ships back and kept them in port. From then on, nothing went as planned for the conspirators. Those in Kent rose prematurely on 10th October, their aim being to march on London. Unfortunately for the rebels, Norfolk was in the capital, and hearing of their advance he speedily raised a force and blocked the Thames crossing at Gravesend, thwarting their plans. The Duke then sent an urgent letter to the King in Lincolnshire, warning him what was afoot and breaking the news of Buckingham's treachery, which had been disclosed to him by captured rebel leaders, along with details of the planned rebellion.

Richard III entered Lincoln on 11th October and there, the next day, he received Norfolk's letter. Its contents shocked him deeply: he had not guessed that Buckingham had abandoned him, and the news came as a blow. Croyland says Richard received more information 'by means of spies', and in a very short time 'the whole design of this plot became perfectly well-known to [him], who exerted himself in no drowsy manner, but with the greatest alacrity and vigilance'. Thanks to the premature rising in Kent, Richard had time to take effective measures against the rebels. He 'contrived that, throughout Wales, armed men should be set in readiness around the Duke, as soon as ever he had set foot from his home, to pounce upon all his property'.

On 12th October Richard sent to Lord Chancellor Russell in London for the Great Seal, informing him that 'here is all well and truly determined, for to resist the malice of him that had best cause to be true, the Duke of Buckingham, the most untrue creature living. We assure you there never was false traitor better purveyed for.' Three days later Buckingham was publicly proclaimed a rebel and a traitor; on the same day violent gales swept across Wales and the West Country.

Buckingham was not yet aware that the King had learned of his treachery. On 18th October, the day on which Henry Tudor again sailed from France, the Duke raised his standard and, defying the gales, marched south towards the River Severn, planning to cross it and link up with the conspirators in the South-West, who had also risen as planned on that day. The next day the King sent proclamations to the South and West, advising the people that £1,000 would be given as a reward for the capture of Buckingham, and naming Morton, Dorset and others traitors. Meanwhile, Buckingham's neighbour, Sir Thomas Vaughan, had seized the Duke's stronghold at Brecknock for the King. Further proclamations were issued by Richard from Leicester on 23rd October: one, typically, accused Dorset of immorality and adultery with 'Shore's wife'. At around this time in Bodmin, Cornwall, it appears that a group of rebels actually proclaimed Henry Tudor king. Certainly, from this time on he adopted the royal style, signing his letters '*Henricus Rex*' or 'H.R.'. On 24th October, Richard III left Leicester with an army and marched south, hoping to intercept Buckingham's forces and prevent them from meeting up with the rebels in the South West.

The gales, however, had accomplished his task for him. Ten days of storms and torrential rain had left the countryside flooded, with houses and bridges swept away; many people had drowned. Buckingham's men, who were mostly unwilling Welsh conscripts who bore him several grudges, grew demoralised and resentful and eventually deserted him. Left alone in the Forest of Dean he took shelter with one of his tenants, Ralph Banastre, who betrayed him. The Duke, says Croyland, was 'discovered in the cottage of a poor man', and was delivered to the King's men at Salisbury on 1st November by the Sheriff of Shropshire.

By then, the rebellion had collapsed; some leaders were taken, and the rest fled, either abroad or to sanctuary. In the confusion, Morton had escaped from Brecknock, later making his way secretly to Henry Tudor in Brittany. Buckingham's five-year-old son Edward was smuggled to safety by his nurse, who shaved his head and dressed him as a girl. On 2nd November, two of Henry Tudor's ships landed at Plymouth, but when Henry learned of the collapse of the rebellion he sailed back to Brittany at once, there to meet up with Dorset, the Courtenays and a considerable number of other refugees from England, including Lionel Wydville, who died soon afterwards.

Buckingham was not so lucky. Croyland says that the King came to Salisbury with a very large army. A trial took place and Buckingham was sentenced to death. He begged an audience of the King before he died, but Richard refused to see him. Many years later the Duke's son alleged that his father had planned to stab Richard III with a hunting knife. Croyland, as a churchman, was outraged that the King gave the order for the execution to go ahead that same day, a Sunday: 'Notwithstanding the fact that it was the Lord's day, the Duke suffered capital punishment in the market place of that city.'

Vergil states that the King had several other conspirators executed, 'even of his own household', but only six are known to have perished at Tyburn as well as St Leger, Richard's brother-in-law, at Exeter. When Parliament met in 1484 it passed so many Acts of Attainder that, says Croyland, 'we do not read of the like being issued by the Triumvirate of Octavius, Antony and Lepidus. What immense estates and patrimonies were collected into the King's treasury in consequence of this measure!' A hundred people, including Henry Tudor and Buckingham retrospectively, were attainted, representing one-quarter of all attainders passed in fifty years. One-third were later pardoned by the King; their offices, however, were distributed amongst at least 100 of 'his northern adherents, whom he planted in every spot throughout his dominions, to the disgrace and lasting and loudly-expressed sorrow of all the people in the South, who daily longed more and more for the hoped-for return of their ancient rulers rather than the present tyranny of these people'. This was one of the chief factors prompting a steady trickle of defectors to join Henry Tudor in Brittany, a trend that would escalate as time went on.

Although Richard punished Yorkists formerly loyal to Edward IV, Wydville partisans and Lancastrian diehards, he made no move against Elizabeth Wydville and her kinsfolk; in fact he offered clemency to Dorset, Morton and Richard Wydville. This may, however, have been a trap, and they wisely stayed in Brittany. Margaret Beaufort fared worse. She was attainted, but the Rolls of Parliament record that 'the King, of his especial grace, remembering the good and faithful service that Thomas, Lord Stanley, has done and intends to do for him', and not daring to offend Stanley, for he now needed all the support he could muster from the peers, 'for his sake remits the great punishment of attainder on the said Countess that she deserves'. Instead, her servants were removed from her, she was disabled in law from owning any property, her estates were declared forfeit to her husband and she was placed under his jurisdiction. Henceforth she was known merely as Lady Stanley. These strictures, however, did not prevent Margaret Beaufort from continuing to work in secret against the King by spreading further rumours, nor from embarking on a campaign to convert Stanley to her way of thinking and win his support for her son.

Stanley was given Buckingham's former office of Lord High Constable and remained in favour. However his wife's persuasions eventually had the desired effect and brought about his gradual alienation from the King. Richard, obviously, did not trust him; indeed, he would shortly have cause to regret his clemency to Lady Stanley.

On 25th November, 1483, Richard returned in triumph to London. He now appeared invincible, but this was largely an illusion: the rumours about the princes had cost him many supporters, high and low, and he could not rely on the loyalty of those left to him. Buckingham's fall had brought to prominence three great magnates, Norfolk, Stanley and Northumberland, and the King meant to retain their support, even if he had to buy it. Towards those who had opposed him in the past he would from now on adopt a policy of conciliation, winning over some with lucrative offices and grants. It was also essential to gain, if not the love, then the approval of the people, and to this end Richard made, in the months ahead, strenuous efforts to present an image of himself as a sovereign worthy of respect, a man of high morals and political integrity, keen to uphold the liberties of Church and State, a man whose patronage it would be worth seeking. Richard hoped to establish himself as a popular ruler before his enemies had time to retrench for a further attack on him.

Nevertheless he was acutely aware of the insecurity of his position and conscious of the fact that there were two potential focuses for rebellion: the former Queen and her daughters in sanctuary and Henry Tudor in Brittany. Of the two, Henry Tudor was the more dangerous, for the rebellion had greatly strengthened his position as the Lancastrian pretender to the throne and his presence in Brittany was acting as a magnet to all those who were dissatisfied with Richard III, a steadily increasing number. Already Henry had established a court in exile, and it seemed certain that one day he would make another bid for the crown, perhaps with the aid of a European power hostile to Richard.

This was exactly what Henry Tudor intended. To establish his position clearly in the eyes of his supporters and the world at large, on Christmas Day, 1483, as Richard III was keeping the festival of the Nativity with great solemnity and splendour at Westminster, Henry made a solemn vow in Rennes Cathedral that as soon as he should be king he would marry Elizabeth of York. Afterwards his supporters, many of them prominent Yorkists, swore to be loyal to each other before kneeling to Henry and paying him homage as though he had been already crowned king. They then swore they would one day return to England and overthrow the tyrant Richard. This ceremony was intended to inspire others to join Henry's cause and to bring over to his side those Yorkists who were loyal to the line of Edward IV, thus uniting them with the Lancastrian faction.

It was a masterful move, but it would not, and could not, have happened if Henry and-his supporters had not by then been certain that the Princes in the Tower were in truth dead.

16

An Especial
Good Lord

By January, 1484, it was widely believed, not only in England but in France also, that Richard III had murdered his nephews. The new French king, Charles VIII, was a minor, as Edward V had been, and his elder sister, Anne de Beaujeu, had been appointed Regent. However, certain French nobles were reluctant to accept her as such and on 15th January the Estates General met at Tours for the purpose of bringing them to heel. On that day Guillaume de Rochefort, Chancellor of France, a grave and learned man not given to flights of fancy, addressed the assembly, and these nobles in particular, warning them of the perils of a minority, reminding them of what had happened in England:

> Look, I pray you, at the events that have taken place in that country since the death of King Edward. Think of his children, already big and strong, murdered with impunity and the crown transferred to their murderer by the will of the people.

Rochefort was obviously reminding the French government of what they already knew, and his statements may have been based not only on the gossip then infiltrating the court of Europe but also on high-level intelligence that has not survived. It is also possible that he had spoken with Mancini, who is known to have been his friend. Mancini had stayed at Beaugency in December 1483 when Rochefort had been nearby on the King's business. It is likely that the two men met and that Mancini passed on what information he had about the Princes; the subject was highly topical just then on account of the rumours seeping in from England. However, when Mancini wrote his account of Richard III's usurpation that December he referred only to rumours current in London before mid July 1483. Rochefort must therefore have had something more to go on, but it is notable that he assumed that the murder had taken place before Richard's accession. There is no doubt that he spoke with conviction, not only because he believed he was speaking the truth, but also because he welcomed the opportunity to vilify Richard III, who had been unpopular in France since he had advocated the revival of England's dynastic claims to that kingdom.

In England, on 23rd January, 1484, the only Parliament of Richard III's reign met at Westminster and passed the Act of Settlement known as 'Titulus Regius', formally confirming the King's title to the crown. Its purpose was to remove 'all doubts and seditious language' and to quieten men's minds, but many were strongly critical of its legality. Croyland, a canon lawyer himself, wrote: 'Although that lay court found itself unable to give a definition of his rights, since matrimonial law was at issue, this body of laymen was not qualified to pronounce on the matter; nevertheless, even the stoutest were so swayed by fear that Parliament presumed to do so, took that power upon itself, and did so pronounce.' The difficulty was that Parliament had no jurisdiction to determine the validity of Edward IV's marriage: only an ecclesiastical court could do that. But the members were cowed into overturning all legal precedent for fear of the King's vengeance. After the Act was passed, Edward, Prince of Wales was recognised by Parliament as heir to the throne.

The legislation passed by Richard III's Parliament was seen retrospectively as wise and beneficial. In 1525 Cardinal Wolsey was informed by the Lord Mayor of London that 'although the King did evil, yet in his time were many good Acts made'. Francis Bacon called Richard 'a good law maker' who legislated 'for the ease and solace of the common people'. However, it is not known how far Richard was personally responsible for these laws, which provided for the first legal-aid system in England, bail for offenders, the reform of oppressive land-tenure laws, the regulation of qualifications for jury service, and the abolition of livery and maintenance practices and of the hated 'benevolences', the system whereby wealthy men were forced to make financial gifts to the Crown. This last was a very popular measure, enacted in response to public opinion and Richard III may well have intended it to be a placatory measure to keep the magnates in check and boost public support and his own popularity. But the people who benefited most from the majority of the new laws were the lower orders of society and this left the magnates, on whom Richard depended, disgruntled and dissatisfied, and the King no more popular than he had been before.

Richard III was an energetic and efficient ruler with many qualities of leadership. In 1484 he proclaimed to the men of Kent that he was 'utterly determined that all his true subjects shall live in rest and quiet and peaceably enjoy their lands, according to the laws of this, his land'. Rous, writing in Richard's reign, called him 'an especial good lord. He ruled his subjects in his realm full commendably.' Other commentators also praised his abilities as a sovereign. He was hard-working and generally lenient. Because of his preoccupation – or obsession – with security, he was forced to employ conciliatory policies and to make constant bids for popularity, doubtless hoping that in time he might overcome the prejudices of his subjects. But it was already too late for this. Public feeling was against him, fuelled by the promotion of northerners and the dark rumours about the Princes. Men imputed a cynical motive to whatever he did, and late in 1484 he became even more unpopular when, short of money, he was obliged to extort forced loans from his wealthier subjects, which were equivalent to the benevolences he himself had declared illegal. Croyland thought this scandalous because the King had 'openly condemned' such practices in Parliament. Now he was being 'careful to avoid any use of the word benevolence'. 'Oh, God,' lamented Croyland, seizing the opportunity to enlarge upon Richard's shortcomings, 'why should we any longer dwell on this subject, multiplying our recital of things so distasteful and so pernicious in their example that we ought not so much as to suggest them? So, too, with other things which are not written in this book, and of which I grieve to speak.' Was Croyland, that most discreet of chroniclers, referring here to the Princes?

Elizabeth Wydville, meanwhile, remained in sanctuary with her daughters. The failure of Buckingham's rebellion had extinguished her hopes of a return to power, and the punishment of her allies had left her isolated and demoralised. She had now been confined for nine months and must have found her life tedious in the extreme. Even so, she undoubtedly regarded sanctuary as a place of safety and showed no sign of leaving it. This caused embarrassment to the King, who was doing his best to convince his people that his rule was benevolent and conciliatory. He was also aware that many of his subjects regarded Elizabeth of York as the rightful Queen of England, and he was consequently determined to obtain custody of her. Besides, if she was at court he could arrange a suitable marriage for her and thus put her beyond the reach of Henry Tudor. Elizabeth Wydville's refusal to leave sanctuary was a constant thorn in Richard's side, and early in 1484 he made up his mind to do something about it. However, his cause was prejudiced from the first because not only had Parliament just enacted a Statute confiscating Elizabeth Wydville's property, leaving her penniless, but also, says Vergil, because the 'grave men' sent by the King to persuade the former Queen to leave Westminster Abbey with her daughters upset her by referring to the death of her sons, which amounted to official confirmation that they were dead.

Croyland states that Richard's emissaries used 'frequent entreaties and threats' and 'strongly solicited' Elizabeth Wydville to comply with the King's wishes, while Rous says she was 'harassed by repeated intercessions and dire threats'. It soon became alarmingly clear that the Sanctuary could no longer be regarded as a place of refuge, since Richard would obviously not hesitate to use force to remove her and her daughters if she resisted him. This was the main reason why, in the end, the Queen agreed to compromise by sending her daughters 'from the Sanctuary at Westminster to King Richard', but only, says Vergil, after being promised 'mountains' by him after she had shown signs of weakening. In striking such a bargain she showed herself to be both a realist and a pragmatist.

The revisionists constantly argue that Elizabeth Wydville would never have agreed to transfer her daughters into the care and control of the man who had murdered her sons. But this is exactly what she did do, knowing that he had not only done away with the Princes but had also murdered another of her sons, Sir Richard Grey, who had been executed without justification or a proper trial. The fact of the matter was that in view of Richard's threats, Elizabeth had no choice but to surrender her daughters: had she not agreed to do so, force would have been used to make her. While the King was still hoping for an amicable conclusion to the impasse, she seized her advantage and drove a hard bargain, knowing that Richard was anxious to maintain his public image: she insisted that he swear a solemn public oath to protect and care for her daughters. Elizabeth was well aware of the value that her contemporaries placed on such oaths, and that the publicity generated by one would serve as protection for the young girls when they left her care.

Richard agreed to take an oath, and he also offered Elizabeth a generous pension of 700 marks, which she accepted. Agreement was reached on all these matters by the end of February, and on 1st March the King summoned to Westminster his magnates and princes of the Church, as well as the Lord Mayor and chief citizens of London, and in their presence placed his hand on sacred relics of the Four Evangelists and swore the following oath:

I, Richard, by the Grace of God King of England etc., in the presence of my lords spiritual and temporal, promise and swear on the word of a king that if the daughters of Dame Elizabeth Grey, late calling herself Queen of England, will come to me out of the Sanctuary at Westminster, and be guided, ruled and demeaned after me, then I shall see that they be in surety of their lives, and also not suffer any manner hurt by any manner person, nor any of them imprison within the Tower of London or any other prison, but that I shall put them in honest places of good name and fame, and them honestly and courteously shall see to be entreated and to have all things requisite and necessary as my kinswomen, and every one of them give in marriage to gentlemen born. And such gentlemen as shall hap to marry with them I shall straitly charge, from time to time, lovingly to love and entreat them as their wives and my kinswomen, as they will avoid and eschew my displeasure.

This oath was undoubtedly based on stipulations made by Elizabeth Wydville, and it proves that she was very suspicious indeed of Richard's motives. The reference to the Tower is significant: without mentioning what had happened to the Princes there, Richard undertook that the same fate should not befall their sisters. It was a comprehensive oath covering all contingencies, and the fact that Richard agreed to swear it in public is an indication of how anxious he was to bring Edward IV's daughters under his control and be seen to have reached an understanding with their mother. To some extent the oath had a beneficial effect on the King's public image: even today, as we have seen, there are those who will not believe that Elizabeth Wydville would have relinquished her daughters to the murderer of her sons. However, one cannot escape the thought that had she not believed Richard to be guilty of that deed there would have been no occasion for such an oath.

The King had also told Elizabeth that he would pardon her son Dorset if he returned to his allegiance, abandoned Henry Tudor and came home to England. Elizabeth wrote to Dorset, urging him to do just that and promising him that Richard would 'treat him well'. She also ordered him to break off negotiations for the marriage between Elizabeth of York and Henry Tudor. Dorset secretly left the Pretender's court but was intercepted by Henry's spies and warned not to go back to England. He complied, but for a long time afterwards Henry Tudor would not trust him.

The daughters of Edward IV left the Sanctuary in early March. There is probably no factual basis for the statement in *The Song of the Lady Bessy* that Elizabeth, the eldest, went to live in Lord Stanley's London house: Margaret Beaufort was there, and it is hardly likely that the King would have countenanced his niece fraternising with the woman who had tried to marry her to Henry Tudor. It is much more likely that the girls all went initially to court and accompanied the King and Queen to Nottingham in April, returning to London at the end of July. There is confusion over what happened to Elizabeth Wydville. Clearly she did not leave sanctuary with her daughters, for the King authorised payment of her pension via John Nesfield, the man he had placed in charge of security at the Abbey and whose duty it was 'to attend upon the former Queen'. But by the summer of 1484 Nesfield was serving as a naval captain, fighting the French, and we may assume that Elizabeth Wydville had at last emerged from sanctuary.

Where she went is a mystery. Possibly she was given an apartment at court, but this is unlikely given the bad feeling between herself and the King. Croyland says that at Christmas 1484 she sent her daughters to court, implying that they were then living with her away from it, having probably been sent by the King to her after she left sanctuary and they returned from the Midlands. We do not know where this was: Elizabeth's properties had been confiscated, so the King must have provided them with accommodation.

In April, Richard III, gratified that he had achieved his objective, went with the Queen and the court to Nottingham Castle. Here, says Croyland, 'it was fully seen how vain are the thoughts of a man who desires to establish his interests without the aid of God'. For the Prince of Wales, 'this only son of his, in whom all the hopes of the royal succession, fortified by so many oaths, were centred, was seized with an illness of but short duration'. Dr Saxon Barton suggested in the 1930s that this could have been appendicitis because the Prince, he alleged, suffered violent stomach pains, though no contemporary source for this evidence is quoted. Whatever the illness, the child, aged only seven or eight, met what Rous calls 'an unhappy death' on 9th April, 1484, one year to the day after the death of Edward IV. He died at Middleham Castle and was probably buried in Sheriff Hutton Church, where a tomb bearing a much-damaged alabaster effigy of a little boy, beneath a window containing fragments of fifteenth-century glass showing the Yorkist Sun in Splendour emblem, may mark his final resting place.

Croyland says that when the news reached Nottingham on 20th April, 'you might have seen his father and mother in a state almost bordering upon madness by reason of their sudden grief'. Not only had they lost their only child, but Richard had also lost his heir, and this left his realm vulnerable to a disputed succession in the event of his early death. It also undermined his own position and prompted some nobles to reflect upon whether the hand of God was evident in this latest circumstance, a consideration which led some of their number to transfer their loyalty to Henry Tudor.

On a personal level Richard was devastated by his son's death. For ever after he would refer to Nottingham as his 'Castle of Care', and it may be that his personal prayer dedicated to St Julian was composed for him at this time. He may also have seen the death of his son as a judgement on him for murdering the Princes, a predictable reaction in those superstitious times: nothing else could have brought home to him more forcibly the extent of his guilt, a cross he had to bear alone. It has even been claimed by some modern writers that Richard was a little deranged after his son died, though there is no evidence to substantiate this.

We cannot, of course, be certain that Richard himself saw the loss of his child as a divine punishment; nevertheless, that is how the majority of his subjects viewed it. More says that when they heard of Prince Edward's death, 'Englishmen declared that the imprecations of the agonised mother [Elizabeth Wydville] had been heard'. And naturally the event provoked a fresh crop of rumours about the Princes in the Tower. These rumours may also have been the consequence of the emergence from sanctuary of Edward IV's daughters, and some of them certainly filtered into England from the court of exiles surrounding Henry Tudor in Brittany.

The *Great Chronicle of London* states that 'all the winter season the land was in good quiet, but after Easter much whispering was among the people that the King had put the children of King Edward to death, of whom as then men feared not openly to say that they were rid out of this world, but of their death's manner was many opinions, for some said they were murdered between two feather beds, some said they were drowned in Malmsey, and some said they were sticked with a venomous potion. But howsoever they were put to death, certain it was before that day they were departed this world, of which cruel deed Sir James Tyrell was reported to be the doer. But others put that weight upon an old servant of King Richard's named . . . ' Here there is a blank space in the manuscript. In the margin the chronicler has written two headings: 'Innocents' and 'Death of the Innocents'.

The contents of this and other London chronicles are a genuine record of the events of their time. Here, therefore, is confirmation that in April 1484 Tyrell's involvement in the murder was known or suspected in the City of London. This section of the *Great Chronicle* covers the period ending in 1496 and it was written between then and 1501–2 at the latest, certainly before Tyrell is said to have confessed to the murder and long before More wrote his history.

The widespread rumours lost Richard III 'the hearts of the people' once and for all. The *Great Chronicle* says that 'the more in number grudged so sore against the King for the death of the innocents that as gladly would they have been French as to be under his subjection' – to be French was the worst fate imaginable to an Englishman at that time. The Milanese ambassador recorded in 1496 that Richard's subjects 'abandoned' him, 'taking the other side because he put to death his nephews, to whom the kingdom belonged'. Public feeling against Richard was not limited just to the lower and middle classes. Croyland says that the King 'fell in great hatred of the more part of the nobles of his realm, insomuch as such as before loved and praised him and would have jeopardised life and goods with him if he had remained still Protector, now murmured and grudged against him. Few or none favoured his party, except it were for dread or the great gifts that they received of him.' Many crossed to Henry Tudor in Brittany, increasingly a focus for the disaffected in England. Even now, though, Richard could have won back the loyalty of his people and pre-empted Henry Tudor's designs on the throne had he been able to produce the Princes alive. It was the fact that he did not that, more than anything else, prompted an increasing number of his subjects to look to Henry Tudor for deliverance.

In June 1484 Richard took advantage of the temporary mental illness of the Duke of Brittany and persuaded Pierre Landais, the Treasurer of Brittany who was acting for his master, to extradite Henry Tudor. Just in time, Henry received a warning from Bishop Morton and fled to France, where he was warmly welcomed by the Regent, Anne de Beaujeu, who was happy to add to Richard III's many problems and thus prevent him from pursuing an aggressive policy towards her country.

Thwarted of his prey, Richard, says Croyland, 'took all necessary precautions for the defence of his party'. He strengthened England's defences, issued a series of proclamations branding 'Henry Tydder' a traitor, put all his commissioners of array on special alert, and made friendly overtures to foreign princes, hoping to prevent them from giving aid to his enemy. The French, in turn, encouraged Henry Tudor to expedite plans for an invasion of England, realising that Richard might at any time marry off Elizabeth of York to someone else. If this happened, Henry's cause would be irretrievably lost.

With French backing Henry posed a dangerous threat to Richard's future security, which was even less certain now that the King had no son to succeed him. Richard was much preoccupied with the problem of the succession. Rous states that 'Not long after the death of the Prince, the young Earl of Warwick was proclaimed heir-apparent in the royal court, and in ceremonies at table and chamber he was served first after the King and Queen.' Richard, however, made no move to have Clarence's attainder reversed, not wishing perhaps to draw attention to the fact that Warwick's claim to the throne was better than his own. Many writers have questioned Rous's statement but, as mentioned before, he had close links with Middleham and the Warwick family and made it his business to record the deeds of its members. It has been said that Richard would hardly have named someone with a better right to be king than himself as his heir, but Warwick was a child of nine and no-one in that turbulent period was likely to revolt in favour of a child.

Warwick was probably in Richard's train when he travelled to Durham that May and thence to York in June, and the King had an opportunity to get to know him. In 1499 it was inferred by Vergil that Warwick was either mentally retarded or intellectually feeble. It may have been this that made Richard change his mind about naming the boy his successor. In July ordinances were drawn up for the regulation of the King's Household in the North, to be established at Sheriff Hutton Castle under the rule of Richard's nephew, John de la Pole, Earl of Lincoln. Sheriff Hutton was designated by the King to be the official residence of his northern representative and a nursery establishment for the younger members of the House of York. Rous hints that Warwick was 'placed in custody' there in the summer of 1484; here, too, came his sister Margaret, Richard's bastard children and, later on, the daughters of Edward IV. Now a ruin, Sheriff Hutton was then a luxurious royal castle with excellent facilities and defences, set in a deer park. Its very impregnability was why the King, obsessed with security, had chosen it.

Rous says that after Warwick was sent there Lincoln was designated Richard's heir: certainly on 21st August Richard appointed Lincoln Lieutenant of Ireland, a post held by former heirs apparent of the House of York. It was a wise choice. Lincoln was the King's nearest adult male heir, an energetic man of good intellect and ability who was admired for his knightly prowess and conduct. He had always been a loyal supporter of his uncle, and had in July been appointed President of the newly-established Council of the North. He also received lands, an annuity from Duchy of Cornwall revenues, and the reversion of Margaret Beaufort's estates.

On 9th November Richard returned to London. It was not a happy home-coming for the Queen was unwell, and there remained the ever-present problem of Henry Tudor. Against such a backdrop would be enacted the last scandal of Richard III's reign.

17
An Incestuous Passion

In 1484 Elizabeth of York was eighteen. In looks she resembled her mother, but her long red-gold hair was inherited from her Plantagenet forebears. Of medium height, she had 'large breasts', according to one Portuguese ambassador, and extant portraits of her show that she must have been very comely in her youth: a Venetian envoy to the court of Henry VII called her 'very handsome'. Vergil later described her as 'a woman of such character'. She was intelligent, pious and literate, could speak French and a little Spanish, delighted in music, card games and gardens, and was renowned for her skill at embroidery. Of gentler nature than her mother, she had nevertheless inherited her father's sensual and passionate nature, and at eighteen she was long past the age at which princesses were usually married. Commines records a rumour circulating in 1484 that Richard III had considered marrying Elizabeth to Bishop Stillington's bastard son, but this almost certainly had no basis in fact, nor would such a marriage have complied with the terms of the King's undertaking to Elizabeth Wydville.

By the end of 1484 it was clear that Queen Anne was a sick woman, unlikely to have any more children, and probably not long for this world. Elizabeth Wydville, following her usual pragmatic instincts, and having now abandoned her hopes of Henry Tudor, saw some advantage for her daughter and herself in this situation, for if Anne died, as seemed likely, the King would be expected to marry again in the hope of providing for the succession. In such circumstances, who better to mate with him than the Lady Elizabeth, regarded by many as the rightful heiress of the House of York? Marriage to her would place Richard III in an unassailable position: as husband of the woman many people regarded as the lawful Queen of England he would enjoy the unchallenged right to wear the crown. Elizabeth would be accorded her rightful rank and dignity and, even more to the point, Elizabeth Wydville could expect to be restored to power and influence as the mother of the Queen Regnant. For all the former Queen's ambition, it must have cost her dearly to contemplate marrying her daughter to the man who had murdered her sons, but with such advantages in view, scruples had to be suppressed.

In December, says Croyland, 'the lady Elizabeth was, with her four younger sisters, sent by her mother to attend the Queen at court at the Christmas festivals kept with great state in Westminster Hall. They were received with all honourable courtesy by Queen Anne, especially the Lady Elizabeth, who was ranked familiarly in the Queen's favour, who treated her as a sister. But neither the society that she loved, nor all the pomp and festivity of royalty, could heal the wound in the Queen's breast for the loss of her son.'

With Anne ill and preoccupied with her grief, Richard – himself in need of comfort – began to look to his attractive, buxom niece for solace. The sensual streak in his nature perhaps recognised something similar in hers, and it was only a matter of days before a passionate attraction was kindled between the two of them. Elizabeth may have initially approached her uncle with feelings of distaste: later chroniclers all assure us she had been devoted to her brothers. But she was also ambitious, like her mother, and she had recently been thwarted of her chance of a crown as the wife of Henry Tudor. Now the prospect of queenship was opening up once again. Not only was the Queen ailing but there was also talk of the King having their marriage annulled in order to remarry and beget more sons. He might soon be a free man. On a personal level, Richard had the charisma and appeal of one who enjoys and wields power, an older and experienced man who well knew how to charm a young girl. When courtiers observed how things stood between the King and his niece, the rumours of an impending royal annulment proliferated.

Richard's interest in Elizabeth of York was not purely sensual: he, too, had perceived the enormous advantages of a union with her. Henry Tudor's determination to marry her and claim the crown through her, ignoring the provisions of 'Titulus Regius', could not have failed to bring these advantages to Richard's notice. If Henry could strengthen his claim to the throne by marrying Elizabeth, so could he, Richard, even if it meant reversing his own Act of Settlement and legitimising her. The King's determination to marry his niece is virtual proof, if any were needed, that the precontract story on which his title was based was pure invention. Had it been true, Richard would not now have been contemplating the marriage to strengthen his position. His pursuit of Elizabeth was not only a tacit acknowledgement of the widespread recognition of her as the rightful queen, but also amounted to confirmation that the Princes were dead. Marriage to her would crush Henry Tudor's pretensions once and for all, and it would hopefully silence the ever-present rumours about her brothers. It would stabilise Richard's tenure of the throne, enlist the Wydvilles on the side of the Crown, and in every way make sound political sense.

It is clear from the evidence available that Elizabeth attracted the attentions of her uncle in a remarkably short time, and that by January 1485 this was apparent to observers at court. Croyland tells us that 'the Feast of the Nativity was kept with due solemnity at the Palace of Westminster and the King appeared with his crown on the day of the Epiphany' (6th January). Then a note of clerical disapproval creeps in:

> It must be mentioned that, during this Feast of the Nativity, immoderate and unseemly stress was laid upon dancing and festivity, vain changes of apparel of similar colour and shape being presented to Queen Anne and the Lady Elizabeth, a thing that caused the people to murmur and the nobles and prelates greatly to wonder thereat. It was said by many that the King was bent, either on the anticipated death of the Queen taking place, or else by means of a divorce, for which he supposed he had quite sufficient grounds, on contracting a marriage with Elizabeth, whatever the cost, for it appeared that no other way could his kingly power be established or the hopes of his rival put an end to. There are also many other matters which are not in this book because it is shameful to speak of them.

Croyland, writing in 1486, would not have committed to paper anything compromising about the new Queen of England, Elizabeth of

York. Instead, he would represent Richard III as the villain of the piece and, ever discreet, was probably implying in this last sentence there was more to the relationship between uncle and niece than political advantage. With the passage worded as it is it appears that the chronicler is trying to convey that there was already a sexual relationship of some nature. Croyland's reticence leads us to believe that there were more grounds for conjecture than just the similar gowns given by Richard to his wife and niece, for this by itself would hardly have provoked such disapproval. And Croyland's statement that Richard supposed he had sufficient grounds for divorce is indicative that the matter had already been discussed, perhaps in Council.

Whilst the King 'was keeping this festival with remarkable splendour' in Westminster Hall and the court hummed with speculation, 'news was brought to him from his spies beyond the sea that, notwithstanding the potency and splendour of his royal estate, his adversaries would, without question, invade the kingdom during the following summer'. Richard answered that, 'than this, there was nothing that could befall him more desirable'.

News of the coming invasion made the idea of marriage with his niece not only desirable but urgent, and in the days after the Epiphany the King's courtship became more ardent. Buck believed his desire was 'feigned', but most of the evidence is to the contrary and shows that he had every intention of making Elizabeth his wife as soon as he was free to do so. Croyland would later refer to Richard's 'incestuous passion' for her and throughout strongly implies that the King was motivated by passion as much as ambition. Molinet even alleged that Elizabeth bore a child by him, though there is no evidence for this, but it may well have been at this time that Richard gave Elizabeth his copy of *The Romance of Tristan* (now in the British Library), which bears not only his name but her motto and signature also: '*Sans removyr, Elizabeth*'. The book cannot have come into her possession later on because when she was queen she always signed herself 'Elizabeth ye Queen', while her usual signature before 1486 was 'Elizabeth Plantagenet'.

Elizabeth was under considerable pressure from her mother and her half-brother Dorset to respond to the King's advances, but there is good evidence that this pressure was unnecessary and that she had already become emotionally involved. How she reconciled this with the fact that Richard had murdered her brothers is not known; the simplest explanation must be that he somehow convinced her that he was innocent of the deed, a lie that a girl in the throes of infatuation would be only too willing to believe. The fact that she could contemplate such a marriage shows her to have been as much of a pragmatist as her mother and confirms that her ambition to wear a crown was greater than her grief for brothers who might never have been close to her.

Croyland says that 'the King's determination to marry his niece reached the ears of his people, who wanted no such thing.' Vergil states that when Henry Tudor, in France, learned what was afoot, the news 'pinched him to the very stomach', and he was even more downcast when he heard that Richard proposed to marry Elizabeth's sister Cecily to an unknown knight so that Henry should be baulked of yet another Yorkist princess. The three youngest girls, Anne, Katherine and Bridget, were too young to be considered seriously as prospective brides, and while Elizabeth of York lived the dynastic claims of her sisters were secondary to hers anyway. Henry, in desperation, now made a bid to marry Maud Herbert, daughter of his former guardian, hoping thereby to enlist Welsh support for his cause, but Maud could not bring Henry a crown as her dowry and was therefore a poor substitute for the Yorkist heiress.

Contrary to popular belief, at that time a marriage between uncle and niece was permitted by the church provided a dispensation was obtained beforehand. When Richard III's contemporaries condemned his intended marriage as unlawful and incestuous, it became clear that the path to wedded bliss would be littered with obstacles, though people anticipated that Richard would sweep these aside and have what he wanted. But, says the chronicler Hall, 'one thing withstood his desires. Anne, his queen, was still alive.'

As the affair between Richard and Elizabeth progressed, so did Anne's illness. Croyland writes that a few days after Epiphany 'the Queen fell extremely sick, and her illness was supposed to have increased still more and more because the King entirely shunned her bed, claiming that it was by the advice of his physicians that he did so. Why enlarge?'

The Queen's illness was terminal and was probably caused by either tuberculosis or cancer. It conveniently freed Richard from his marital obligations and left him with more opportunities to pursue Elizabeth.

hallmarks of authenticity.

Two versions of Buck's history exist, each with the letter worded differently. In 1646 Buck's nephew and namesake published a savagely abridged and inaccurate edition of his uncle's work, the only one available until 1979, when the eminent historian A.N. Kincaid produced a fine version faithful to Buck's original text. This second version, from which the above letter is quoted, shows two significant amendments to the 1646 text of it, which show that the nature of the relationship between Richard III and Elizabeth of York was far different from what historians had assumed up until 1979.

Firstly, the 1646 edition states that Elizabeth required Norfolk to be a mediator 'to the King in respect of the marriage propounded between them', which led many writers mistakenly to conclude that Richard was an unwilling participant in the affair and that his feigned pursuit of his niece was only a ploy to discountenance Henry Tudor. Buck's original text actually reads that Elizabeth prayed Norfolk, 'as before, to be a mediator for her in the cause of the marriage to the King', and does not specify with whom he was to mediate: because of her previous request, Elizabeth assumes that Howard will know to whom she is referring. Clearly it is not the King, for the letter is proof that her feelings were very much reciprocated, as Croyland confirms; it was likely to have been either one of several prominent doctors of divinity and canon law whom we know were summoned by the Council to pronounce on the feasibility of a dispensation, or one of the councillors close to the King who were known to be violently opposed to the marriage, seeing it conflicting with their own interests. Elizabeth was hoping to put pressure on these men and thereby ensure a happy outcome.

The second amendment concerns the intimate nature of her relationship with the King, and indicates that Elizabeth was already a willing partner in an adulterous liaison. In the 1646 version she states that 'she was his in heart and thought', but the original text shows 'that she was his in heart and thought, in body and in all', proof that the relationship was a sexual one. It was not unusual then for couples to live together quite honourably on the strength of a formal promise to wed followed by sexual intercourse, but in this case Richard had a wife still living and that arrangement could not apply. Elizabeth's relationship with him was at best adultery. Her telling comment that Richard was her 'only joy and maker in this world' implies that she was otherwise at a very low ebb, which is understandable considering how circumscribed her life had been during the previous two years. Maybe the stigma of bastardy had caused her to lose sight of her own worth. Whatever the reason for her surrender, it had brought her both joy and pain, and now she was so deeply involved that she could view the continuing existence of Richard's sick wife as no more than an obstacle to her own future happiness and the fulfilment of her ambitions.

Anne was now very ill indeed. It is possible that the King, spurred on by his dynastic ambitions, his passion for his niece, and the knowledge that Henry Tudor would invade in the summer, took steps to hasten her end. The man who had murdered two children would not have hesitated to dispose of an ailing and unwanted wife, especially when she was known to be dying anyway and there was little chance of anyone proving his guilt.

On 16th March, 1485, Anne died during a great eclipse of the sun. Nine days later she was buried in Westminster Abbey, says Croyland, 'with no less honour than befitted the interment of a queen' in an unmarked grave in front of the sedilia by the ancient tomb of Sebert, King of the East Saxons. Croyland says her husband wept openly by her grave.

But London was vocal with rumours. The Acts of Court of the Mercers Company record that there was 'much simple communication among the people, by evil-disposed persons, showing how that the Queen, as by consent and will of the King, was poisoned, for and to the intent that he might then marry and have to wife Lady Elizabeth'. The *Great Chronicle of London* states there was 'much whispering among the people that the King had poisoned the Queen his wife, and intended with a licence purchased to have married the eldest daughter of King Edward'. It goes on to say that even the King's northern stalwarts, 'in whom he placed great reliance', willingly imputed 'to him the death of the Queen', and there was much 'whispering of poison' among them. These are authentic reports of rumours circulating at the time of the Queen's death; given his previous notoriety, people had no difficulty in believing that Richard had murdered his wife. Later allegations of poison were therefore based on what was regarded as credible at the time and not on so-called Tudor propaganda.

John Rous, who devotedly chronicled all the deeds of the Neville family, believed the rumours: 'Lady Anne, his queen, he poisoned,' he wrote. Commines, in France, heard the rumours and later recorded how 'some said he had her killed'. *The Song of the Lady Bessy* also alleges that Richard poisoned and 'put away' his wife. Vergil, having heard how he had tried to hound her to death by other means, wrote: 'But the Queen, whether she was despatched by sorrowfulness or poison, died.' And Edward Hall, years later, stated: 'Some think she went her own pace to the grave, while others suspect a grain was given her to quicken her in her journey to her long home.'

After Anne's death, says Croyland, Richard's 'countenance was always drawn'. More tells us that a mutual acquaintance told him that, from this time onwards, the King 'was never quiet in his mind, never thought himself secure, his hand ever on his dagger. He took ill rest at nights.' He was now more hated and distrusted by his subjects than ever before, and had alienated most of the nobility and gentry. His courtiers found his dogged attention to business tedious; he had the reputation of being over-meticulous and some, such as Sir William Stanley, disparagingly referred to him as 'Old Dick' behind his back. The majority of his contemporaries regarded him as a treacherous hypocrite of whom they were wise to be fearful.

The marriage between Richard III and Elizabeth of York never took place. The rumours that Richard had poisoned his queen so that it could be accomplished made it impossible for him to carry through his plans. The rumours perturbed him deeply, for he had seen their effect in the past and knew that his throne was too unstable to survive another scandal. If he made Elizabeth his queen it would only serve to fuel the rumours and might lose him valuable support when he most needed it.

The majority of Richard's Council were violently opposed to the marriage. Croyland says that when 'the King's purpose and intention [was] mentioned to some who were opposed thereto, the King was obliged to summon a Council and exculpate himself by denying profusely that such a thing had ever entered his mind. There were some persons however, present on that Council, who very well knew the contrary' – including, presumably, Croyland himself:

Those who were most strongly against the marriage were two men whose views even the King himself seldom dared oppose: Sir Richard Ratcliffe and William Catesby. By these persons the King was told to his face that if he did not abandon his intended purpose and deny it by public declaration, all the people of the north, in whom he placed the greatest trust, would rise in rebellion and impute to him the death of the Queen, through whom he had first gained his present high position, in order that he might gratify his incestuous passion for his niece, something abominable before God.

Again, Croyland is implying a sexual relationship. 'For good measure they brought him 12 doctors of divinity who asserted that the Pope could grant no dispensation in the case of such a degree of consanguinity.' This was not strictly true but in the climate of the time people were willing to believe it.

Croyland says there were other, more personal, reasons for the objections of Catesby and Ratcliffe. 'It was widely assumed that these two, and others like them, raised so many obstacles out of fear, because if Elizabeth became queen, it would be in her power sooner or later to avenge the deaths of her uncle, Earl Rivers, and her brother Richard [Grey]', and punish those, such as Ratcliffe, who had been involved in their deaths. The very real fear felt by Ratcliffe and Catesby is testimony to the general belief of the councillors that Elizabeth of York was capable of such vengeance. After all, she had not scrupled to involve herself with the King while his wife lay dying. Some councillors feared her because of her Wydville mother and would have placed any obstacle in the way of that faction's return to favour. Some northern councillors had been given confiscated Wydville lands by the King and feared to lose them. Vergil says that the Council was opposed to the marriage mainly because 'the maiden herself opposed the wicked act', but contemporary evidence does not bear this out. Vergil, writing in Tudor times under royal patronage, could hardly have accused the wife of Henry VII and mother of Henry VIII of having wished to marry Richard III; his job as official historian was to exonerate her from all culpability.

Richard, says Croyland, followed the advice of his councillors. Two weeks after Anne's death, 'a little before Easter, in the great hall of St John's [Hospital at Clerkenwell] and before the Mayor and citizens of London, the King totally repudiated the whole idea in a loud, clear voice.' The Acts of Court of the Mercers Company record that he 'showed his grief and displeasure and said it never came in his thought or mind to marry in such manner-wise, nor willing nor glad of the death of his queen, but as sorry and in heart as heavy as man might be'. He then commanded his subjects to cease all discussion of the matter on pain of his displeasure and imprisonment, while he investigated whence the rumours originated. Letters reiterating his public denial were sent to major towns and cities such as York and Southampton.

The King's statement was seen as a public humiliation. Few were deceived by it; Croyland says 'people thought it was more because of his advisers' wishes than his own'.

Hell, it is said, hath no fury like a woman scorned. Richard's public denial that he had ever planned to marry her deprived Elizabeth of York of her lover, her matrimonial prospects, and the crown which she felt was hers by right. Richard probably made it clear that their affair could not continue because of the scandal it would create. She was abandoned and dishonoured with no immediate prospect of ever regaining her rights. Within an indecently short time the King was considering other matches for her, with the Earl of Desmond or the Portuguese Duke of Beja, while he himself was negotiating to marry Juana of Portugal. It was as if the close relationship between them had never existed.

Not for nothing her mother's daughter, Elizabeth was both ambitious and determined. Twice she had aimed for a crown and twice she had been thwarted, but this second disappointment was made all the more bitter by Richard's rejection of her. Now her infatuation for her uncle metamorphosed into vengeful hatred, and she firmly resolved to place her hopes once more in Henry Tudor and do all in her power to ensure the success of his planned enterprise.

According to *The Song of the Lady Bessy*, Elizabeth waylaid Lord Stanley at court and asked him to come secretly to her rooms at night. He refused, whereupon Elizabeth staged a dramatic swoon which made him realise that it might be wiser if he went along with her request. Accompanied only by his esquire, Humphrey Brereton, the author of the poem, he visited Elizabeth in secret and began plotting with her on Henry Tudor's behalf. Elizabeth Wydville, baulked of a restoration to power, joined the conspirators, and together with Margaret Beaufort persuaded Elizabeth to send Henry a letter and a ring to signify that she was still willing to become his wife, should he take the crown. *The Song of the Lady Bessy* may exaggerate Elizabeth of York's role in the conspiracies that preceded Henry Tudor's invasion, but there is no reason to doubt that she took part in them. It also portrays her as revolted by the idea of marriage with Richard III, and that is probably the impression she desired people to gain, to save her honour and reputation.

Richard III may well have discovered that Elizabeth was now working against him. Sometime between the end of March and June he sent her to live at the royal household at Sheriff Hutton in Yorkshire. In that secure stronghold she would be out of Henry Tudor's reach should he attack in the South, and away from those persons of whom Richard was suspicious.

The King now prepared to face his enemy. In June he moved to Nottingham Castle and made it his military headquarters. From there he commanded his magnates to raise armies on his behalf. He was painfully aware that his success in the field would depend on those same magnates staying loyal. In July he dismissed Lord Chancellor Russell and appointed in his place a northerner, Thomas Barrow, Master of the Rolls.

Many people in England were preparing to support Henry Tudor. Most came from the ranks of the gentry families who had supported Buckingham's rebellion in 1483. Others were Wydville supporters and several Welshmen of note. Those members of the nobility who meant to support Henry were already in France with him, preparing to invade, and the French government was providing financial support.

On 1st August, 1485, Henry Tudor sailed from Harfleur. He landed at Milford Haven in Wales six days later and marched unopposed via Welshpool, Shrewsbury and Stafford to Lichfield, arriving on 19th August. Richard III learned of the invasion whilst hunting in Sherwood Forest; Croyland says he 'rejoiced' and summoned his forces, promising them they would triumph with ease 'over so contemptible a faction'. On 19th August he left Nottingham and set up his headquarters at Leicester.

On Sunday 21st August, says Croyland, 'the King left Leicester with great pomp, wearing his diadem on his head'. Knowing that Henry Tudor's army was approaching he set up camp near Ambien Hill, overlooking Redmore Plain, not far from the little town of Market Bosworth. Here, he spent a miserable night. Vergil says he was troubled by nightmares, which Croyland corroborates, telling us of the inauspicious beginning to the day on which battle would be joined. 'At dawn on Monday morning the chaplains were not ready to celebrate mass for King Richard, nor was any breakfast ready with which to revive the King's flagging spirit. The King, so it was reported, had seen that night, in a terrible dream, a multitude of demons apparently surrounding him, just as he attested in the morning when he presented a countenance which was always drawn but was then even more pale and deathly, and affirmed that the outcome of this day's battle, to whichever side the victory was granted, would totally destroy the kingdom of England.' Diego de Valera, the Spanish envoy, says that a Spanish mercenary warned the King that he had not a hope of winning the battle for those whom he trusted had betrayed him. He answered, 'God forbid that I yield one foot. This day I will perish as king or have the victory.'

The Battle of Bosworth, which took place that day, 22nd August, 1485, was, says Croyland, 'a most savage battle'. No eyewitness accounts survive, but the evidence we have shows that it was fought on Redmore Plain below Ambien Hill, where the King took up his position and directed his army. The conflict lasted two hours. Henry Tudor did not engage in the fighting but remained under his standard behind the lines. The Stanleys stood off with their forces to the north, to see which way the battle was going before joining it; Richard waited in vain for their support. When the royal forces appeared to be losing the day, Northumberland, who should have intervened with his men on the King's behalf, did nothing. Seeing that his soldiers were struggling, and realising that he had been deserted by those in whom he had trusted, Richard gathered round him a small band of loyal adherents and made one final, desperate charge, bearing down on the red dragon banner of Henry Tudor. He cut down the standard bearer and was about to swoop on Henry himself, but at that point the Stanleys came to Henry's aid, which turned the tide of the battle. Rous says of Richard: 'Let me say the truth to his credit, that he bore himself like a noble soldier and honourably defended himself to his last breath, shouting again and again that he was betrayed, and crying, "Treason! Treason! Treason!"' Croyland records that 'during the fighting, and not in the act of flight, King Richard was pierced with many mortal wounds, and fell in the field like a brave and most valiant prince'. 'King Richard alone,' says Vergil, 'was killed fighting manfully in the thickest press of his enemies.' 'The children of King Edward,' commented Croyland, had been 'avenged' at last.

Vergil says that when the news spread that the King was slain, 'all men forthwith threw away their weapons and freely submitted themselves to Henry's obeisance'. 'Providence,' wrote Croyland, 'gave a glorious victory to the Earl of Richmond.' The crown was found where it had rolled under a hawthorn bush – later a popular Tudor emblem – and one of the Stanley brothers placed it on Henry Tudor's head, proclaiming him King Henry VII, the first sovereign of the Tudor dynasty. With the death of Richard III, 331 years of Plantagenet rule had come to an end.

There had been many casualties. Norfolk, Ratcliffe, Brackenbury and nearly 1,000 soldiers were killed. Surrey and Catesby were taken prisoner. Lovell fled and led the life of a fugitive for the next two years. Northumberland offered his allegiance to King Henry.

When the news of Richard's death and Henry Tudor's accession reached Westminster, London burst into celebration. But in York, the clerk to the City Council recorded that 'King Richard, late mercifully reigning upon us, was, through the great treason of many that turned against him, piteously slain and murdered, to the great heaviness of this city.' The available evidence shows, however, that very few other than the prosperous burghers and local gentry whose relationship with Richard had been mutually beneficial, mourned him in York. When he had sent a plea for military aid against Henry Tudor, the city Council sent only eighty men, an insignificant offering from the second greatest city in the realm. Croyland states also that many northerners in whom Richard had placed his trust also deserted at Bosworth.

Hated though Richard III had been, every chronicler expresses outrage at what happened to his corpse. Croyland says that it 'was found among the slain and many insults were heaped on it, and it was removed to Leicester in an inhuman manner, a halter being put about the neck, as was the custom with condemned felons'. The *Great Chronicle* says that the King's body was 'despoiled to the skin and, nought being left about him so much as would cover his privy member, he was trussed behind a pursuivant' – his own herald, Blanche Sanglier – 'as an hog or other vile beast'. Vergil described the body's 'arms and legs hanging down both sides' of the horse. And so, recounts de Valera, 'all besprung with mire and filth', Richard was brought to Leicester when Henry VII entered the town in triumph that evening. The new King ordered the body to be taken to the conventual church of the Franciscan or Grey Friars, where, says de Valera, it was 'covered from the waist downward with a black rag of poor quality [and] exposed there three days to the universal gaze', for all men 'to wonder upon'. Croyland commented acidly that this usage of a human corpse was 'not exactly in accordance with the laws of humanity'.

Two days later, says the *Great Chronicle*, Richard III was 'indifferently buried' in an unmarked grave in the choir of the Collegiate Church of St Mary, by the charity of the friars and without, says Vergil, 'any pomp or solemn funeral'. In 1496 Henry VII paid £10.1s, a paltry sum, for a coloured marble tomb and alabaster effigy to be placed above his rival's grave. This bore a Latin inscription proclaiming that Richard had come to the throne by betraying the trust placed in him as Protector during his nephew's reign.

During the Reformation of the 1530s the monastery of the Franciscan friars was dissolved and the church despoiled. Richard's tomb was destroyed and his bones disinterred and thrown into the River Soar. They were either lost at that point or recovered and reburied at Bow Bridge: the evidence is conflicting. Richard's coffin is said to have been used as a horse trough in Leicester but had been broken up by 1758 and its pieces used to build the cellar steps in the White Horse Inn. Some ruined walls and foundations are all that is left of the monastery; a car park now occupies most of its site. However, there is a modern memorial stone to Richard III in Leicester Cathedral, put up by the Richard III Society.

The fall of the House of York and the Plantagenet dynasty may be attributed directly to the fatal effects of Richard III's ambition: his usurpation and the murder of the Princes. Had these events not occurred there would have been no need for an opposition party to focus its hopes on Henry Tudor.

The view of Richard's contemporaries was that God had delivered His judgement upon the King at Bosworth: Richard's death was seen as divine punishment for his crimes. 'In spite of being a powerful monarch,' wrote de Valera, 'Our Lord did not permit his evil deeds to remain unpunished.' 'Thus ended this man with dishonour as he that sought it,' commented the *Great Chronicle*, 'for had he continued still Protector and had suffered the children to have prospered according to his allegiance and fidelity, he should have been honourably lauded over all, whereas now his fame is darkened and dishonoured as far as he was known.' 'No killing was more charitable,' wrote the Welsh bard Dafydd Llywd. Rous was scathing: 'This King Richard, who was excessively cruel in his days, reigned in the way that antiChrist is to reign. His days were ended with no lamentation from his groaning subjects.'

Hall, writing over fifty years after Richard's death, acknowledged his qualities of courage and leadership and his early loyalty to Edward IV, but commented that his character was perverted by his overweening ambition. More's analysis was even more damning to Richard's reputation, for he held that his ambition had warped all his fundamentally decent feelings and turned him into the tyrannical monster of the 'Black Legend'.

But for the murder of his nephews, Richard III might have been a successful king, despite his acts of tyranny and his ruthless seizure of the throne. It was the murder of the Princes that gave Henry Tudor his opportunity and which brought down the House of Plantagenet. Thus the murder may be viewed in its wider context as a single event that dramatically changed the course of history.

18

A Dark Prince

Henry VII made it clear from the first that he came to the throne with the intention of reconciling both Lancastrians and Yorkists and putting old quarrels behind him. His first act as king was to send Sir Robert Willoughby to Sheriff Hutton to pay his respects to Elizabeth of York and escort her to Westminster. Henry meant to keep his oath and marry her, thus bringing about the longed-for alliance between Lancaster and York. He was aware that Elizabeth was widely regarded as the rightful Queen of England and the legitimate heiress of the House of York, and he meant to turn this to his own advantage. Once 'Titulus Regius' was repealed and he was married to her, his title could not be disputed.

Henry and Elizabeth, both descendants of Edward III, were within the forbidden degrees of consanguinity, however, and until a dispensation for the marriage could be granted, Henry was vulnerable to potential conspiracies on behalf of the Earl of Warwick, the last direct descendant in the male line from Edward III. Although there was no Salic Law in England, the concept of a female sovereign was repugnant to most people, and there were those who might look to the heir male of the House of York in preference to the man whom Richard III had aptly described as 'an unknown Welshman'. Henry VII knew he was by no means secure on the throne, and therefore entrusted Willoughby with a second mission, that of secretly escorting the ten-year-old Warwick to the Tower of London to forestall would-be abduction attempts. Deprived of the society of all save his gaolers the boy was to grow to manhood uneducated, isolated, and imprisoned so securely that rumours of his death abounded.

Henry VII also had Bishop Stillington arrested for unspecified 'heinous offences imagined and done' by him. Henry may have held him responsible for concocting the precontract story that had led to the bastardising of Elizabeth of York. With Stillington in custody there was no danger of any contention when Parliament met to repeal 'Titulus Regius'. Significantly, it was only after that had been done that Stillington was pardoned and released. Henry would not allow anyone to impugn Elizabeth of York's title.

Three days after Bosworth Henry had Catesby executed. He also took into custody Richard III's bastard, John of Gloucester. No-one who had adhered to Richard's cause was allowed to remain at large as a focus for opposition to the new régime. Henry entered London in triumph on 3rd September, receiving a warm welcome from the Mayor and citizens. He then gathered together his first Council, constituted in part from those who had shared his exile or supported him in England, notably the Stanleys, Bishop Morton and Reginald Bray.

Henry VII was twenty-eight, tall, lean and fair, with thinning yellow hair, grey-blue eyes and bad teeth. He was, said the Venetian ambassador, 'a man of great ability'. He was ambitious, unscrupulous, devious, avaricious, astute, cautious and highly intelligent. Not violent by nature, he preferred to adopt a policy of reconciliation and pacification, but he could be ruthless when crossed. He loved money to excess, but, like Richard III, he possessed great qualities of leadership and was an able administrator. As king, his aims were to establish his dynasty firmly on the throne, amass wealth, promote law and order, preserve peace, and raise England to the status of a great European power. In order to consolidate the position of the monarchy, he intended to curb the power of the nobility, having seen what havoc it could wreak within the state: the age of the over-mighty subject was drawing to a close.

All these things Henry VII achieved in time. He gave his realm strong government and peace and brought to it the political stability it had lacked during the Wars of the Roses. In fact, what Henry achieved during his reign was to lay the foundations of the modern state of Great Britain.

Henry VII was formally crowned on 30th October, 1485, in West-minster Abbey with great pomp, while the Lady Margaret Beaufort wept with joy. Although she herself had a better claim to the throne than her son, she rejoiced in his triumph, and henceforth she would play no further part in politics, confining her considerable influence to the domestic sphere and living a life filled with religious observances, benefactions and good works until her death in 1509.

When the first Parliament of his reign met on 11th November, Henry was hailed as the new Joshua, come to save his subjects from tyranny. When it came to the matter of his dubious title to the throne, therefore, Parliament was accommodating. Doubts had been expressed as to whether an attainted traitor could actually inherit the crown, but Henry's judges pronounced that his accession had automatically nulli-fied his attainder. Henry ensured, however, that Parliament did not appear to bestow or confirm his sovereignty. A new Act of Settlement merely declared that the inheritance of the Crown had come as of right to Henry VII and the heirs of his body. After so many changes of monarchs, what really mattered was that the King of England should be able to hold on to his throne. Much was made by Henry and his supporters of the fact that God had endorsed his right to rule by granting him the victory at Bosworth, an argument that held great weight with their contemporaries. It also obscured Henry's shaky hereditary claim. Henry was *de facto* king.

Croyland commented drily that 'the sovereignty was confirmed to our lord the King as being his due, not by one but by many titles, so that we are to believe that he rules most rightfully over the English people, and that not so much by right of blood as of conquest'. He tells us that Parliament next debated the King's proposed union with Elizabeth of York, 'in whom it appeared to all that every requisite might be supplied which was wanting to make good the title of the King himself'. But Henry had no intention of being looked upon as Elizabeth's consort – he would not, he said, be his wife's 'gentleman usher'. Nor did he apply for a papal dispensation for their marriage until after the Act of Settlement had become law, even though his councillors were strongly advising an early wedding.

Of course, there were a number of people who had a better claim to the throne than Henry VII, a fact of which he was painfully aware. A few believed that Elizabeth of York should be Queen Regnant, yet while many were prepared to argue for her rights no-one envisaged her ruling alone. Richard III had designated the Earl of Lincoln as his heir but few regarded him as a serious contender, despite his pedigree and obvious aptitude for leadership. The Earl of Warwick was seen as the most obvious claimant and despite his youth and imprisonment he was the hope of a number of diehard Yorkists in 1485 and for many years after. Other male heirs of the House of York, such as Lincoln's younger brothers, were too young at that time to represent any serious threat. Henry VII brought Lincoln to court and looked after his family, intending thereby to win his loyalty, or at least keep a watchful eye on him. He also extended his protection to Buckingham's heir, who was restored to his father's dukedom by Parliament. But because he too was descended from Edward III the young Duke represented yet another potential threat to the new dynasty.

Sir Francis Bacon describes Henry VII as 'a dark prince and infinitely suspicious, and his time full of secret conspiracies'. He also states that Henry's unwavering policy was 'the discountenancing of the House of York, which the general body of the realm still affected', and that he had 'a settled disposition to depress all eminent persons' of that house. This policy was in time carried on by his son Henry VIII, but what happened to the last of the Plantagenets during his reign is a tale beyond the scope of this book. It suffices to say that the Tudors, conscious of the frailty of their own dynastic title, were obsessed with security and seized any opportunity to eliminate or neutralise those whom they regarded as a threat. Since Henry VII was not a bloodthirsty man he counteracted the claims of Elizabeth of York's sisters by marrying them to men staunchly loyal to himself, and adopted a policy of conciliation towards Lincoln and young Buckingham. Only to Warwick was he merciless, an indication of how seriously people took Warwick's claim to the throne.

As soon as the Act of Settlement was passed, 'Titulus Regius' was repealed. Parliament thereby recognised the validity of Edward IV's marriage to Elizabeth Wydville and the legitimacy of their children, including Henry VII's future queen. Thus it was acknowledged, not only that Edward V had been the rightful King of England, but also that he and his brother were dead. Perhaps significantly, Parliament made no reference to them: the Act was repealed with only the sketchiest of references to its sensitive contents. The King's judges regarded 'Titulus Regius' as so objectionable that they were reluctant to recite its contents in case they should become notorious, and both they and the King, after studying the contents of the Act, concluded that Bishop Stillington had been the inspiration behind it. The judges offered to question Stillington but Henry refused because he had resolved to pardon the Bishop and desired no adverse publicity about Elizabeth of York's title, being of the opinion that 'least said, soonest mended'.

It might have been expected that, prior to his marriage, Henry would ask Parliament to consider the whole question of the precontract story and issue some statement refuting it, but he apparently considered it sufficient to have 'Titulus Regius' repealed and then suppressed. Whether he liked it or not, most people were of the view that his title to the throne would be greatly strengthened by marriage to Elizabeth of York, and the last thing Henry wanted was an enquiry into her legitimacy, in case it provided his enemies with grounds for denying her title and threatening his own future security. Nor did he wish to revive talk of the fact that earlier that year Elizabeth had been on the brink of marriage to Richard III and the affair between them had been the subject of furious court gossip. The least said about Elizabeth's status and her past the better, as far as Henry was concerned.

In November 1485 Henry VII commanded that 'Titulus Regius' be deleted from the Statute Books in the interests of his policy of reconciliation. The Parliament Roll of 1484 was suppressed and all official documents referring to the Act destroyed. By royal command, anyone having in their possession a copy of it was required to relinquish it to the Lord Chancellor by Easter 1486 on pain of imprisonment and a fine, 'so that all things said and remembered in the said Act may be for ever out of remembrance and forgot'. The text of 'Titulus Regius' was, of course, incorporated into the *Second Continuation of the Croyland Chronicle*, which was completed in the spring of 1486. Several copies of the *Chronicle* were made but nearly all of these, and the original, were destroyed. Thus, when Tudor historians came to write their versions of recent events, they had no access to this valuable source. Neither André, Carmeliano, Rous, Vergil or More ever saw Croyland, although they often corroborate it. So effective had the suppression of 'Titulus Regius' been that very few people had any idea what it had contained.

Vergil, Henry VII's official historian, may have known more than the rest, for he made special efforts to refute the idea that the legitimacy of Edward IV's children had ever been called into question, saying there was 'common report that in Shaa's sermon Edward's children were called bastards, and not King Edward himself, which is devoid of any truth'. According to Vergil, the precontract story was the product of rumour and Richard III had never used it to justify his usurpation.

This re-writing of history meant that Eleanor Butler's name disappeared from the records for more than a century. More knew of the precontract story but he was under the impression that Edward IV's partner in it had been Elizabeth Lucy, his mistress for a time. But in 1533 the Spanish ambassador to England, Eustache Chapuys, told the Hapsburg Emperor Charles V: 'People here say you have a better title than the present king [Henry VIII], who only claims by his mother, who was declared, by sentence of the Bishop of Bath [*sic*], a bastard, because Edward IV had espoused another wife before the mother of Elizabeth of York.' Chapuys may well have received his information from Yorkist families with long memories and a grudge against the Tudors.

During the early seventeenth century the historian George Buck unearthed the only surviving copy of the *Croyland Chronicle*, and for the first time in over 130 years the contents of 'Titulus Regius' were revealed to the public in print. Buck's discovery brought to his attention the fact that certain details, such as the identity of Eleanor Butler, had been censored by Henry VII, and he mistakenly concluded that this was because the contents of the Act were the true record of the facts. He did not view his discovery in the context of Henry VII's tenuous hold on the throne in 1485 when it was first suppressed and when most people believed that marriage to Elizabeth of York would ensure Henry's security as king. Buck did not realise that it was hardly surprising that Henry should wish to destroy such sensitive material, given that he might not be able to disprove its veracity without raising a dangerous debate or providing his enemies with grounds for rebellion. Upon such misconceptions was the revisionist movement founded.

Henry VII was resolved to have his predecessor attainted by Parliament even though it was not legally possible for an English monarch to be convicted of treason: to attaint Richard III would be to accuse him of committing a crime against himself. To circumvent this anomaly,

Henry announced that he was dating his reign from the day before Bosworth. Eyebrows shot up and many members registered their opposition to such a move. 'Oh, God!' exclaimed Croyland, 'what security shall our kings have henceforth, that in the day of battle they may not be deserted by their subjects?' But Henry was adamant. Parliament calmed down and did as it was bid, then obligingly attainted 'Richard, late Duke of Gloucester, and 28 others', most of whom had died at Bosworth.

The attainder against Richard was not specific when it came to detailing his crimes, which were listed as 'unnatural, mischievous and great perjuries, treasons, homicides and murders in shedding of infants' blood, with many other wrongs, odious offences and abominations, against God and man'. The Princes in the Tower were not mentioned by name, nor was Richard directly accused of their murder.

When Henry VII came to the throne, he might have been expected to expose the true facts about the murder of the Princes and to blazon Richard III's guilt before the world. It would have made good political capital to do so. However, he did nothing of the kind. After his accession, says Rous, 'the issue of cruel death of the sons of King Edward flared up again'. Henry himself was aware of this and it seems that, very early on, he ordered a 'diligent search' to be made in the Tower and elsewhere for the bodies of the Princes. John Rastell, writing in 1529, says the King had 'all places open and digged [but] the bones of the said children could never be found buried, neither in the Tower nor in none other place'. If Sir James Tyrell was questioned – and there is no evidence that he was, although it would have been logical to do so – he could either have denied any involvement with the murder, or he could have answered truthfully that he did not now know where the bodies were – the last he had heard was that Brackenbury had had them reinterred. For Henry to admit publicly that there was no trace of the bodies could only have had adverse effects: either it would have given rise to speculation that the Princes still lived, or it would provoke uprisings on behalf of imposters. Either way, Henry's throne would be placed in jeopardy.

Thus the King extended his policy of 'least said, soonest mended' to the Princes. He and many others involved in Buckingham's rebellion of 1483 had received intelligence that the boys had been murdered, and their subsequent disappearance coupled with the rumours circulating that year had been taken as confirmation of that information. Confident that they were dead, Henry had sworn to marry their sister and claim the crown through her, and in 1485 he had declared her and her siblings legitimate, something he would never have dared to do had he any suspicion that the Princes might be alive, for if so, Edward V would be the rightful king and York his heir. Henry believed that the Princes were dead, but he could not prove it: there were no bodies.

This placed the King in a dilemma. Had the bodies been found, he could have exhibited them, provided them with honourable royal burial and denounced Richard III as their murderer. Without the bodies he could do none of these things; instead, he was to be haunted throughout his reign by the fear that perhaps the intelligence fed to him in 1483 had been false or inaccurate, and that one or the other or both the Princes would turn up alive somewhere, or that some clever imposter would successfully impersonate one of them and wrest his crown from him.

Because of these factors, Henry never directly accused Richard III of murdering the Princes, nor could he be specific when it came to the wording of Richard's attainder: the phrase 'shedding of infants' blood' was a stock one in such documents, and the rumours about the Princes' fate were so notorious that it was doubtless assumed by Henry that people would know to what it referred and that no qualification was necessary. The King felt it was time that this old scandal died the death – brought to public debate, it might easily ruin him. There was to be no official Tudor version of the fate of the Princes, just a tacit assumption that rumour spoke the truth. Thus, when Henry VII addressed his troops before the Battle of Stoke in 1487 and told them, according to André, that Margaret of York, Duchess of Burgundy, was 'not unaware that her dynasty had been destroyed by her brother Richard', his remark could be taken to refer either to the House of York generally or to the Princes.

Many writers over the centuries have viewed Henry Tudor's silence on the matter of the Princes with suspicion, and concluded that he himself was responsible for their murder. There is, however, no evidence to support such a theory. Henry's behaviour convincingly suggests that he did not know what had happened to the Princes. He chose to play down the scandal of regicide that had tainted his future wife's family in the interests of hoped-for alliances with foreign powers, though this left him vulnerable to the threats posed over the next decade by a succession of pretenders purporting to be one of the Princes. As Yorkist malcontents regrouped and conspired against the new régime, Henry's inability to prove that the Princes were dead lent plausibility to their claims and his frantic efforts to trace the real identities of each of these pretenders is confirmation that he did not know for certain what had befallen the sons of Edward IV.

Nor did Henry go out of his way to blacken Richard's reputation – he did not need to. Much that is written about so-called Tudor propaganda is a myth. In modern times, when reviewing written accounts of recent history, such as the two World Wars or the lives of members of the present British royal family, we can clearly perceive what was originally written under strict codes of censorship and the authors' own discretion because changing times have enabled us to see earlier events in a new perspective, and the constraints of the past are no longer relevant. How much greater then would the constraints have been in an age when kings were all-powerful and '*ira principis mors est*' (the wrath of the prince is death)? Nowadays we expect history books to be objective and to cast new light upon a subject, revealing it 'warts and all'. Thus it was after Bosworth, when the constraints of a tyrannical régime were lifted and men were at last free to speak and write the truth as they perceived it. There was certainly a good deal of evidence and opinion derogatory to Richard III that was never committed to paper during his lifetime, but now it was possible for people to express the moral outrage they had for so long been obliged to keep to themselves. There is plenty of evidence that Richard's reputation was bad two years before his death, when his deeds were already notorious. Much of what was written under the Tudors certainly served as propaganda against Richard, but for propaganda to succeed it must be believable: it only works if it is based on fact, and there were many people still living who had known Richard III well.

From 1483 onwards rumour had nourished the belief, at home and abroad, that Richard III had murdered his nephews. By January 1486 this belief was accepted as the truth by most people, and Richard's death at Bosworth was seen by his contemporaries as a divine judgement. No Tudor propaganda could have fostered such widespread acceptance of Richard's guilt in the four months after Henry Tudor's accession. The fresh spate of rumours that followed that event was fuelled by stories already circulating before Richard's death. The difference now was that people were no longer afraid to speak the truth.

Late in 1485 King Henry rewarded those who had supported him: Morton, who later became Lord Chancellor of England and a cardinal; Stanley, who was created Earl of Derby; Jasper Tudor, who was created Duke of Bedford and married to Buckingham's widow, Katherine Wydville. Dorset, Sir Edward and Richard Wydville were all restored to their lands and honours, and Elizabeth Wydville had her widow's jointure and the rights and privileges of a dowager queen restored to her. The Act of Parliament confiscating her property was repealed, but Henry VII did not immediately return it to her; instead, he granted her an income of £400 per annum from more than seventy manors.

On 10th December, the day before Parliament went into recess for Christmas, the Commons petitioned the King to unite 'two bloods of high renown' and marry Elizabeth of York without further delay, 'which marriage they hoped God would bless with a progeny of the race of kings for the comfort of the whole realm'. The Lords seconded the request and the King was pleased to consent. A papal dispensation had already been applied for.

Since Henry's accession Elizabeth had been deferred to as the future Queen of England. On 11th December the King gave orders for the wedding preparations, including a great tournament, to be put in hand. It seems likely that Henry and Elizabeth were already sharing a bed: their first child was born eight months after their wedding, seemingly a full-term baby, whose early arrival excited comment.

In January 1486 the papal legate in England advised the King that the dispensation was on its way and that the marriage might go ahead. The famous union of the red and white roses took place on 18th January at Westminster Abbey amidst great celebrations and rejoicing and a welter of propaganda about the significance of the event. The marriage brought Henry the support of all but the most committed Yorkists as well as the indisputable right to the crown, and the rejoicing of the people at the marriage was proof indeed that few had ever doubted that the new queen was the true representative of the Yorkist line. And great was the King's satisfaction when he received the Pope's dispensation and found that His Holiness had threatened with excommunication any person daring to challenge his title.

Little is known of the relationship between Henry and Elizabeth. Henry was a faithful husband but apparently reserved and distant. Bacon says 'he showed himself no very indulgent husband towards her, though she was beautiful, gentle and fruitful. But his aversion towards the House of York was so predominant in him as it found place not only in his wars and councils but in his chamber and bed.' This aversion may have had its roots in Henry's awareness of Elizabeth's earlier infatuation with Richard III. She, continues Bacon, 'could do nothing with him. To her he was nothing uxorious. But, if not indulgent, he was companionable and respective, and without personal jealousy.' The Spanish ambassador was of the opinion that the Queen was in need of 'a little love'. He noted that she resented the influence wielded over the King and the royal household by her mother-in-law, the Lady Margaret Beaufort. The Prior of Santa Cruz states that because of this Elizabeth 'suffered under great oppression and led a miserable and cheerless life'. Nevertheless there developed over the years a certain affection between the royal couple, as evinced in 1502 when they consoled each other most movingly after the death of a child.

Both were good and loving parents. Vergil states they had eight children, four boys and four girls. Only three lived to adulthood: the future Henry VIII, Margaret, who became Queen of Scots, and Mary, who became Queen of France. Arthur was the eldest child, born, says Bacon, 'in the eighth month, as the physicians do prejudge', but 'strong and able'. Fuller, in his *Church History*, says Arthur was '*partus octomestris*, yet vital and vigorous, contrary to all the rules of physicians'. His father created him Prince of Wales and spent many years negotiating a brilliant marriage for him with Katherine of Aragon, daughter of the Spanish sovereigns, Ferdinand and Isabella.

Busily occupied with successive pregnancies and her children, Queen Elizabeth took no part in political life. 'The Queen is beloved because she is powerless,' observed the Spanish ambassador; 'she is kept in subjection by the mother of the King.' This was a deliberate policy of Henry VII, designed to keep Elizabeth from meddling in politics as her mother had done. He endowed her with a mere two-thirds of the estates Elizabeth Wydville had enjoyed, and kept her pitifully short of money, so that she was always in debt and was forced to pawn her plate or borrow funds from her servants. Her household accounts bear witness to the fact that her gowns were repeatedly mended, turned and re-trimmed, and her shoes adorned with cheap tin buckles. Evidence in royal letters shows that Margaret Beaufort even made all the important decisions concerning the royal children. Small wonder that Elizabeth of York chose as her motto the legend 'Humble and Penitent', or that her innate sensuality was dissipated by a passionless marriage, religious observances and charitable works. She had achieved her ambition to become queen, but it is doubtful if she had much joy of it.

19

Pretenders

Henry VII's obvious alarm at the advent of successive pretenders to his throne in the course of his reign is evidence enough that he did not know the details of the Princes' fate. He had believed them to be dead – but was it just possible that one of them had survived?

Had Henry been able to parade the Princes through London, as he once did with the Earl of Warwick after the pretender Lambert Simnel had claimed to be Clarence's heir, then he would have effectively crushed all such pretensions. Instead, the King and his advisers spent considerable time and effort in painstakingly tracing the identity of each of these pretenders, of whom the most prominent were Lambert Simnel and Perkin Warbeck.

Lambert Simnel's origins are still shrouded in some mystery. André says that when the rumours about the Princes flared up again, 'seditious men hatched another novel evil. They maliciously put up a certain boy as the son of Edward IV.' This conspiracy was hatched in the summer of 1486 in the vicinity of Oxford, and was almost certainly the brainchild of John de la Pole, Earl of Lincoln, who lived at nearby Ewelme, not far from Minster Lovell, the seat of the fugitive Lord Lovell, who became a party to the conspiracy. Both men had little cause to love Henry VII. It appears that they had made contact with an Oxford priest of lowly birth, one Richard Symonds, who had in his care a boy of about eleven allegedly called Lambert Simnel. The priest had reared and educated the boy and instructed him in courtly manners.

Symonds' loyalties were with the children of Edward IV. Vergil hints that he had purposed to 'represent the lad as being born of royal stock' during Richard III's reign. Now Symonds conspired with Lincoln and his associates to present Simnel to the English people as the younger of the two Princes, Richard, Duke of York. It is probable, however, that Lincoln's true intention was to seize the crown for himself, as the nephew of Edward IV and Richard III, once the planned coup met with success.

Simnel was duly coached in his role and prepared to impersonate York. Late in 1486 he was sent to Ireland where many people were sympathetic to the Yorkist cause: for thirty years members of the House of York had served as Lieutenants of Ireland, and their rule had brought benefits to the Irish. At the same time, doubtless prompted by an urgent request from Lincoln, Margaret of Burgundy, the sister of Edward IV and Richard III, began raising money and troops in the Low Countries in support of the conspiracy.

By early 1487 Henry VII had learned what was happening, but by then Simnel was no longer pretending to be York. He now claimed to be the Earl of Warwick, who was, of course, a prisoner in the Tower. Henry and his advisers rightly regarded Simnel, young as he was, as a dangerous threat to the throne and the security of the realm.

On 2nd February the Council met to discuss the crisis. Amongst other matters the affairs of Elizabeth Wydville also came under scrutiny and, says Vergil, it was resolved 'that [she] should lose and forfeit all her lands and possessions because she had voluntarily submitted herself and her daughters to the hands of King Richard, whereat there was much wondering' – understandably, since she had committed this misdemeanour three years before and Henry had made no move against her for eighteen months: indeed, up to now he had behaved towards her with courtesy and respect and had chosen her as a sponsor for Prince Arthur. Certainly her surrender of her daughters to Richard III had been a major setback to Henry Tudor's cause, but she had had no choice at the time. Henry must have known this, and it is likely that the real reason for Elizabeth Wydville's disgrace was something quite different. What this was has been the subject of considerable conjecture.

Bacon says that Elizabeth was 'at this time extremely discontent with the King, thinking her daughters not advanced but depressed'. This attitude may have communicated itself to Henry VII who, ever suspicious, became convinced that the Queen Dowager was plotting against him, or was even involved in the Simnel conspiracy. As Bacon observed, 'None could hold the book so well to prompt and instruct this stage play as she could.' Yet there is no evidence that Elizabeth Wydville was an accomplice in the Simnel rebellion. She was hardly likely to espouse the cause of the son of Clarence or take any action that might prejudice her daughter's position or the future of her grandson.

On 20th February Parliament declared her estates forfeit and granted Elizabeth Wydville a pension of 400 marks per annum. Later that spring warrants were issued to officers of the Royal Exchequer to pay all issues from the confiscated estates to Elizabeth of York. In this we may perceive the real reason why Henry VII had disparaged his mother-in-law: while she was enjoying the revenues from properties normally used to dower a queen consort, his wife was being deprived of the property appertaining to her estate. Henry had no intention of supporting two queens, and by depriving Elizabeth Wydville of her lands he rid himself at a stroke of this inconvenience. He had also deprived the Queen Dowager of funds she might use against him. That he had his suspicions about the Wydvilles is confirmed by his imprisonment of Dorset in the Tower until after the rebellion. His later treatment of Elizabeth Wydville is evidence that he had probably believed her to have been culpable.

Having learned that she was deprived of her estates and the income from them, Elizabeth had no choice but to retire to a nunnery. Around 12th February 1487 she moved to Bermondsey Abbey, a fourteenth-century foundation long favoured by royal ladies. A beautiful, peaceful place, the abbey had elegant gardens and commanded a site on the Surrey shore of the Thames opposite the Tower of London. From its windows the ageing Queen could see across the river to the fortress wherein lay, she believed, the bodies of her sons. At Bermondsey she was assigned apartments once reserved for the use of the earls of Gloucester, and registered as a boarder.

Some revisionists have asserted that Elizabeth was 'banished' to Bermondsey – though there is nothing to suggest that she went there under duress – because she had discovered that Henry had been responsible for the murder of the Princes; it is said he wanted to silence her. Bacon alleges that during her retirement it was hazardous for any person to see or speak with her, but the circumstances of her life at Bermondsey from 1487 until her death give these assertions the lie. In no sense was Elizabeth a prisoner. Henry VII continued to refer to her as his 'right dear mother' and she visited court from time to time. In 1489 she was present when the Queen bore a daughter, Margaret, and afterwards she helped Elizabeth of York host a reception for foreign ambassadors. In 1490 her pension was increased to £400 per annum, and over the years she was given various grants by the Exchequer, such as payment for Christmas sundries and wines. Elizabeth Wydville died at Bermondsey, with her daughters round her, on 8th June, 1492, and was buried beside Edward IV in St George's Chapel, Windsor.

Henry's spies soon discovered the truth about Lambert Simnel's identity and he was proclaimed an imposter on 17th February, 1487. A few days later Lincoln fled in secret to Margaret of Burgundy in Flanders. On 29th February Henry had Warwick paraded through London, to demonstrate the falsity of Simnel's claim. After high mass at St Paul's, Warwick was allowed to converse with courtiers who had known him before being returned to the Tower. In March, Henry mobilised his forces in preparation for an invasion.

Many people were nevertheless duped by Simnel's supporters into believing in him. Some, of course, found it politically desirable to acknowledge his claims – Lincoln was one of them. By Whitsun 1487, when Lincoln landed in Ireland with an army provided by his aunt, there was panic in England at the prospect of another dynastic war. The Earl publicly recognised Simnel as his cousin Warwick, and played a prominent part when the boy was crowned 'Edward VI' in Dublin Cathedral on 24th May. Early in June, the rebel forces, led by Lincoln, crossed to England, but on 16th June they were massacred by Henry VII's army at the bloody Battle of Stoke. Lincoln was killed, and Simnel was taken prisoner. Lovell disappeared; over 200 years later a skeleton thought to be his was found sitting at a desk in a walled-up room at Minster Lovell.

The King's victory at Stoke was seen by his contemporaries as reaffirmation by the Almighty of the divine judgement made manifest at Bosworth. It left him in a much stronger position and he could afford to be merciful to the hapless boy who had been at the centre of the conspiracy. Simnel was put to work in the royal kitchens and later promoted to be the King's falconer, dying in 1525.

Who *was* Lambert Simnel? Born around 1475, he was described in Lincoln's attainder as the son of an Oxford joiner and organ-maker called Thomas Simnel. Henry VII, in a letter to the Pope, claimed he was illegitimate. However, there is no trace in fifteenth- and sixteenth-century English records of anyone by the name of Simnel, except for Richard Simnel, a canon of St Osyth's Priory, Essex, in the reign of Henry VIII who was probably Lambert's son. An account of the Battle of Stoke was written in 1487–9 by one of Henry VII's heralds: in the original manuscript, now in the British Library, reference is made to the pretender 'whose name was indeed John'. In a later transcription by the antiquarian John Leland that name has been changed to 'Lambert'. It seems likely that the boy's real name was not Lambert Simnel and that that name was chosen as a pseudonym, probably to find favour with the people of Flanders, one of whose favourite saints was St Lambert, whose reliquary in Liège Cathedral had been a gift from the late Duke of Burgundy, Margaret of York's husband. There is no reason to believe that 'Simnel' had any genetic connection with the royal family, nor that he was any other than 'common in all respects', as he himself admitted under interrogation.

One person who was certainly involved in the Simnel conspiracy, and suffered for it, was Bishop Stillington. He was apprehended and questioned in March 1487 but, despite not being charged with any crime, was kept under house arrest at Windsor Castle until his death in May 1491 to keep him from further mischief.

After Stoke, Henry VII set about consolidating his position. He had his queen crowned at last – her first pregnancy and then the rebellion had obliged him to defer this, much to his subjects' annoyance. In March 1488 he opened negotiations with Spain for the marriage of Katherine of Aragon to Prince Arthur, an alliance that would considerably increase the standing of the Tudor dynasty in Europe. But Henry was still by no means secure on his throne at this date: there is evidence that from 1488 onwards disaffected Yorkists were conspiring against him. In 1489, just as the marriage alliance with Spain was being successfully concluded, Henry began to be troubled by a new wave of rumours – probably originating with these Yorkist malcontents – that one of the Princes in the Tower still lived. Henry did not know it then but this was the opening fanfare for yet another pretender.

This second, more serious, conspiracy probably originated with Margaret of Burgundy. In the autumn of 1491 a young man called Perkin Warbeck appeared in Ireland, calling himself the Earl of Warwick. But almost immediately, on the advice of prominent White Rose loyalists, he changed his identity to that of Richard, Duke of York, the younger of the Princes in the Tower. The pro-Yorkist Irish soon rallied to support him.

News of this new imposture caused Henry VII the greatest concern. 'This lad who calls himself Plantagenet', as he referred to Warbeck, with his strong White Rose backing, posed a serious threat to the crown as more and more Yorkist partisans offered him their loyalty. In time, Warbeck would secure the recognition of most of the princes of Europe, which made him even more of a danger. In March 1492 he was welcomed as a visiting sovereign at the French court and lorded it there for several months. But in November, when England and France signed the Treaty of Etaples, Charles VIII undertook not to grant political asylum to any more pretenders to the English crown. Warbeck fled to Flanders where Margaret of Burgundy whole-heartedly acknowledged him as her long-lost nephew and fêted him as the rightful King of England. Her stepson-in-law, the Archduke Maximilian, ruler of the Low Countries, followed suit.

News of these events came, says Bacon, 'blazing and thundering into England', causing people to take the pretender rather more seriously and to wonder whether the Princes in the Tower had been murdered after all. Many chose to believe that Warbeck was in fact York and attached themselves to his cause. But by July 1493, Henry VII's spies had uncovered Warbeck's true identity, and the King was able to write to Sir Gilbert Talbot that the pretender was just 'another feigned lad, called Perkin Warbeck, born at Tournai in Picardy, which at his first [coming] into Ireland called himself the bastard son of King Richard, and after that the son of the Duke of Clarence, now the second son of our father, King Edward the Fourth, whom God assoil.'

Armed with this knowledge, Henry made a formal protest to the government of Flanders about harbouring an imposter to his throne, and when this was ignored, he risked England's commercial prosperity by imposing a ban on trade with the Low Countries. At this time English supporters of Warbeck were still making the journey to

Flanders to offer him their allegiance. Maximilian ignored Henry's remonstrances and took Warbeck to Vienna with him to represent England at his own father's funeral. After his return to Flanders in 1493, Warbeck crossed to Ireland, intending to use it as a spring-board for an invasion of England. In October 1494, Henry VII sent the redoubtable Sir Edward Poynings to Ireland with instructions to eject the pretender. A month later the King pointedly created his second son Henry, aged three, Duke of York, in a very public ceremony.

Meanwhile, Henry's agents had discovered and rounded up Warbeck's chief supporters in England. Most were arrested late in 1494, but the biggest fish of all, Sir William Stanley, brother of the Earl of Derby, and brother-in-law to the king's mother, was netted in January 1495 and executed the following month. This deprived the pretender of any cohesive support in England.

By March 1495 Maximilian was beginning to grow weary of his guest, who had been forced to return from Ireland to Flanders, and he urged Warbeck to invade England and take what he claimed was his birthright. That summer, Henry VII had his realm placed on invasion alert, and in July Warbeck's pathetic attempt to land at Deal was foiled by soldiers guarding the coast. After returning for a short while to Flanders, Warbeck attempted Ireland once more, but was driven away by Poynings at Waterford in late July, 1495.

James IV of Scotland now expressed himself sympathetic to Warbeck's cause, glad to have an opportunity of embarrassing Henry VII. In November the pretender took refuge at the Scottish court where he was royally received and given one of the King's kinswomen as his wife, though in February 1496 Maximilian withdrew his support under the terms of a treaty, the 'Magnus Intercursus', he had signed with Henry VII, which restored trade between the two countries.

By now, Warbeck's credibility had been badly impaired. In 1496 James planned an invasion of England, not so much on Warbeck's behalf but to suit his own ends. In the event, Scots incursion, mounted in September, turned out to be no more than a border raid, over in twenty-four hours. James was disgusted when the squeamish Warbeck expressed outrage over the needless pillaging and destruction of English property, and thereafter made it clear to the pretender that his presence in Scotland was not welcome.

In June 1497 Henry VII successfully quelled a rebellion by the men of

Cornwall against the harsh taxes levied to finance the country's defences against the Scots. To avoid war, Henry instructed his envoys in Scotland to press for Warbeck's extradition, and a day after they did so he was expelled from Scotland with his wife, and sailed to Cork in Ireland. On 7th September, having dodged Poynings' forces, he landed at Cornwall and marched with his supporters on Exeter, gathering an army of yeomen and country folk on the way. Henry VII, learning of his advance, sent a great force against him, following behind himself with reinforcements. On 17th September Warbeck laid siege to Exeter but the city was ably defended by the Earl of Devon, and he was driven off the next day. Three days later he moved to Taunton, where he learned that the royal army was bearing down on him, and, abandoning his ragged force to their fate, he escaped and galloped south for the coast, but was apprehended on 5th October and brought before King Henry.

Henry was remarkably lenient with Warbeck. He sent him to London, extracted a confession from him without resorting to torture, and initially placed him in the Tower. After a short time he allowed him to live under guard at court, but not to sleep with his wife, who lived under the Queen's protection. Warbeck was at court for eighteen months, but by June 1498 the silken chains that bound him had begun to chafe and he tried to escape. He was caught within hours, and this time Henry VII was not so forbearing. He had Warbeck placed in close confinement in the Tower, cut off from the light of day. Men who saw him a year later were shocked at how the experience had aged him.

Yet still it did not sap his penchant for intrigue. In a cell near him the Earl of Warwick lived out his dreary existence. It seems almost certain that in August 1499 an *agent provocateur* was planted amongst the gaolers by the government to lure both Warbeck and Warwick into conspiracy, with a view to annihilating two threats to the security of the realm. Why else should Warwick, who had been kept so solitary and close that it was rumoured he was dead be housed in close proximity to the perilous Warbeck and allowed to communicate with him?

The government's ploy worked: the two prisoners plotted to escape and overthrow the King. On 12th November, 1499, the Council were told of this and ordered the arrest of both men. Four days later Warbeck was tried and condemned to death. Warwick was arraigned and sentenced on 19th November. Of him, it was said by Vergil that he could not tell a goose from a capon, and it was believed by many that he had not had the wits to resist being led into the conspiracy, nor had he had any treasonous intent.

Warbeck was executed on 23rd November, 1499, at Tyburn, after publicly swearing that he was not the son of Edward IV. His scaffold confession was afterwards printed and widely circulated by order of the King. Warwick was beheaded on Tower Hill a few days later, although most people believed him innocent. His death was deemed necessary, not so much because of his involvement with Warbeck, but because Ferdinand of Aragon was refusing to allow his daughter Katherine to come to England while he lived, a potential threat to the crown. The deaths of Warwick and Warbeck certainly removed the worst menaces to Henry VII's security. There were no more imposters after 1499.

The fact that Perkin Warbeck managed to maintain his imposture for so long has, over the years, led many writers to assert that he was indeed Richard of York, or at least a scion of the House of York. 'This,' wrote Bacon, 'was a finer counterfeit stone than Lambert Simnel. He was a youth of fine favour and shape. He had been from his childhood such a wanderer it was hard to hunt out his nest and parents.' Bacon felt sure that some hushed-up scandal was attached to Warbeck's birth; he had learned that Edward IV had stood godfather to the son of a converted Jew, and assumed that this son was really the King's bastard, fostered on a Jewish family. The truth of the matter was that the King had stood godfather to the Jewish Sir Edward Brampton on his conversion to the Christian faith, and Sir Edward was later Warbeck's employer. On the false assumption that Warbeck was Edward IV's bastard, Bacon wrote: 'It was ordained that the winding ivy of a Plantagenet should kill the true tree itself.'

What impressed people about Warbeck were his dignity, his regal bearing, his knowledge of court matters and of the royal house. His acceptance by a succession of European crowned heads led many to believe that he must indeed be York, or at least a bastard of the house of York. His appearance seemed to confirm this: a drawing of him survives in the French manuscript known as the '*Receuil d'Arras*' and shows a young man with long fair hair, a minor squint or cast in one eye and features bearing a strong resemblance to those of Edward IV. In 1497 the Venetian ambassador saw Warbeck at Henry VII's court and described him as a 'well-favoured young man, 23 years old', thus placing his birthdate around 1473–4 – York was born in August 1473. But the Milanese ambassador thought him 'not handsome; indeed, his left eye rather lacks lustre, but he is intelligent and well-spoken'. His attributes were all, alas, skin deep, for while he was clever enough to maintain his imposture for several years, when it came to prosecuting his claims he showed himself inept and cowardly, faults that would bring about his ruin.

Warbeck, posing as York, was ever ready to recount the tale of what had happened to him in the Tower. In the autumn of 1493 he described this in a letter to Ferdinand and Isabella of Spain, in which he declared that he was indeed the son of Edward IV, that his name was Richard Plantagenet, and that he had been secretly spared by the murderers of his brother, Edward V. He was careful not to accuse either Richard III or Henry VII of the murder. Once his brother was dead, he said, he had been entrusted 'to a gentleman who had received orders to destroy him but who, taking pity on his innocence, had preserved his life and made him swear on the sacrament not to disclose for a certain number of years his birth and lineage'. From 1483–91 he had lived abroad in a variety of places and been in the care of two guardians, until one died and the other – Sir Edward Brampton – returned to England, leaving him at a loose end in Portugal. It was at this point that he went to Ireland and was recognised as the long-lost Duke of York. How the Irish recognised York, who had spent his life until the murder in England and was not well-known even there, is not satisfactorily explained.

This unsubstantiated account received short shrift from the Spanish sovereigns, who did not believe it, as is proved by a note to that effect written on the letter. Nevertheless, other monarchs did recognise Warbeck as York, affirming they had seen birthmarks that satisfied them of his identity.

The possibility that Yorkist blood did flow in Warbeck's veins cannot be discounted, although the evidence for it is tenuous. Recognition by other princes was not proof of his identity, since they undoubtedly found it to their advantage politically to acknowledge his claim, given the fact that all of them, at one time or other, desired to embarrass Henry VII.

It is hardly conceivable that Warbeck could have been York. He, himself denied it with his dying breath, and his earlier account of his escape from his brother's murderers does not bear close scrutiny. Nor is it likely that he was a bastard son of Edward IV conceived during the King's exile in the Low Countries in 1470–71 and fostered with the Warbeck family, as Margaret of Burgundy, in 1498, and Warbeck himself, in 1497 and 1499, admitted that he was not the son of Edward IV. The future Richard III was also in exile in Flanders in 1470–71 – he could conceivably have fathered Warbeck, who claimed first of all to be his bastard son.

The Calendar of State Papers in the archives of the Spanish government states that the Archduke Maximilian alleged in later years that Warbeck was actually the bastard son of Margaret of Burgundy by the Bishop of Cambrai. In 1492 Margaret had done her utmost to convince 'all that he was indeed Richard, son of her brother Edward'. She would have been able to do this with plausible conviction in the knowledge that the boy was of Plantagenet blood, and it is true that the people of Flanders and many others believed her. But in 1498, when Margaret learned that Warbeck had sworn that she knew as well as himself that he was not the son of King Edward, the Duchess wrote in secret to Henry VII and craved his pardon for having supported the pretender, whom she now acknowledged an imposter. Her emissary was the Bishop of Cambrai, who, by a series of diplomatic manoeuvres, managed to negotiate a reconciliation. During his visit he asked to see Warbeck, who was by then a prisoner in the Tower, and was appalled at the change in the young man, who might have been his son.

In his confession of 1497, Warbeck himself declared he was the son of John Warbeck, or Osbeck, and Katherine de Faro, his wife, both converted Jews living in Tournai where John was a minor official. When Peter (or Peterkin, as he was known) was small, the family had lived for a time in London, where John Warbeck earned a living by supplying carpets to the royal court, by means of which employment he may have gained information that his son would later find useful.

In 1484–5, according to his confession, Warbeck was sent to Antwerp to learn Flemish. After war forced him to return home to Tournai for a time, he went back to Antwerp to look after the market stall of a local merchant, but was struck down by illness for five months. His career as a salesman then continued until the summer of 1487, when he agreed to escort the wife of Sir Edward Brampton, a prominent Yorkist exile, to Portugal. He stayed there a year in the service of a knight before leaving of his own accord to see the world. A few months later he entered the employ of a Breton merchant called Pregent Meno. Meno dealt in luxury fabrics and Warbeck's job was to model these for customers. This was how he came to be in Ireland in 1488–9. Shortly afterwards, the plot to impersonate Warwick was hatched.

By his own admission, Warbeck was not Richard of York. Margaret of Burgundy admitted he was not the son of Edward IV. He could, conceivably, have been her bastard son or Richard III's. But most probably he was the son of John and Katherine Warbeck of Tournai, a man of straw used by unscrupulous men for their own ends.

Significantly, none of the pretenders in Henry VII's time – and Simnel and Warbeck were by no means the only ones – ever claimed to be Edward V. This was not so much because rumour had long proclaimed him to be dead, but because he was too well-known both at court and in London to be successfully impersonated. York was not well-known at all, and was a far safer target for imposters.

After the execution of Warbeck, no-one else claimed to be one of the Princes. Henry VII's summary justice had ensured that, and even if it had not, the King would soon have been able to deal with such persons speedily and effectively, for in 1502 Henry discovered the truth about the fate of the Princes.

20

Tyrell's Confession

Sir James Tyrell was in France when Bosworth was fought. Henry VII, on his accession, deprived him of his offices and Welsh estates, but restored them in February 1486, by which time Tyrell had crossed from Calais to offer the new King his allegiance.

He fared much better than most of those who had faithfully served Richard III. In the summer of 1486 the King, of his own volition, ordered two pardons to be issued to Tyrell; there is no evidence that these related to the murder of the Princes, as has sometimes been suggested, and they were probably concerned with his misplaced loyalty to Richard III. In July Tyrell was reappointed Governor of Guisnes in the Pale of Calais and left England, having accepted lands in France in lieu of his Welsh estates.

He remained in Guisnes for sixteen years, rendering faithful service to the King. He served as Henry's emissary on several diplomatic missions to the courts of Europe, and was created a Knight of the Body, a royal councillor and Constable of Guisnes. He visited England on occasion and took part in a tournament held in 1494 in celebration of Prince Henry's creation as Duke of York. Tyrell also refused to become involved with any pretender, and was praised by the King for his faithfulness.

But in the summer of 1501, Tyrell stepped out of line. The late John de la Pole, Earl of Lincoln, who had died fighting at Stoke in 1487, was the eldest of several sons born to Elizabeth Plantagenet, sister of Edward IV and widow of the Duke of Suffolk. Lincoln's next brother,

Edmund, was allowed by Henry VII to inherit the earldom of Suffolk but not the dukedom, because he had not the means to support it, and this rankled. The new Earl was a hot-headed, impetuous fool with grand designs on the throne of England, and in July 1501 he went voluntarily into exile in Flanders with his brother Richard, hoping to obtain support for their cause from Maximilian. On their way they visited Sir James Tyrell, who had probably known them as children during Richard III's reign and earlier and he unwisely offered them assistance.

Sir Richard Nanfan, Deputy Lieutenant of Calais, found out what Tyrell had done and that he had done it in the full knowledge that Suffolk was planning to overthrow Henry VII. This was treason of the first order and Nanfan duly reported what he knew to the Council in London, though Henry VII at first refused to believe it and others accused Nanfan of maliciously seeking to do Tyrell harm. However, when Sir Robert Curzon, described by Vergil as an agent of the King, laid before the Council information which corroborated Nanfan's allegations, Henry had to accept that Tyrell was guilty, and not only Tyrell, because there was now evidence that Lord William Courtenay (husband of the Queen's sister Katherine), William de la Pole (Suffolk's brother) and others were involved. The King suspected a far-reaching conspiracy against him, and in October 1501 ordered the arrest of all concerned, who were then publicly proclaimed traitors. Suffolk and his brother Richard were out of reach: Suffolk was not arrested until he was extradited to England in 1506, and not executed until 1513, and Richard de la Pole remained abroad, a thorn in the side of the Tudors until he was killed at the Battle of Pavia in 1525. But William de la Pole was incarcerated in the Tower and remained there, in relative comfort, until his death thirty-eight years later. Other conspirators, including Courtenay, were also imprisoned. A luckless few were executed.

Early in 1502 Henry VII, angry because Tyrell was still at liberty in Guisnes Castle, insisted that he be apprehended without delay. Tyrell refused to surrender to the King's officers and began to prepare the castle for a siege as the Calais garrison, loyal to Henry VII, took up its position outside the walls. Then Richard Fox, Bishop of Winchester and Lord Privy Seal, asked to speak with Tyrell, and was admitted to the castle, where he promised him, in the King's name, a safe-conduct to England, assuring him he was in no danger. Tyrell at length agreed to go with him, but he refused to surrender the castle, leaving his son Thomas to hold it against the King's force.

In Calais harbour a battleship waited to convey Tyrell to England. He boarded it under escort and was soon in conversation with John, Lord Dynham, the Lord Treasurer, when the Captain of the Guard informed him that, unless he ordered his son to surrender Guisnes Castle, he would be thrown overboard without delay. Tyrell complied, and both he and his son were arrested on board ship and put in chains. On arrival in England both were sent to the Tower.

'Very truth it is,' writes More, 'and well known that at such time as Sir James Tyrell was in the Tower for treason, both Dighton and he were examined and confessed the murder [of the Princes], but whither the bodies were removed they could nothing tell,' for they too had been misled by tales of a reburial.

No official record or transcript of Tyrell's confession survives today, but it must have existed at one time because More describes it as his chief source, implying that he had seen it, and the details in his account, which occur nowhere else, argue its authenticity. More may also have obtained some information from Mary Tyrell and other inmates of the Minories and from John Dighton. Bacon says that, after being interrogated, Dighton was set at liberty and granted a pension on condition that he left England and took up residence in Calais. He also states that Dighton was 'the principal means of divulging this tradition'. More, writing in the reign of Henry VIII, seems to have traced Dighton, for he knew he 'yet walks alive and in good possibility to be hanged ere he die', which suggests he had either returned from exile without permission, or was living a life of crime. Dighton's interrogation could only have taken place if Tyrell had revealed details of the murder and his accomplices under questioning. Otherwise, why would the government have gone to the trouble of tracing and examining Dighton also?

More implies in his account that Henry VII himself had divulged the contents of Tyrell's confession and had disclosed that Dighton was still alive and free. Bacon says the King 'gave out' that the statements of Tyrell and Dighton corroborated each other. However, there is no extant record of any public statement being made by the King about the death of the Princes, which argues that Henry VII probably 'gave out' his information to his trusted advisers only, many of whom were known to More.

More's account became accepted as the truth by every Tudor writer on the subject. Thanks to More, we have a good idea of what was in the confession, and the striking thing about More's account is that it substantiates many of the rumours, from as far back as 1483, and also the circumstantial evidence dating from Richard III's reign.

The revisionists have frequently disputed the fact that Tyrell ever made such a confession, but without backing their claim by convincing arguments. Here, after all, was an eye-witness account of the murder of the Princes, and it was believed to be the truth by a man of great learning and integrity who was in a position to check its veracity. Such powerful evidence cannot easily be ignored. It has been suggested that Tyrell was forced into making a confession to suit Henry VII's purposes. If so, why did he involve Dighton? It is far more likely that Tyrell, facing death, with nothing to lose and the hope of absolution and thereafter Heaven, was only too relieved to unburden himself. He was not necessarily looking for a reward, nor coerced by fear, but perhaps seeking the salvation of his soul. It is also significant that he was never charged with collusion in the murder.

It has been suggested that Henry VII fabricated this confession. If so, why did he not use it for propaganda purposes? Why bother to go to such trouble for nothing? There are very good reasons for accepting Tyrell's confession as genuine, but the fact remains that Henry VII did not publicise or make use of it. It would seemingly, for many reasons, have been to his advantage to accord the widest publicity to the information he had received, which he had after all been seeking for years: nevertheless there were equally compelling reasons why the confession should be suppressed.

Firstly, it would be in keeping with Henry's general policy of 'least said, soonest mended' with regard to the history of the House of York. Secondly, the King was hoping to preserve the precious alliance with Spain. Prince Arthur had just died and Henry was hoping to marry his widow, Katherine of Aragon, to the young Duke of York, now heir to the throne. But her father, King Ferdinand, had in the past expressed deep concern over the insecurity of the English crown; it was because of this that Henry had had Warwick executed. Therefore in the spring of 1502 the last thing that Henry wanted was adverse publicity about the fate of the Princes, especially since his son was not yet eleven and he himself was beginning to suffer symptoms of the disease, either cancer or tuberculosis, that was later to kill him.

Thirdly, the murder of the Princes had been very much to Henry's own advantage. Should he publicise Tyrell's involvement, people would view Tyrell's previous steady advancement under Henry VII as highly suspicious, seeing it as a reward for carrying out the murder on Henry's behalf. Henry had suffered enough public opprobrium for the killing of Warwick, and he dared not now accuse Tyrell, his faithful servant for sixteen years, for fear that people would lay the murder at his own door. He had seen what such rumours had done to Richard III's reputation. It was one thing to learn that the Princes were really dead, but quite another to be known to have favoured their murderer.

Lastly, Henry's chief motive in having Tyrell questioned had probably been his desire to trace the bodies of the children. Had he been able to do this he could have made out that the discovery of their remains had resulted from a search that he himself had ordered, and Tyrell's involvement need never have been referred to. But Tyrell, of course, firmly believed that the bodies had been removed to an unknown grave or even, if rumour spoke the truth, buried at sea. It is unlikely, therefore, that Henry ordered a search to be made at the original burial site, as the bodies of the children were not found. Hence the confession was virtually worthless to Henry – without the bodies he was still no further forward.

The fact that Henry VII made no use of Tyrell's confession therefore argues its authenticity. Its absence from official records and Vergil's history proves how politically sensitive the issue still was. Only years later was More able to find out the truth about it, and even then his sources were reluctant to be identified. Clearly the issue was still a sensitive one when More's book was written, and this may well be the reason why it was written for private circulation only.

On 2nd May, 1502, Sir James Tyrell was arraigned on a charge of high treason; his indictment specified that his crime was his traitorous association and correspondence with Suffolk. No mention was made of the murder of the Princes. Tyrell was found guilty, and on 6th May was beheaded on Tower Hill, apparently without making any speech to the watching crowd. A day later his son Thomas was also condemned to death, though Henry VII was merciful and spared his life. Three years later Thomas Tyrell managed to secure the reversal of the attainder on his father and himself.

21

The Skeletons in the Tower

Because Tyrell's confession was suppressed and More's account of it remained long unpublished, the fate of the Princes in the Tower remained a matter for speculation during the reigns of Henry VII and Henry VIII. More himself says that their deaths had 'so far come into question that some remain yet in doubt whether they were in King Richard's days destroyed or no'. It appears then that there were some who believed that the Princes were not dead and others who believed that Henry VII had murdered them. As we have seen, More, who had no reason to like Henry VII, was firmly of the opinion that Richard III was the guilty party. After More's book was published it rapidly gained acceptance as the most veracious account of what had actually happened and became the basis of all subsequent memoirs on the subject of the Princes written during the Tudor and early Stuart periods. Shakespeare's play, *Richard III*, derived its plot from Holinshed, who based his chronicle on Hall's, who used More's history almost word for word in his own chronicle.

Between them, More and Shakespeare did more than any other writers to publicise Richard III's evil reputation. By Shakespeare's time Richard had become the arch villain, capable of any crime, however terrible. More's history is a moral tale about tyranny; Shakespeare's play is a study of evil.

No further searches were made in the Tower for the bones of the Princes. Yet Edward V and York were not the only children to disappear in that grim fortress during a turbulent age. In November

249

1539, when Henry VIII sent his cousins, Henry Courtenay, Marquess of Exeter, and Henry Pole, Lord Montagu, to the Tower on a charge of conspiring to overthrow him, he ordered also the imprisonment of all the other members of their families including their sons, Edward Courtenay and Henry Pole, both aged twelve. Both Exeter and Montagu went to the block. Afterwards, the King ordered that Lady Exeter, her son Henry Pole and Henry's aged grandmother, Margaret Pole, Countess of Salisbury – daughter of Clarence and mother of Lord Montagu – remain in the Tower.

His Yorkist cousins had been a thorn in Henry's side for many years, and his former warmth towards the family had changed rapidly to bitter loathing after Cardinal Reginald Pole, Montagu's brother, had written a virulent tract denouncing his marriage to Anne Boleyn. Where the Pole family was concerned, Henry VIII now acted like a man obsessed, and this explains why he extended his vindictiveness to the innocent sons of Exeter and Montagu, who had played no part in any treasonable conspiracy, and why, because he was a Pole, young Henry fared worse than Edward Courtenay.

In 1541 a northern rebellion against the King gave Henry the excuse he needed to execute the ageing Countess of Salisbury, who was informed of her impending doom only a short time beforehand and whose sentence was carried out with horrific butchery. Henry Pole, then aged fourteen, was expected to follow her to the block, but even Henry VIII dared not risk alienating public opinion – already shocked at the fate of Lady Salisbury – by putting so young a person to death. Instead he ordered that the boy be placed in solitary confinement, and refused to allow him a tutor, although his cousin Edward Courtenay enjoyed such a privilege. The King intended that Henry Pole be 'poorly and strictly kept, and not desired to know anything'. Such treatment was not dissimilar to that meted out by Henry VII to Warwick half a century earlier.

Edward Courtenay remained a prisoner until he was released by Mary I in 1553, but it is certain that Henry Pole never left the Tower. He was alive in 1542, as a record of payment for his meals attests. But after that, he disappears from the records, and it can only be assumed that he died in the Tower, an event that would without doubt have been welcomed by Henry VIII.

Henry Pole may have died from natural causes or as a consequence of the rigours of his imprisonment – it has been suggested by several modern writers that he was starved to death. Certainly there was no-one close to him left alive to ask awkward questions, and it may well be that Henry VIII, once the furore about the execution of Lady Salisbury had died down, decided to be rid of her grandson. However he died, there were now at least three children buried in the Tower; for all we know, Henry Pole's bones may lie there still.

More than sixty years passed. Henry Pole was forgotten, but the tale of the Princes became an established part of Tudor folklore. The Tudor dynasty ended with the death of Elizabeth I in 1603, to be replaced by the Scottish Stuarts in the person of James VI and I, great-grandson of Henry VII's daughter Margaret.

Between 1603 and 1614, during the time that Sir Walter Raleigh and Lord Grey de Wilton were prisoners in the Tower, a man called John or Jonathan Webb found, in an underground pipe or tunnel within the Tower, what were thought to be the bones of the Princes. However, it was quickly established that the bones were those of an ape from the Tower menagerie, who had somehow climbed into the tunnel, become trapped there, and perished.

The French chronicler Molinet had stated in the late fifteenth century that the Princes had been walled up in a secret chamber within the Tower and left there to starve to death. A statement made by a Mr Johnson and preserved in Volume LXXXIV of *Archaeologia*, records not only the finding of the bones of the ape but also the discovery in 1647 of the skeletons of two children, aged about six and eight and thought to be male, in a small room 7 or 8 feet square, which was found behind a wall in the passageway of the King's Lodging in the royal apartments of the Tower. The room had been sealed and the children apparently left there to perish. Those present when the discovery was made assumed that the bones were those of the Princes, although the estimated ages of the children appears to make this unlikely. Unfortunately there is no way of proving or disproving the theory because there is no further mention of these bones in the records.

During the 1650s Oliver Cromwell ordered that the old mediaeval royal apartments to the south of the White Tower be demolished. The job, however, was only half completed at his death, and the ruins stood undisturbed until 1674, when Charles II decided to have the site cleared 'of all contiguous buildings'.

In an upper storey of the White Tower may be found the Chapel of St John the Evangelist, one of the most perfectly preserved examples of Norman architecture in existence. It was a favourite place of worship of the mediaeval kings of England, who had their own private means of access to it by way of an external castellated turret on the left hand corner of the White Tower, facing the river. This turret, estimated to have been about 20 feet square and to have stood at two-thirds of the height of the keep, housed a stairway, lit by two lancet windows, which led up to a door 14 feet above ground level; this is the door through which visitors to the White Tower enter today. The door used to open on to a landing from which arose a spiral staircase leading to the chapel; today, this staircase is walled up. In 1674 this turret or 'fore-building' was crumbling, and the workmen engaged by Charles II demolished it. Then they began to dismantle the staircase, the foundations of which went very deep.

On 17th July, 1674, just as this task was nearing completion, the workmen made an astonishing find. The contemporary accounts of what they discovered are not as precise as we could wish, but they make it clear that whilst digging at the base of the staircase, or in or near its foundations, the workmen came upon a wooden chest at a depth of 10 feet below the ground. Inside the chest were the skeletons of two children: the taller child lay on its back, the smaller face down on top of it.

It was immediately assumed that these were the bodies of the Princes in the Tower. An anonymous eyewitness wrote: 'This day I, standing by the opening, saw working men dig out of a stairway in the White Tower the bones of those two Princes who were foully murdered by Richard III. They were small bones of lads in their teens, and there were pieces of rag and velvet about them.' They were, he adds, 'fully recognised to be the bones of those two Princes'. Twenty years later, the 1695 edition of Camden's *Britannia* carried the note that the bodies of the Princes, 'though some have written they were put into a leaden coffin and cast into the Black Deeps by the Thames Mouth by Sir Robert Brackenbury's priest, were found on July 17, 1674, by some workmen who were employed to take up the steps leading to the Chapel of the White Tower, which in all probability was the first and only place they were deposited in'.

The discovery provided the most compelling corroboration of Sir

Thomas More's account of the Princes' first burial: the bones had been found exactly where he had described, 'at the stair foot, meetly deep under the ground, under a great heap of stones'. Of course, there would have been a degree of subsidence of the ground over a period of 200 years, and it is not likely that the chest was originally buried as deep as 10 feet below the surface. Nevertheless, the common practice of mediaeval stonemasons was to fill in the hollow beneath a staircase with stones and rubble. This place of burial was probably chosen because of the privacy of the turret enclosing the stairs, which was a private way for the monarch's use. Tyrell's assistants had apparently dug a hole in the ground and then made a recess inward into the foundations of the staircase.

If these skeletons were not those of the Princes, then their discovery in this particular place was an astonishing coincidence. In the light of later forensic evidence it has been claimed by several revisionists that these bones could have belonged to any historical period: in the 1970s it was suggested that they could even have been Roman, given the Tower's long history. This cannot be so. The bones were discovered with 'pieces of rag and velvet about them'. According to information given to the author by a textile expert contacted through the Archaeological Resource Centre in York, velvet was invented in the 1400s in Renaissance Italy, and was not made in England before the sixteenth century. In the 1480s the wearing of imported velvets was restricted to persons of the highest rank, not only because it was so expensive but also because of the social conventions then prevailing. Even in the seventeenth century, velvet was a costly material available only to the well-to-do. The children whose bones were found in 1674 must therefore have been well-born and must have died in the fifteenth century at the earliest. They could not have been Roman because no material resembling velvet existed at that time. As no other pair of well-born children had disappeared in the Tower during the previous 200 years, it is a fair assumption – forensic evidence aside – that these were indeed the bones of the Princes.

The eyewitness who saw the bones unearthed says that on that day 'they were carefully put aside in a stone coffin or coffer'. It is thought that they had been damaged to some extent by the tools used by the workmen during their exhumation. Then it seems they were left alongside a pile of builders' rubbish on the site for a time, whilst news of their discovery was sent to King Charles II. It also appears that several people removed some of the bones as souvenirs at this time, and replaced them with animal bones from the rubbish heap.

Eventually, the King ordered that the skeletons be examined by the royal surgeon and a panel of experienced antiquaries, all of whom declared they were satisfied that the remains were indeed those of the Princes. According to Camden's *Britannia* (1695 edition), the bones remained in the Tower for four years, except for some few that were secured as curiosities by Elias Ashmole and sent to the Ashmolean Museum in Oxford. In 1678 Charles II asked Sir Christopher Wren 'to provide a white marble coffin for the supposed bodies of the two Princes'. The bones were translated from the Tower to Westminster Abbey and decently interred, according to Camden, 'under a curious altar of black and white marble' which may still be seen today, bearing the inscription:

> Here lie interred the remains of Edward V, King of England, and Richard, Duke of York, whose long desired and much sought after bones, after above an hundred and ninety years, were found by most certain tokens, deep interred under the rubbish of the stairs that led up to the Chapel of the White Tower, on the 17th of July in the year of our Lord 1674. Charles the Second, a most merciful prince, having compassion upon their hard fortune, performed the funeral rites of these unhappy Princes among the tombs of their ancestors, anno Domini 1678.

It is not known what the 'most certain tokens' that facilitated the identification of their bodies were, only that they were accepted as sufficiently convincing by those most qualified to judge at the time.

Those bones that had been sent to the Ashmolean Museum were recorded in a seventeenth-century catalogue of the museum's treasures. But in 1728, when the celebrated antiquarian Thomas Hearne went there and asked to see the bones, the keeper, Mr Whiteside, could not find them. All he could say was that he had seen them and remembered them as being 'very small, particularly the finger bones'. In 1933 a search was made in the museum for the bones, but they were not found.

During the first part of the twentieth century, strong pressure was brought to bear upon the authorities of Westminster Abbey to have the urn containing the supposed bones of the Princes opened and its contents re-examined in the light of new advances in medical science. The Abbey was – and still is – a Royal Peculiar, which means that both the Sovereign and the Home Secretary have to give permission for any of the tombs to be opened. In 1933, George V, bowing to public opinion, finally authorised the opening of the urn, and an examination of the bones therein was carried out in the Abbey precincts by Dr Lawrence E. Tanner, an eminent physician, archivist and Keeper of the Monuments at Westminster Abbey, and Professor W. Wright, a dental surgeon who was President of the Anatomical Society of Great Britain. Tanner's report on their findings was published in *Archaeologia* in 1934.

Tanner and Wright found, to begin with, that the urn contained all kinds of bones including animal bones which probably came from the rubbish heap on the excavation site at the Tower. Once the human bones were separated from these, Tanner and Wright discovered they had the incomplete skeletons of two children, the elder 4 foot 10 inches tall, and the younger 4 foot 6½ inches tall; both were of slender build with very small finger bones. Using dental evidence, they estimated that the elder child was twelve to thirteen years old (Edward V had been twelve years and ten months in September 1483) and the younger nine to eleven years old (York was ten in September 1483). Because the bones were pre-pubertal their sex could not be established. Nor could the age of the bones.

Wright stated that the elder child had certainly suffered from extensive, chronic bone disease – probably osteomyelitis – affecting both sides of the lower jaw; this 'could not fail to have affected his general health', causing painful swelling and inflammation of the lower gums, making the patient miserable and irritable. In the light of this evidence it is significant that Dr Argentine was attending Edward V shortly before his disappearance; both Argentine and More confirmed that the boy was then sunk in apathy and depression, which may have been partly due to the discomfort in his jaw.

Wright stated also that the structure of the jaws and bones in each skeleton indicated a familial link, and further claimed that a red stain on the facial bones of the elder child was a blood stain caused by suffocation.

Tanner and Wright felt that there were too many coincidences between the evidence of the bones and the evidence of history: who else could these bones belong to but the Princes? Wright thought the evidence 'more conclusive than could, considering everything, reasonably have been expected'. This was a blow to those revisionists who had questioned the seventeenth-century identification of the skeletons. For, as the report concluded, if they were those of the Princes, 'by no possibility could either or both have been still alive on August 22nd 1485', the day of Bosworth. In other words, on the basis of the children's ages at the time of their death, it was likely that they had died in 1483 and that More's account of their deaths came very near to the truth since 'the evidence that the bones in the urn are those of the Princes is as conclusive as could be desired'.

Since 1934 there have been several attempts to discredit the findings of Tanner and Wright. In the 1970s and 1980s the Richard III Society made several unsuccessful attempts to persuade the Dean and Chapter of Westminster Abbey to apply for royal permission to re-exhume the bones for further tests, on the grounds that significant scientific advances since 1933 could now establish the ages of the children with greater accuracy, new chemical tests could perhaps determine their sex, radio-carbon dating could estimate the age of the bones to within twenty-five years, and biochemical analysis could resolve the vexed question of whether the facial stain on the elder child's skull is in fact blood. The Dean and Chapter, however, are reluctant to disturb the royal bones within their precincts and do not consider a new examination either desirable or worthwhile.

Medical experts called upon in recent years to examine the forensic evidence for the identification of the skeletons have therefore had to rely on the report and photographs of Wright and Tanner. Within these constraints, there now exists a substantial body of medical opinion on the subject. In 1955 Richard III's revisionist biographer Paul Murray Kendall enlisted the assistance of four experts: Dr W. M. Krogman, Professor of Physical Anthropology in the Graduate School of Medicine of the University of Pennsylvania; Dr Arthur Lewis, an orthodontist of Dayton, Ohio; Professor Bertram S. Kraus of the Department of Anthropology of the University of Arizona; and Dr Richard Lyne-Pirkis of Godalming, Surrey. Professor A. R. Myers, the eminent mediaeval historian, canvassed the opinion of Professor R. G. Harrison, Professor of Anatomy at the University of Liverpool. In

1978 Elizabeth Jenkins, author of *The Princes in the Tower*, obtained an opinion from Mr F. M. Lind, BDS Lond., LDS, RCS Eng., while in 1981 the late Professor Charles Ross, author of the most outstanding biography of Richard III, sought the opinions of Dr Juliet Rogers, a specialist in the study of ancient bones, Dr J. H. Musgrove, an anatomist, and Professor E. W. Bradford, a professor of dental surgery. Dr Jean Ross, senior lecturer in anatomy at Charing Cross Hospital Medical School, gave 'evidence' at the television trial of Richard III in 1984, and in 1987 there was a lively debate between *The Times'* archaeology correspondent Norman Hammond, Dr Theya Molleson and a Mr William White in the correspondence columns of *The Times* on the subject of the bones in the urn.

The findings of the experts were in all cases consistent with the bones being those of the Princes in the Tower. Although some questioned the findings of Tanner and Wright they did not discredit them; indeed, their conclusions substantiated them.

With regard to the age of the children, most of the experts preferred to rely on the dental evidence, which mostly showed that the age of the elder child was at least eleven years and at most thirteen years. The age of the younger child was more difficult to determine, but was within the range of seven to eleven and a half years. These findings were consistent with the deaths of the children occurring in September 1483.

Dr Ross found indications of a blood relationship between the skeletons in the bones of the skull, and the number and type of permanent teeth missing, a condition known as hypodontia. Dr Molleson agreed that these factors were strongly suggestive of kinship because of the rarity of such bone formations; William Wright disputed this on the grounds that research showed this was true of modern skeletons but not of seventeenth-century Londoners, but Dr Molleson had compared her findings with tests carried out on mediaeval skeletons found in Winchester, in which the incidence of hypodontia was the same as it is today. Dr Molleson also concluded that there was every likelihood of a blood relationship with Anne Mowbray, York's wife and a third cousin of the Princes, whose bones had been subjected to forensic tests in 1965, and whose permanent teeth were also incomplete.

Dr Molleson was the only expert to pronounce on the sex of the children, it being agreed by the rest that it was extremely hard to ascertain the gender of pre-pubertal skeletons. She compared the dental and skeletal maturity of Anne Mowbray's bones with the bones in the urn and concluded that the latter were probably both pre-pubescent boys.

All the experts agreed that the age of the bones could not be determined from the evidence available to them. Dr Juliet Rogers stated that the most that could be said was that the children died before 1674, and added that they could even be Roman. As we have seen, if one accepts the textile evidence, this could not have been so.

None of the experts were able to determine the cause of death. Dr Ross and Dr Lyne-Pirkis could find no evidence of any facial blood-stain on the elder child, but Dr Krogman did concede that the mark there could have been blood resulting from the rupturing of vessels during suffocation, even though it was usually only facial tissues that were damaged in such circumstances. Dr Musgrove agreed that there might be a blood stain, but stated that proof could only be obtained by biochemical analysis.

The weight of medical evidence may not be conclusive, but it in no way excludes the likelihood that these bones were those of the ill-fated Princes in the Tower; indeed, it corroborates Sir Thomas More's evidence and the findings of Wright and Tanner, and in its own right strongly suggests that the original identification of the bones in the seventeenth century was correct. No other pair of boys of rank disappeared in the Tower between 1483 and 1674: to suggest otherwise is really to stretch coincidence too far. It is true that the medical evidence presently available does not identify the cause of death of the children, nor their murderer. Nevertheless, it confirms that, if these were the Princes -- and there is no reason to suppose otherwise -- then they were dead by the end of 1483. And if that is the case, given all the other evidence already discussed in previous chapters, then only one man could have been responsible for their deaths: Richard III.

Genealogical Table:
Lancaster and York

Lancaster and York: A Simplified Genealogy

† = murdered
✗ = killed in battle
ex. = executed

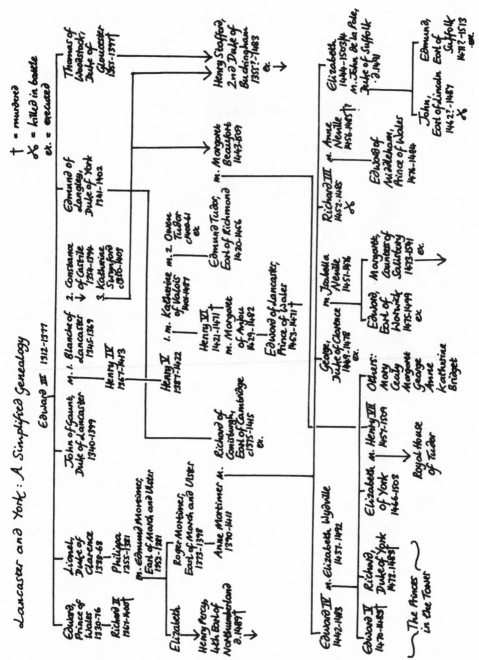

Edward III 1312-1377

Select Bibliography

Primary Sources

General Works

Annals of Ulster (4 vols, ed. William Hennessey and B. MacCarthy, Belfast, 1888–1901)

Archaeologia, or Miscellaneous Tracts relating to Antiquity (102 vols, Society of Antiquaries, 1773–1969)

Calendar of Close Rolls, Edward IV–Richard III (3 vols, Rolls Series, HMSO, 1927–54)

Calendar of Documents Relating to Scotland, Vol IV, 1357–1509 (ed. J. Bain, 1888)

Calendar of Papal Registers relating to Great Britain and Ireland (HMSO, 1960)

Calendar of Patent Rolls Preserved in the Public Record Office:
Edward IV, 1461–1467 (Rolls Series, HMSO, 1897)
Edward IV, Henry VI, 1467–1477 (Rolls Series, HMSO, 1900)
Edward IV, Edward V, Richard III, 1476–1485 (Rolls Series, HMSO, 1901)

A Collection of Ordinances and Regulations for the Government of the Royal Household made in divers reigns from King Edward III to King William and Queen Mary (Society of Antiquaries of London, 1790)

A Collection of Wills of the Kings and Queens of England from William the Conqueror to Henry VII (ed. J. Nichols, Society of Antiquaries, 1780)

The Complete Peerage of England, Scotland, Ireland, Great Britain and the United Kingdom (13 vols, ed. V. Gibbs, H. A. Doubleday, D. Warrand, Thomas, Lord Howard de Walden, and G. White, St Catherine's Press, 1910–59)

English Historical Documents, Vol. IV, 1327–1485 (ed. A. R. Myers, Eyres & Spottiswoode, 1969)

Excerpta Historica (ed. S. Bentley, 1831)

The Great Chronicle of London (ed. A. H. Thomas and I. D. Thornley, 1938)

The Harleian Miscellany (ed. W. Oldys and T. Park, 1810)

Letters and Papers illustrative of the Reigns of Richard III and Henry VII (2 vols, ed. J. Gairdner, Rolls Series, 1861–63)

Letters of the Kings of England (ed. J. O. Halliwell, 1846)

Original Letters illustrative of English History (11 vols, ed. H. Ellis, 1824–46)

The Popular Songs of Ireland (ed. T. Croker, 1839)

The Registers of Robert Stillington, Bishop of Bath and Wells (1466–91) and Richard Fox, Bishop of Bath and Wells (1492–94) (ed. C. Maxwell-Lyte, Somerset Record Society, 52, 1937)

Rotuli Parliamentorum (The Rolls of Parliament) (7 vols, ed. J. Strachey, Record Commissioners, 1767–1832)

Statutes of the Realm, 1101–1713 (Record Commissioners, 1810–28)

Sources before 1483

Historie of the Arrivall of Edward IV in England and the final Recoverye of his Kingdomes from Henry VI, AD MCCCCLXXI (ed. J. A. Bruce, Camden Society, 1838)

Three Chronicles of the Reign of Edward IV (ed. Keith Dockray, Alan Sutton, 1988)

Warkworth, John, Master of Peterhouse College, Cambridge: *A Chronicle of the First Thirteen Years of the Reign of King Edward the Fourth* (to 1473; written c.1483; ed. J. O. Halliwell, Camden Society, 1839)

William of Worcester: *Annales Rerum Anglicarum* (ed. T. Hearne, 1728, and J. Stevenson in *Letters and Papers illustrative of the Wars of the English in France*, 2 vols, Rolls Series, 1861–64)

Ricardian Sources

Acts of Court of the Mercers' Company, 1453–1527 (ed. L. Lyell and F. D. Watney, Cambridge, 1936)

British Library Harleian Manuscript 433 (ed. R. E. Horrox and P. W. Hammond, 4 vols, Alan Sutton, 1979–83)

A Castilian Report on English Affairs, 1486 (ed. Anthony Goodman and Angus Mackay, *English Historical Review*, LXXXVIII, 1973)

The Cely Letters, 1472–1488 (ed. Alison Hanham, Early English Texts Society, 1975)

Chronicles of London (ed. C. L. Kingsford, Oxford, 1905)

The Coronation of Richard III (ed. Anne F. Sutton and P. W. Hammond, Alan Sutton, 1983)

The Croyland Chronicle Continuation, 1459–1486 (ed. N. Pronay and J. Cox, 1986)

A Descriptive Catalogue of the Manuscripts bequeathed unto the University of Oxford by Elias Ashmole (includes Humphrey Lluyd's Latin manuscript; Oxford, 1845)

Extracts from the Municipal Records of the City of York during the Reigns of Edward IV, Edward V and Richard III (ed. R. Davies, 1843)

Grants etc. from the Crown during the Reign of Edward the Fifth (ed. J. G. Nichols, Camden Society, 1854)

Gregory's Chronicle, or the Historical Collections of a Citizen of London in the Fifteenth Century (ed. J. Gairdner, Camden Society, 1876)

Historiae Croylandensis Continuato in Rerum Anglicarum Scriptores Veterum (ed. W. Fulman, Oxford, 1684)

Historiae Croylandensis in *Ingulph's Chronicle of the Abbey of Croyland* (trans. and ed. H. T. Riley, 1854)

Historical Notes of a London Citizen, 1483 to 1488 (being the fragment discovered in the College of Arms in 1980) (ed. Richard Firth Green, *English Historical Review*, Vol. 96, 1981)

Household Books of John, Duke of Norfolk, and Thomas, Earl of Surrey (ed. J. Payne-Collier, Roxburghe Club, 1844)

Mancini, Dominic: *De Occupatione Regni Anglie per Riccardum Tercium* (trans. and ed. C. A. J. Armstrong, 2nd edition, Oxford University Press, Oxford, 1969)

Rous, John: *The Rous Roll* (ed. C. R. Ross and W. Courthope, Alan Sutton, 1980)

Select Bibliography

'A Spanish Account of the Battle of Bosworth' (ed. E. M. Nokes and G. Wheeler, *The Ricardian*, No. 36, March, 1972)

The Stonor Letters and Papers 1290–1483 (2 vols, ed. C. L. Kingsford, Camden Series, 1919)

York Civic Records, Vols. I and II (ed. Angelo Raine, Yorkshire Archaeological Society, Record Series CIII, 1939–41)

Tudor Sources

André, Bernard: *Vita Henrici VII* (in *Memorials of King Henry VII*, ed. J. Gairdner, Rolls Series, 1858)

Bull of Pope Innocent VIII on the Marriage of Henry VII with Elizabeth of York (ed. J. Payne-Collier, *Camden Miscellany I*, 1847)

The Chronicle of Calais in the Reigns of Henry VII and Henry VIII (ed. J. G. Nichols, Camden Society, 1846)

English Historical Documents Vol. V, 1485–1588 (ed. C. H. Williams, 1967)

Fabyan, Robert: *The Concordance of Histories: The New Chronicles of England and France (1516)* (ed. H. Ellis, 1811)

Grafton, Richard: *Grafton's Chronicle, or History of England* (2 vols, ed. H. Ellis, 1809)

Grafton, Richard: *The Chronicle of John Hardyng . . . Together with the Continuation by Richard Grafton* (ed. H. Ellis, 1812)

Hall, Edward: *The Union of the Two Noble and Illustre Families of Lancaster and York* (London, 1550; ed. H. Ellis, 1809; facsimile edition of the original published 1970)

Holinshed, Raphael: *Chronicles of England, Scotland and Ireland* (6 vols, ed. H. Ellis, 1807–8)

Leland, John: *Collectanea* (6 vols, ed. T. Hearne, Oxford, 1770–74)

Letters and Papers, Foreign and Domestic, of the Reign of Henry VIII (21 vols, ed. J. S. Brewer, J. Gairdner and R. H. Brodie, 1862–1932)

A London Chronicle in the Time of Henry VII and Henry VIII (ed. C. Hopper, Camden Society, *Camden Miscellany IV*, 1839)

Materials for a History of the Reign of Henry the Seventh (2 vols, ed. William Campbell, Rolls Series, 1873–7)

Memorials of King Henry VII (ed. J. Gairdner, Rolls Series, 1858)

More, Sir Thomas: *The History of King Richard the Third* (in *The*

Complete Works of Sir Thomas More, Vol. II, ed. R. S. Sylvester and others, Yale, 1963, London, 1979)

The Reign of Henry VII from Contemporary Sources (3 vols, ed. A. F. Pollard, 1913; reprinted New York, 1967)

Rous, John: *Joannis Rossi Antiquarii Warwicensis. Historia Regum Angliae* (ed. T. Hearne, Oxford, 1716 and 1745)

The Song of the Lady Bessy (in *English Historical Literature in the Fifteenth Century,* ed. C. L. Kingsford, Oxford, 1913)

State Papers of King Henry VIII (11 vols, 1830–52)

Stow, John: *A Survey of London* (2 vols, ed. C. L. Kingsford, Oxford, 1908, and H. B. Wheatley, Dent, 1987)

Tudor Royal Proclamations. Vol. I: The Early Tudors (ed. P. L. Hughes and J. F. Larkin, New Haven, 1964)

Vergil, Polydore: *The Anglica Historia of Polydore Vergil, AD 1485–1573* (trans. and ed. D. Hay, Camden Series, 1950)

Vergil, Polydore: *Three Books of Polydore Vergil's English History* (ed. H. Ellis, Camden Society, 1844)

Seventeenth-Century Sources

Bacon, Sir Francis: *The History of the Reign of Henry VII* (1622; ed. J. R. Lumby, Cambridge, 1881, and F. Levy, Indianapolis, 1972)

Buck, Sir George: *History of the Life and Reign of Richard III* (5 vols, ed. G. Buck (nephew), 1646; included in White Kennett's *History of England,* 1710; ed. A. N. Kincaid, Alan Sutton, 1979)

Cotton, Sir Robert: *A Brief Abridgement of Records in the Tower of London* (London, 1657)

Foreign Sources

Basin, Thomas: *Histoire de Charles VII* (2 vols, ed. C. Samaran, Paris, 1933 and 1944)

But, Adrien de: *Chroniques relatives à l'Histoire de la Belgique sous la Domination des Ducs de Bourgogne, Vol. I* (ed. Kervyn de Lettenhove, Académie Royale de Belgique, Brussels, 1870)

Calendar of Letters, Despatches and State Papers relating to the Negotiations between England and Spain, preserved in the Archives of Simancas and elsewhere (13 vols, ed. G. A. Bergenroth, P. de Gayangos, G. Mattingley, M. A. S. Hume and R. Taylor, 1862–1965)

Calendar of State Papers and Manuscripts existing in the Archives and Collections of Milan (ed. A. B. Hinds, HMSO, 1912)

Calendar of State Papers and Manuscripts relating to English Affairs existing in the Archives and Collections of Venice and in other Libraries of Northern Italy (38 vols, ed. Rawdon Brown, G. Cavendish-Bentinck, H. F. Brown and A. B. Hinds, 1864–1947)

Clercq, J. du: *Mémoires sur le Règne de Philippe le Bon, Duc de Bourgogne* (ed. M. le Baron de Reiffenberg, 1835–36)

Commines, Philippe de: *Mémoires* (ed. Andrew Scobie, 1900, and by J. Calmette and G. Durville, 3 vols, Paris, 1924–25)

Journal des États Généraux de France tenus à Tours en 1484 (ed. J. Masselin and A. Bernier, Paris, 1835)

Marche, Olivier de la: *Mémoires d'Olivier de la Marche* (ed. H. Beaune and J. d'Arbaumont, Paris, 1883)

Molinet, Jean: *Chroniques des Ducs de Bourgogne, 1476–1506* (5 vols, ed. J. A. Buchon, Paris, 1827–28)

Molinet, Jean: *Chroniques de Jean Molinet, 1476–1506* (3 vols, ed. J. Doutrepont and O. Jodogne, Académie Royale de Belgique, Brussels, 1935–37)

Scriptores Rerum Silesiacarum (3 vols, ed. G. A. Stenzel, Breslau, 1847)

Waurin, Jean de: *Anchiennes Chroniques d'Engleterre* (3 vols, ed. Mlle E. Dupont, Paris, 1858–63)

Secondary Sources

General and Miscellaneous Works

Armstrong, C .A. J.: *The Inauguration Ceremonies of the Yorkist Kings* (Transactions of the Royal Historical Society, 30, 1948)

Armstrong, C. A. J.: *The Piety of Cecily, Duchess of York* (in *For Hilaire Belloc*, ed. D. Woodruffe, 1942)

Brooks, F. W.: *The Council of the North* (Historical Association Pamphlet, 1966)

Cust, Mrs *Henry: Gentleman Errant: Gabriel Tetzel of Nuremburg* (1909)

Dart, John: *The History and Antiquities of the Abbey Church of West-minster* (2 vols, 1723)

Davies, C. S. L.: *Peace, Print and Protestantism: 1450–1558 (The Paladin History of England*, Hart-Davis, MacGibbon, 1976)

The Dictionary of National Biography (63 vols, ed. L. Stephen and S. Lee, 1885–1938)

Fletcher, Brian: 'Tree-Ring Dates for Some Paintings in England' (*Burlington Magazine*, cxvi, 1974)

Fowler, Kenneth: *The Age of Plantagenet and Valois* (Ferndale, 1980)

Green, V. H. H.: *The Later Plantagenets* (Edward Arnold, 1955)

The Handbook of British Chronology (ed. F. M. Powicke and E. B. Fryde, Royal Historical Society, 1961)

Harvey, John: *The Plantagenets* (Batsford, 1948)

Hassall, W. O.: *They Saw it Happen, 55 BC to 1485* (Blackwell, Oxford, 1957)

Hassall, W. O.: *Who's Who in History, Vol. I: 55 BC to 1485* (Blackwell, Oxford, 1960)

Howard, Maurice: *The Earl Tudor Country House: Architecture and Politics, 1490–1550* (George Philips, 1987)

Jacob, E. F.: *The Fifteenth Century, 1399–1485* (Oxford University Press, Oxford, 1961, 1969)

Kendall, Paul Murray: *The Yorkist Age* (Allen and Unwin, 1962)

Lander, J. R.: *Conflict and Stability in Fifteenth-Century England* (Hutchinson, 1969)

Lane, Henry Murray: *The Royal Daughters of England* (2 vols, Constable, 1910)

Lindsay, Philip: *Kings of Merry England* (Howard Baker, 1936)

Macdougall, Norman: *James IV* (John Donald, Edinburgh, 1989)

Minster Lovell Hall: Official Handbook (Department of the Environment, HMSO, 1977)

Palmer, Alan: *Princes of Wales* (Weidenfeld and Nicolson, 1979)

Palmer, Alan and Veronica: *Royal England: A Historical Gazeteer* (Methuen, 1983)

Peck, F.: *Desiderata Curiosa* (1799) (for the tale of Richard Plantagenet of Eastwell)

Platt, Colin: *The National Trust Guide to Late Mediaeval and Renaissance Britain* (National Trust, 1986)

Platt, Colin: *The Traveller's Guide to Mediaeval England* (Secker and Warburg, 1985)

Poole, Austin Lane: *Late Mediaeval England* (2 vols, Oxford University Press, Oxford, 1958)

Rae, Dr John: *Deaths of the English Kings* (1913)

Robinson, John Martin: *The Dukes of Norfolk: A Quincentennial History* (Oxford University Press, Oxford, 1982)

Royal Britain (The Automobile Association, 1976)

Weinreb, Ben and Hibbert, Christopher: *The London Encyclopaedia* (Macmillan, 1983)

Westminster Abbey: Official Guide (various editions)

Wickham, D. E.: *Discovering Kings and Queens* (Shire Publications, 1973)

Wilkinson, B.: *The Late Middle Ages in England, 1216–1485* (1969)

For the Wars of the Roses

Alderman, Clifford Lindsey: *Blood Red the Roses: The Wars of the Roses* (1971)

Chronicles of the Wars of the Roses (ed. Elizabeth Hallam, Weidenfeld and Nicolson, 1988)

Cole, Hubert: *The Wars of the Roses* (Hart-Davis MacGibbon, 1973)

Goodman, Anthony: *The Wars of the Roses: Military Activity and English Society, 1452–1497* (Routledge and Kegan Paul, 1981)

Kinross, John: *The Battlefields of Britain* (David and Charles, Devon, 1979)

Lander, J. R.: *The Wars of the Roses* (Alan Sutton, 1990)

Pollard, A. J.: *The Wars of the Roses* (Macmillan, 1988)

Ross, Charles: *The Wars of the Roses* (1976)

Rowse, A. L.: *Bosworth Field and the Wars of the Roses* (Macmillan, 1966)

For Edward IV and His Family

Clive, Mary M.: *This Sun of York: A Biography of Edward IV* (Macmillan, 1973)

Davies, Katharine: *The First Queen Elizabeth* (Lovat Dickson, 1937)

Select Bibliography

Falkus, Gila: *The Life and Times of Edward IV* (Weidenfeld and Nicolson, 1981)
Hicks, M. A.: *False, Fleeting, Perjur'd Clarence* (Alan Sutton, 1980)
Ross, Charles: *Edward IV* (Eyre Methuen, 1974)
Scofield, Cora L.: *The Life and Reign of Edward the Fourth* (2 vols, 1923, reprinted by Frank Cass and Co. 1967)
Simons, Eric N.: *The Reign of Edward IV* (1966)

For Richard III

Cheetham, Anthony: *The Life and Times of Richard III* (Weidenfeld and Nicolson, 1972) (revisionist)
Drewett, Richard and Redhead, Mark: *The Trial of Richard III* (Alan Sutton, 1984)
Given-Wilson, Chris and Curteis, Alice: *The Royal Bastards of Mediaeval England* (Routledge and Kegan Paul, 1984) (for details of Richard III's bastard children)
Hammond, P. W. and Sutton, Anne F.: *Richard III: The Road to Bosworth Field* (Constable, 1985)
Hanham, Alison: *Richard III and his Early Historians* (Oxford University Press, Oxford, 1975)
Kendall, Paul Murray: *Richard the Third* (Allen and Unwin, 1955) (revisionist; for many years, the definitive biography, but now largely discredited)
Lamb, V. B.: *The Betrayal of Richard III* (The Research Publishing Company, 1959) (revisionist)
Markham, Sir Clements: *Richard III: His Life and Character* (1906) (revisionist)
Potter, Jeremy: *Good King Richard?* (Constable, 1983) (revisionist)
Ross, Charles: *Richard III* (Eyre Methuen, 1981) (traditionalist; the definitive biography)
St Aubyn, Giles: *The Year of Three Kings: 1483* (Collins, Glasgow, 1983)
Seward, Desmond: *Richard III: England's Black Legend* (Country Life Books, 1983) (traditionalist)
Tudor-Craig, Pamela: *Richard III* (National Portrait Gallery, 1973, 1977)
Woodward, G. W. O.: *King Richard III* (Pitkin, 1972)

The Princes in the Tower

Crawford, A.: 'The Mowbray Inheritance' (*The Ricardian*, June, 1981)

Jenkins, Elizabeth: *The Princes in the Tower* (Hamish Hamilton, 1978)

Molleson, Theya: 'Anne Mowbray and the Princes in the Tower: a Study in Identity' (*The London Archaeologist*, Vol. 5, no. 10, Spring 1987)

Richard III and the Princes in the Tower (ed. Langdon-Davies, Jackdaw Series, 1965)

Tanner, L. E., and Wright, W.: 'Recent Investigations Regarding the Fate of the Princes in the Tower' (*Archaeologia*, LXXXIV, 1934)

Williamson, Audrey: *The Mystery of the Princes* (Alan Sutton, 1978)

The Tower of London

Charlton, John: *The Tower of London: Its Buildings and Institutions* (HMSO, 1978)

Hibbert, Christopher: *The Tower of London* (Readers' Digest, 1971)

Mears, Kenneth J.: *The Tower of London: 900 Years of English History* (Phaidon Press, Oxford, 1988)

Minney, R. J.: *The Tower of London* (Cassell, 1970)

Picard, Barbara Leone: *The Tower and the Traitors* (Batsford, 1961)

Rowse, A. L.: *The Tower of London in the History of the Nation* (Weidenfeld and Nicolson, 1972)

Somerset Fry, Plantagenet: *The Tower of London: Cauldron of Britain's Past* (Quiller Press, 1990)

Wilson, Derek: *The Tower, 1078–1978* (Hamish Hamilton, 1978)

Henry VII

Chrimes, S. B.: *Henry VII* (Eyre Methuen, 1972)

Chrimes, S. B.: *Lancastrians, Yorkists and Henry VII* (1966)

Grant, Alexander: *Henry VII* (Methuen, 1985)

Lenz-Harvey, N.: *Elizabeth of York, Tudor Queen* (1973)

Macalpine, Joan: *The Shadow of the Tower: Henry VII and his England* (BBC Publications, 1971)

Rees, David: *The Son of Prophecy: Henry Tudor's Road to Bosworth* (Black Raven Press, 1985)

Williams, Neville: *The Life and Times of Henry VII* (Weidenfeld and Nicolson, 1973)

The Tudor Period

Bennett, Michael: *Lambert Simnel and the Battle of Stoke* (Alan Sutton, 1987)

Durant, Horatia: *Sorrowful Captives: The Tudor Earls of Devon* (Griffin Press, 1960)

Elton, G. R.: *England under the Tudors* (Methuen, 1955)

Mackie, J. D.: *The Earlier Tudors, 1485–1558* (Oxford University Press, Oxford, 1952, 1966)

Morris, Christopher: *The Tudors* (Batsford, 1955)

Plowden, Alison: *The House of Tudors* (Weidenfeld and Nicolson, 1976)

Routh, C. R. N.: *Who's Who in History, Vol. II, England 1485–1603* (Blackwell, Oxford, 1964)

Sir Thomas More

Marius, Richard: *Thomas More* (Dent, 1984)

Ridley, Jasper: *The Statesman and the Fanatic: Thomas Wolsey and Thomas More* (Constable, 1982)

Strong, Sir Roy: *Tudor and Jacobean Portraits* (2 vols, National Portrait Gallery, 1969) (for a discussion on paintings of the More family group)

Trapp, J. B. and Herbrüggen, H. S.: *The King's Good Servant: Sir Thomas More, 1477/8–1535* (National Portrait Gallery, 1977)

Wilson, D.: *England in the Age of Thomas More* (1978)

Index

About the Author

ALISON WEIR is the author of *The Six Wives of Henry VIII* and *Britain's Royal Families: The Complete Genealogy*, the first full genealogy from 800 A.D. to the present. She lives in Surrey with her husband and two children.